FOURTH EDITION

THE CULTURAL DIMENSION OF INTERNATIONAL BUSINESS

Gary P. Ferraro

The University of North Carolina at Charlotte

Upper Saddle River, New Jersey 07458

Library of Congress Cataloging-in-Publication Data

Ferraro, Gary P.
   The cultural dimension of international business / Gary P. Ferraro.—4th ed.
     p. cm.
   Includes bibliographical references and index.
   ISBN 0-13-090327-2
    1. International business enterprises—Social aspects. 2. Intercultural
communication. 3. Technical assistance—Anthropological aspects. I. Title

HD2755.5 .F48 2001
320.3'5—dc21

00-067759

For Avery and Mitchell, with the hope that their generation
will become the best intercultural communicators yet.

VP, Editoral Director: Laura Pearson
AVP, Publisher: Nancy Roberts
Editorial Assistant: Lee Peterson
Project Manager: Merrill Peterson
Cover Director: Jayne Conte
Cover Design: Bruce Kenselaar
Cover Photo: Steve Mason/PhotoDisc, Inc.

Photo Researcher: Sheila Norman
Interior Image Specialist: Beth Boyd
Manager, Rights and Permissions: Kay Dellosa
Director, Image Resource Center: Melinda Reo
Marketing Manager: Chris Barker
Prepress and Manufacturing Buyer: Ben Smith

This book was set in 10/12 Times New Roman by DM Cradle Associates Inc.
and was printed and bound by Courier Companies, Inc.
The cover was printed by Phoenix Color Corp.

© 2002 by Pearson Education, Inc.
Upper Saddle River, New Jersey 07458

Printed in the United States of America

10 9 8 7 6 5 4

ISBN 0-13-090327-2

PRENTICE-HALL INTERNATIONAL (UK) LIMITED, London
PRENTICE-HALL OF AUSTRALIA PTY. LIMITED, Sydney
PRENTICE-HALL CANADA INC., Toronto
PRENTICE-HALL HISPANOAMERICANA, S.A., Mexico
PRENTICE-HALL OF INDIA PRIVATE LIMITED, New Delhi
PRENTICE-HALL OF JAPAN, INC., Tokyo
PEARSON EDUCATION ASIA PTE. LTD., Singapore
EDITORA PRENTICE-HALL DO BRASIL, LTDA., Rio de Janeiro

Contents

Preface

This book is aimed at demonstrating how the theory and insights of cultural anthropology can positively influence the conduct of international business. To date, anthropologists have given embarrassingly little attention to this subject, and writers in the field of international management and marketing, although acknowledging the importance of the cultural dimension, have dealt with it in a cursory and anecdotal fashion. This book—which explores the contributions that cultural anthropology can make to the more effective and humane conduct of international business—can serve the interests of both the international business community and the discipline of anthropology, which is continually searching for new, nonacademic environments in which to make practical contributions. Specifically, the book takes a fourfold approach to understanding the cultural dimension of international business.

I. Culture-General Approach: Making the Connections between Anthropological Theory (Generalizations) and International Business

Chapter 2 provides an in-depth look at the concept of culture, what generalizations hold true for all cultures of the world, and the implications of those generalizations for international business. This chapter is predicated on the notion that it is impossible for anyone to master all of the specific cultural facts about the thousands of cultures found in the world today. Thus, a more conceptual approach is needed. The chapter begins with various definitions of the culture concept, followed by some important generalizations that can be usefully applied to any cross-cultural situation. The importance of these cultural generalizations for the conduct of international business is then discussed.

II. Understanding Communication Patterns—Verbal And Nonverbal

In Chapters 3 and 4 we examine some of the critical dimensions of communication, both verbal and nonverbal, in a cross-cultural business setting. Effective communication between people from the same cultural and linguistic group is often difficult enough, but when one is attempting to communicate with people who speak little or no English—and have different ideas, attitudes, assumptions, perceptions, and ways of doing things—the chances for miscommunication increase enormously. In Chapter 3, we examine the critical importance of language competence in an international business situation, the interrelatedness between language and culture, the situational use of language, and some additional factors (such as slang and euphemisms) that can further complicate verbal communication in an international business context.

In Chapter 4 we discuss the importance of knowing the nonverbal communication patterns prevalent in the international business arena. As important as language is to sending and receiving messages, nonverbal communication is perhaps even more important. Not only do nonverbal cues help us interpret verbal messages, but they are also responsible in their own right for the majority of the messages that make up human communication. Six major modes of communicating nonverbally—posture, hand gestures, facial expressions, eye contact, proxemics, and touching—are discussed in a cross-cultural perspective. The aim of this chapter is to demonstrate how many ways there are to miscommunicate in a cross-cultural business setting unless one is familiar with the nonverbal patterns of communication in addition to the linguistic patterns.

III. Cultural Self-Awareness: Their Values and Ours

Chapter 5, dealing with values, is designed with two purposes in mind. First, it aims to show that people from different cultures view the world from the viewpoint of different cultural assumptions. And second, it encourages Western businesspeople to increase their cultural self-awareness—that is, their ability to recognize the influences of their culture on their thinking and behavior. An increase in cultural self-awareness should make it easier to diagnose difficulties when communicating in a foreign business setting. It should enable the overseas businessperson to discover how a cross-cultural misunderstanding may have arisen from his or her own cultural assumptions rather than from some shortcoming of the culturally different person.

This chapter has undergone extensive revision in this edition. Whereas previous editions had focused on American cultural values, this edition takes a more conceptual approach. Following the lead of such theorists as Florence Kluckhohn, John Condon, and Geert Hofstede, among others, Chapter 5 now presents a framework of values that can be used to analyze cultural differences throughout the world. The model examines such dimensions of values as individualism versus collectivism, equality versus hierarchy, tough versus tender societies, varying levels of uncertainty avoidance, and certain aspects of time, including precise versus loose reckoning of time, past, present, and future time orientations, and sequential versus synchronical aspects of time. Chapter 5 describes each of these dimensions, shows how they play out in different types of societies, and then examines the implications for conducting business.

IV. Culture-Specific Approach: Finding Relevant Cultural Information

The final segment of this four-pronged approach involves a discussion of how and where to find the specific cultural information needed for any particular international business assignment. For example, how does one procure current and pertinent data describing the cultural patterns that exist in Djakarta, Madras, or La Paz? Appendix B explores a number of anthropological and nonanthropological data sources (both documentary and human) that can be useful in developing a profile of any particular culture. This appendix is based on the assumption that if U.S. businesses are to meet the current challenges of a highly competitive world economy, they will need an ever-increasing flow of information about the cultures of those with whom they are conducting business.

Chapter 6 deals with negotiating across cultures. Although it is recognized that no two international negotiating situations are ever identical, some negotiating strategies are generally valid in most situations. Based on the experiences of successful and culturally sensitive international negotiators, this chapter provides such general guidelines as (1) concentrating on long-term relationships, (2) focusing on the interests behind the positions, (3) being attuned to timing, and (4) needing flexibility, careful preparation, and willingness to listen.

Chapter 7 of this book examines culture shock, a phenomenon that can sour an otherwise promising international business assignment. Although there are no ways of totally eliminating this psychologically disorienting experience, there are steps to take before, during, and after an international assignment that can reduce some of the more debilitating symptoms. The chapter concludes with suggestions for minimizing culture shock.

Chapter 8 examines developing global leaders, expatriate excellence, and a number of other important global human resource issues. This chapter argues that expatriate assignments must be managed in a more systematic, holistic, and long-term way than they are currently being managed. This requires international firms to be attentive to all phases of transferring personnel abroad, including selection, cross-cultural preparation, in-country support, repatriation, and the utilization of those skills gained abroad for future assignments.

As a final note, attention should be given to the scenarios appearing at the end of Chapters 2 through 8. The reader is encouraged to analyze these minicase studies in an attempt to determine why a cultural conflict has arisen and how the conflict or misunderstanding portrayed could have been avoided. Although it is impossible to include examples of *every* possible cross-cultural conflict in a business setting, these end-of-chapter scenarios are designed to help the reader gain a greater sensitivity to the wide range of potential conflicts that could arise. Explanations of these scenarios appear in Appendix A.

As with the previous editions of this book, a number of reviewers have made insightful suggestions for improvement. I trust that all reviewers will notice that many of their helpful suggestions have in fact been incorporated into the new edition. In particular, I would like to thank the following reviewers for their helpful suggestions: John P. Staeck, College of DuPage; Thomas E. Durbin, California State University–Stanislaus; R. Boyd Johnson, Indiana Wesleyan University; and John Rhoades, St. John Fisher College.

Gary P. Ferraro

CHAPTER 1

Cultural Anthropology and International Business

How often do we hear people say "The whole argument is academic"? By this statement they mean that, despite the elegance of the logic, the whole line of reasoning makes little or no difference. In other words, the term *academic* has become synonymous with *irrelevant*. In all of academia, it is hard to think of other disciplines generally perceived by the public to be any more irrelevant to the everyday world than cultural anthropology, the comparative study of cultures. The student of biology, for example, can apply his or her skills to the solution of vital medical problems; the student of creative arts can produce lasting works of art; and the political science student, owing to a basic understanding of political dynamics, can become a local, state, or national leader. But according to popular perception, the study of cultural anthropology, with its apparent emphasis on the non-Western cultures of the world, has little to offer other than a chance to dabble in the exotic.

To counter the long-held popular view that cultural anthropology is of little use in helping to understand the world around us, in recent years an increasing number of cultural anthropologists have applied the theories, findings, and methods of their craft to a wide range of professional areas. Professionals in such areas as education, urban administration, and the various health services have been coming to grips, albeit reluctantly, with the cultural environments within which they work; however, those in the area of international business, although having perhaps the greatest need, remain among the most skeptical concerning the relevance of cultural anthropology. There has in fact been little contact between cultural anthropology and the international business sector. According to Erve Chambers, cultural anthropologists have avoided working with the international business community because of "a highly prejudiced ethical stance which associates commercial success and profit taking with a lack of concern for human welfare" (1985, 128). Also, Western multinational corporations have not actively sought the services of cultural anthropologists, whom they generally view as serving little useful purpose other than providing more interesting cocktail-party conversation about the esoteric peoples of the world. In short, both cultural anthropologists and international businesspeople view the concerns of the other as irrelevant, morally questionable, or trivial.

This book rests on the fundamental assumption that to operate effectively in the international business arena one must master the cultural environment by means of purposeful preparation as well as sustained learning throughout one's overseas assignment. Now, as in the past, international businesspeople acquire their international expertise while on the job, and they consider such hands-on factors as business travel and overseas assignments to be the most important experiences. While not minimizing the value of experiential learning, this book argues that, in addition to on-the-job learning (and in most cases, before entering the international marketplace), successful international businesspeople must prepare themselves in a very deliberate manner in order to operate within a new, and frequently very different, cultural environment.

THE ANTHROPOLOGICAL PERSPECTIVE

When the average American hears the word *anthropologist,* two images usually come to mind. The first image is that represented by Harrison Ford in his portrayal of anthropologist Indiana Jones in the film *Raiders of the Lost Ark.* In his search for clues to the secrets of lost civilizations, Indiana Jones spends most of his time being chased by irate cannibals, engaging in hand-to-hand combat with sinister Nazis, and being thrown into pits with thousands of snakes. Although this image is exciting theater, it gives us little insight into what anthropology is all about. The second image of an anthropologist is that of the irrelevant academic who spends every moment out of the classroom interviewing exotic peoples whose cultures are about to become extinct. Anthropology, however, is neither hazardous to the health nor irrelevant. Both these views of anthropology are misleading stereotypes, which obscure both the nature of the discipline and its relevance to the world.

The scientific discipline of anthropology is far less life-endangering than Hollywood would have us believe and far more relevant than most of us imagine. To be certain, anthropologists do travel to the far corners of the world studying little-known cultures (cultural anthropologists) and languages (anthropological linguists). Moreover, some anthropologists unearth fossil remains (physical anthropologists) and artifacts (archaeologists) of people who lived thousands or, in some cases, millions of years ago. Despite the fact that these four subareas of anthropology frequently deal with different types of data, they are all directed toward a single purpose: the scientific study of human cultures in whatever form, time period, or region of the world in which they might be found. According to Carol and Melvin Ember,

> Anthropology is concerned explicitly and directly with all varieties of people throughout the world, not just those close at hand or within a limited area. It is also interested in people of all periods. Beginning with the immediate ancestors of humans who lived a few million years ago, anthropology traces the development of humans until the present. Every part of the world that has ever contained a human population is of interest to anthropologists. (1999, 2)

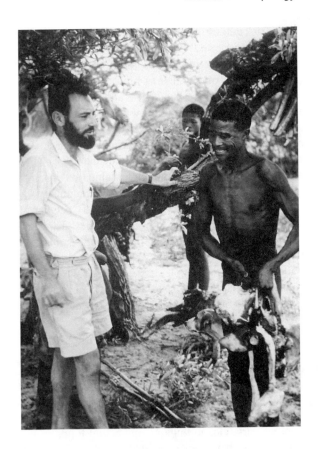

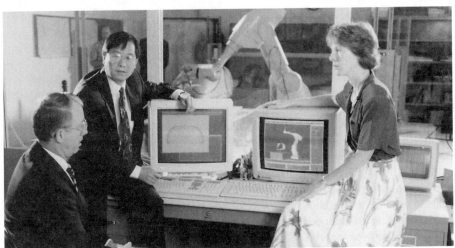

Cultural anthropologist no longer work only in exotic parts of the world, such as southwest Africa.

Anthropology differs from other disciplines that study humans in that it is much broader in scope both geographically and historically. Four distinct yet closely related sub-fields comprise anthropology: (1) *archaeology*, the study of ancient and prehistoric societies; (2) *physical anthropology*, the study of humans as biological entities; (3) *anthropological linguistics*, the comparative study of languages; and (4) *cultural anthropology*, the search for similarities and differences among contemporary peoples of the world. Even though the discipline encourages all anthropologists to constantly integrate these four fields, in recent decades increasing disciplinary specialization has made it virtually impossible for any anthropologist to cover all four fields in a comprehensive way. When we look at the contributions anthropology can make to the more effective conduct of international business, we are looking primarily at cultural anthropology.

Cultural anthropology seeks to understand how and why contemporary peoples of the world differ in their customary ways of behaving and how and why they share certain similarities. It is, in short, the comparative study of cultural differences and similarities found throughout the world. Cultural anthropologists may often appear to be documenting inconsequential cultural facts about little-known peoples of the world, but our learning more about the wide range of cultural variations will serve as a check on those who might generalize about "human nature" solely on observations from their own society. It is not at all unusual for people to assume that their own ways of thinking and acting are unquestionably rational, "natural," or "human." Consider, for example, the nonverbal gesture of negation (found in the United States and in other parts of the world), shaking the head from side to side. In some parts of India, however, people use this very same gesture to communicate not negation but affirmation. In fact, there are any number of different ways of nonverbally communicating the idea of negation, all of which are no more or no less rational than shaking the head from side to side. The study of cultural anthropology provides a look at the enormous variations in thinking and acting found in the world today and how many different solutions have been generated for solving the same problem.

Anthropology does more than simply document the enormous variations in human cultures. If anthropology deserves to be called a science, it must go beyond the mere cataloging of cultural differences. It must also identify and describe the commonalities of humans amid the great diversity—that is, the regularities found in all cultural contexts regardless of how different those contexts might appear at first glance. For example, for any society to continue to exist over the long run, it must solve the basic problem of how to pass on its total cultural heritage—all the ideas, values, attitudes, behavior patterns, and so on—to succeeding generations. Should that complexity of cultural traditions not be passed on to future generations, that society will very likely not survive. Saudis have solved this problem by developing Koranic schools, which pass on the cultural traditions to the younger generations; in parts of West Africa, "bush schools" train young adolescents to become adults; in our own society, we rely on a formal system of compulsory education, complete with books, desks, and teachers. Although the details of these educational systems vary enormously, all societies in the world—today or in the past—have worked out a system for ensuring that new generations will learn their culture. Thus, the science of anthropology attempts to document the great variations in cultural forms while looking for both the common strands that are found in and the general principles that apply to all cultures.

The strong comparative perspective that anthropologists bring to the study of the human condition helps reduce the probability that their theories will be culture bound. Sociologists and psychologists, for example, concentrating as they have on studies of peoples from Western societies, are more likely to construct theories that are based on Western assumptions of reality. The cross-cultural perspective of anthropological studies has frequently served as a corrective to those disciplines that rely more heavily for their theory construction on data from Western societies. According to Clifford Geertz, cultural anthropologists were the first to recognize

> that the world does not divide into the pious and the superstitious; that there are sculptures in jungles and paintings in deserts; that political order is possible without centralized power and principled justice without codified rules; that the norms of reason were not fixed in Greece, the evolution of morality not consummated in England. . . . We have, with no little success, sought to keep the world off balance; pulling out rugs, upsetting tea tables, setting off fire crackers. It has been the office of others to reassure; ours to unsettle. (1984, 275)

In addition to being comparative, the anthropological perspective has another distinctive feature. Unlike other social or behavioral sciences, anthropologists analyze cultural differences and similarities firsthand. For example, psychologists usually study human behavior by using post facto data rather than actually observing the behavior as it is occurring; sociologists generally rely on secondary information gleaned from questionnaires, interviews, and census reports; historians are removed in time from the people and events that constitute their subject matter. Cultural anthropologists, however, use *participant observation* as a major method for collecting culturally comparative information. When anthropologists use participant observation, they share in the everyday activities of the local people while making detailed descriptive observations of people eating, working, playing, conversing, dancing, fighting, or any other activity that might distinguish their cultural patterns.

Given the nature of the anthropological enterprise, it is not surprising that the founders of modern anthropology developed the tradition of firsthand field observations of cultural behavior. If indeed anthropology had set as its task the comparative study of human cultures, it would have to study *all* human cultures, many of which had not been studied before. In the absence of descriptive studies of exotic cultures, early anthropologists had no other choice but to learn the language and spend at least a year immersed in the culture of the people under study. Today, even though libraries are well stocked with descriptive studies of a wide variety of world cultures, participant observation remains a preferred investigative strategy among contemporary anthropologists.

Thus, cultural anthropologists are trained to analyze the social organizations of various types of societies. In the early twentieth century, cultural anthropologists tended to devote their energies exclusively to the analysis of small-scale, technologically simple, and usually non-Western peoples. Within the last several decades, however, cultural anthropologists have become increasingly involved in the study of more complex societies. Yet whether dealing with simple or complex societies, the focus of cultural anthropologists has been the comparative study of sociocultural organizations wherever, or in whatever form, they may be found.

CULTURAL ANTHROPOLOGY AND BUSINESS

Since the 1930s, cultural anthropologists have conducted a modest amount of research in industrial and corporate settings, focusing largely on corporate cultures in the United States. For example, the human relations school of organizational research of the 1930s and 1940s produced a number of ethnographies showing how informal cultural patterns could influence managerial goals (Mayo 1933, Roethlisberger and Dickson 1939, Gardner 1945, Warner and Low 1947, Richardson and Walker 1948). More recent studies of corporate cultures have attempted to show how specific configurations of values contribute to the relative success or failure of meeting corporate goals (Denison 1990, Kotter 1992, Frost et al. 1991, Rhinesmith 1996).

This body of research is predicated on the understanding that, business organizations are like those societies studied by traditional anthropologists. For example, like people found in small-scale, preliterate societies, corporate members engage in rituals; perpetuate corporate myths and stories; adhere to a set of norms, symbols, and behavioral expectations; and use specialized vocabularies. Since business organizations tend to be both differentiated and socially stratified, specific roles and statuses can be identified. Also, business organizations, through dealings with such groups as unions, governments, environmental groups, and consumers, have external relations with other social systems. Given these similarities, cultural anthropologists have made modest contributions to the understanding of domestic business organizations, and they have the potential for making many others.

The anthropological perspective can be useful in the study of purely domestic business organizations, which frequently are composed of many social components that come from different backgrounds, hold contrasting values and attitudes, and have conflicting loyalties. For instance, the company vice president will not likely have much in common with the assembly-line worker, the union representative, the president of the local Sierra Club, the OSHA inspector, the janitor, or many members of that diverse group called the buying public. And yet, if the organization is to function effectively, that high management official needs to know about the values, attitudes, expectations, concerns, and behavioral patterns of all these people, and others as well. This is particularly true today as more and more minorities are brought into domestic workforces under equal opportunity employment laws. In short, domestic business organizations can be viewed as minicultures (composed of different people with different roles, statuses, and value systems) that operate within the wider national cultural context.

In the mid-1990s, approximately 500 doctoral anthropologists were working in the private sector for consulting firms or large corporations (Baba 1994, 178). That number has no doubt increased as we enter the new millenium. Anthropologist John Sherry, who years ago studied communications technology among the Navajo, is now a member of a team of design ethnographers with Intel Corporation. Their purpose is to learn as much as possible (by using anthropological methods) about how people work and use high-tech tools so that Intel can design more efficient tools in the future. Anthropologists are trained to patiently observe human behavior for hours on end while recording those behaviors in minute detail. Intel (along with other high-tech firms like IBM, Hewlett Packard, Motorola, AT&T, and Xerox) is betting that useful insights will emerge from those minute details. To illustrate this application of anthropology, Sherry and his fellow design ethnographers spent large amounts of time in the late 1990s hanging out in teenagers' bedrooms. They talked to over 100 teenagers, analyzed still photos, and studied hours of videos that cataloged how their bedrooms were used. The team concluded that teenagers would like to send photos to each other by transmitting images over telephone lines that would enter a friend's computer and then be displayed in a bedside electronic picture frame. It is not surprising then, that in 2000 the world's first Internet-connected picture frame was on the market (Takahashi 1998).

Failure to consider the cultural context in the domestic organization can, and has, led to misunderstandings, miscommunication, costly marketing blunders, lawsuits, and generally an undermining of organizational goals. When moving into the area of international business, the need to be aware of cultural environments becomes even more critical. Here the magnitude of the cultural differences is vastly greater; consequently, breakdown of communication usually increases geometrically. Although the anthropological perspective is valuable in understanding any business organization, be it domestic or international, this book focuses on the contributions that cultural anthropology can make to the improvement of international business operations, with particular emphasis on the functional areas of international marketing and management.

CULTURAL AND INTERNATIONAL BUSINESS

Whether dealing with issues of marketing, managing, or negotiating, the success or failure of a company abroad depends on how effectively its employees can exercise their skills in a new location. That ability will depend on both their job-related expertise and the individual's sensitivity and responsiveness to the new cultural environment. One of the most common factors contributing to failure in international business assignments is the erroneous assumption that if a person is successful in the home environment, he or she will be equally successful in applying technical expertise in a different culture.

Research has shown that failures in the overseas business setting most frequently result from an inability to understand and adapt to foreign ways of thinking and acting rather than from technical or professional incompetence (Tung 1988; Black, Gregersen, and Mendenhall 1992). At home, U.S. businesspeople equip themselves with vast amounts of knowledge of their employees, customers, and business partners. Market research provides detailed information on values, attitudes, and buying preferences of U.S. consumers; middle- and upper-level managers are well versed in the intricacies of their organization's culture; and labor negotiators must be highly sensitive to what motivates those on the other side of the table. Yet when Americans turn to the international arena, they frequently deal with customers, employees, and fellow workers with a dearth of information that at home would be unimaginable.

The literature on international business is filled with examples of business miscues when U.S. corporations attempted to operate in an international context. Some are mildly amusing; others are downright embarrassing. All of them, to one degree or another, have been costly in terms of money, reputation, or both. For example, when American firms try to market their products in other countries, they often assume that if a marketing strategy or slogan is effective in, say, Cleveland, it will be equally effective in other parts of the world. But problems can arise when changing cultural contexts. The following examples illustrate some miscues. An airline offering service to Brazil advertised that it had comfortable "rendezvous lounges" in its business-class section. Unfortunately, it failed to realize that the word *rendezvous* in Portuguese refers to a room for illicit sexual encounters. Chicken entrepreneur Frank Purdue decided to translate one of his very successful advertising slogans into Spanish, but the new slogan didn't produce the desired results. The slogan "It takes a tough man to make a tender chicken" was translated into Spanish as "It takes a virile man to make a chicken affectionate." And the Dairy Association's wildly successful ad campaign "Got Milk?" had the unfortunate translation "Are you lactating?" when used in Mexico. Although all these cross-cultural advertising blunders cause us to chuckle, they can result in a loss of revenue and even product credibility.

Insensitivity to the cultural realities of foreign workforces can lead to less than desirable results. David Anderson (1985) tells of a U.S. businessperson who rewarded the most outstanding member of a Japanese marketing team by promoting him to head up the group. Rather than being proud and grateful, however, the top performer seemed ashamed, and the others in the group were uncomfortable and demoralized. Contrary to what the American manager had anticipated, performance in the group quickly deteriorated. What the American had not realized was that Japanese feel most comfortable working in teams, with all sharing equally in decisions, workloads, and responsibility for outcomes. As Anderson puts it, "The attempt at motivation, American-style, destroyed a sense of harmonious cooperation the Japanese workers had cherished" (1985, 54–55).

Just as inattention to the cultural context can result in some costly blunders in marketing and management, it also can affect seriously the success of international business negotiations. Time, effort, reputation, and even contracts can be lost because of cultural ignorance. Alison Lanier tells of one American executive who paid a very high price for failing to do his cultural homework:

> A top level, high priced vice president had been in and out of Bahrain many times, where liquor is permitted. He finally was sent to neighboring Qatar (on the Arabian Gulf) to conclude a monumental negotiation that had taken endless months to work out. Confident of success, he slipped two miniatures of brandy into his briefcase, planning to celebrate quietly with his colleague after the ceremony. Result: not only was he deported immediately on arrival by a zealous customs man in that strictly Moslem country, but the firm was also "disinvited" and ordered never to return. The Qatari attitude was that this man had tried to flout a deeply-held religious conviction; neither he nor his firm, therefore, was considered "suitable" for a major contract. (1979, 160–61)

These are only a few of the examples of the price paid for miscalculating—or simply ignoring—the cultural dimension of international business. The most cursory review of the international business literature will reveal many other similarly costly mistakes. In 1974, Ricks, Fu, and Arpan published a compendium of international business miscues appropriately entitled *International Business Blunders*. Less than a decade later, an entirely new collection was published (Ricks 1983), describing only those international business blunders that have occurred since 1974. More recently, Ricks (1993, 1999) has published his latest volumes of new and "improved" international business blunders. The purpose here is not to demonstrate the folly and insensitivity of the American businessperson when operating overseas but to show that the world is changing faster than most of us can calculate. If American businesspeople are to meet the challenges of an increasingly interdependent world, they will need to develop a better understanding of how cultural variables influence international business enterprises. A healthy dialogue between cultural anthropologists and members of the international business community—which this book seeks to initiate—is an important step in achieving that needed understanding.

THE NEED FOR GREATER AWARENESS OF THE CULTURAL ENVIRONMENT

In recent decades, a growing tendency of business and industry has been to become increasingly more globally interdependent. To remain competitive, most businesses, both here and abroad, needed to enter into international/cross-cultural alliances. The overall consequences of this trend have been that more and more companies have engaged in such activities as joint ventures, licensing agreements, turnkey projects, and foreign capital investments. Since the end of the cold war in the late 1980s, however, world economies have experienced dramatic changes, which collectively have been subsumed under the term *globalization*. The term has become one of the most overused and poorly understood words in the English language. To be certain, there have been interconnections between countries and cultures for centuries, but when the Berlin Wall came down in 1989, the world began to change in some dramatic ways. Forces were unleashed that have had and will continue to have profound effects on all cultures of the world.

According to Thomas Friedman (1999), globalization is not just a passing trend but a worldwide phenomenon that has replaced the cold war system. From 1945 until the late 1980s, the nations and cultures of the world were compartmentalized into two major camps, the "communist bloc" and the "free world." However, with the demise of world communism, so powerfully symbolized by the physical dismantling of the Berlin Wall, the world is experiencing (at a very rapid pace) a new type of integration of markets, technology, and information that is oblivious to both national and cultural borders. This post–cold war globalization is driven by free-market capitalism and the idea that the more a country opens up its markets to free trade, the healthier its economy will become. The economics of globalization involves lowering tariff barriers while privatizing and deregulating national economies. The North American Free Trade Agreement (NAFTA)

What follows is just a few illustrations of how extensively the lives of all the world's peoples are interconnected:

- The United States remains highly reliant on other countries for a number of important minerals. For example, the United States imports 100 percent of its graphite, manganese, mica, columbium, and strontium and more than 90 percent of its bauxite and diamonds.
- The hundred largest multinational corporations in the world own nearly $2 trillion of assets outside their home countries.
- The United States has the fourth largest Spanish-speaking population in the world. More than 60 percent of the people of Miami, for example, speak Spanish as their first language.
- In the past quarter of a century, the percentage of the U.S. population that is foreign born has grown from 4.8 percent in 1970, to 6.2 percent in 1980, to 7.9 percent in 1990, and to over 9 percent at the turn of the century.
- A significant number of corporations make more than half their total sales in foreign markets. To illustrate, Coca-Cola sells more of its product in Japan than it does in the United States.
- Direct foreign investments in the United States have increased from $13.2 billion in 1970 to $811.7 billion in 1998, more than a sixtyfold increase in the last quarter of a century (*World Almanac and Book of Facts* 1999).
- U.S. direct investments abroad have increased from $335 billion in 1988 to more than $980 billion in 1998 (*World Almanac and Book of Facts* 1999).
- The near meltdown of many Asian economies in the late 1990s had profound if temporary effects on the economies of the United States and Western Europe.
- Foreign-owned firms operating in the United States employ over 5 million workers, approximately one in ten manufacturing jobs.

and the European Economic Union are two examples of the recent globalization of markets. The result of the globalization of markets is that goods and services from all over the world are making their way into other cultures.

At the same time that world trade barriers are falling, a concomitant revolution is going on in the world of information technology. In the mid-1980s only a handful of people in the world could operate a computer. Today, computers are nearly as common in the home as the radio was in the 1940s. Moreover, the development of digitization, fiber optics, satellite communication, and the Internet now enables people to communicate with one another instantaneously. During the cold war days, grandparents in Pennsylvania had to wait several weeks to see a photograph of a new grandchild born in Istanbul. Today, however, a photo of the new baby can be taken in Istanbul with a digital camera, loaded into your laptop computer, and sent via e-mail to the grandparents in a matter of minutes. With the advent of e-commerce, anyone with a good product, a computer, a telephone, access to the Internet, a website, and a UPS account can become a potential entrepreneur. Globalization has encouraged the participation of large numbers of new players in the world markets. It is now possible to enter the global economy vir-

Anthropologists can serve as cross-cultural trainers for U.S. business people bound for overseas assignments.

tually overnight, with very little capital outlay, and become a global competitor by the next afternoon.

New York Times correspondent Thomas Freidman discusses the various dimensions of globalization in *The Lexus and the Olive Tree* (1999). He provides an insightful glimpse into our very rapidly changing world, a world dominated by global business and the rapid exchange of information. Friedman makes a number of interesting contrasts between the cold war and post–cold war eras.

- The defining symbol of the cold war era was the Berlin Wall, an immovable presence that functioned to separate people and ideas; the hallmark of globalization, on the other hand, is the Internet that functions to integrate people by facilitating communication.
- The concept of weight has been replaced by speed. During the cold war, the operative question was "How big is your missile?" The mantra for the new millenium is "How fast is your modem?"
- The mentality during the cold war was "us" versus "them," but the emerging globalized world sees all people as competitors.
- To make a sports analogy, the cold war era was like two sumo wrestlers trying to knock each other out of the ring; the era of globalization is like sprinters racing one another continually to be the first to get their share of global markets.

Clearly, the end of the cold war helped facilitate this new era of globalization, but it did not, in and of itself, cause it to happen. Several other monumental changes since the late 1980s also have defined globalization. First, the world has experienced a revolution in computer technology, which has made communication faster and cheaper for a rapidly growing segment of the world's population. To illustrate, the speed of computers during the 1990s has doubled every eighteen months, and the space on disks has increased 60 percent every year. Moreover, voice, music, videos, and photos can be digitized and sent cheaply and quickly over fiber-optic cable. Second, fundamental changes have occurred in the way we invest our money. During the cold war era, investing was done by the large banks, insurance companies, and investment firms; today it is, to a much larger degree, in the hands of individuals. At least in the industrialized world, individuals, not multibillion-dollar firms, are managing their own investments through mutual funds and 401K pension accounts. The ability to move one's personal investment funds around has been made even easier by e-trading on the Internet, which eliminates the need for a broker. Third, there has been a fundamental change in the flow of information all over the world. The walls and barriers so prominent during the cold war era allowed governments to control their populations through systematic control of information. As recently as the mid-1980s, copy machines in Russia and China were unavailable to anyone other than government officials because they posed a threat to government monopolies on the flow of information. Today, however, the availability of

The 5th Wave   By Rich Tennant

"He saw your laptop and wants to know if he can check his Hotmail."

the Internet permits the spread of ideas (and ideologies) across national boundaries with little government interference.

It has become a cliché to say that the world is becoming a global village. Rapid technological developments in transportation and communications in recent decades have brought the peoples of the world closer together in ways that we could barely imagine just a decade ago. The globalization of many companies has made it difficult to determine the home country of certain brands. Nike running shoes are made in Taiwan, BMWs are made in South Carolina, and some computer parts are manufactured in as many as a half-dozen different countries. Swissair has moved its entire accounting department to Bombay, India, to take advantage of lower labor costs of a highly educated workforce. Even the Carolina Panthers football team plays in a stadium named after a Swedish cell phone company. Moreover, businesses in a number of countries are gaining prominence in certain markets. To illustrate, India has become the world's leading producer of tractors, just as the French have dominated world markets in glass and the Europeans have taken ownership of most of the publishing industry in the United States. Unfortunately, despite the growing world interdependency, a concomitant revolution in cross-cultural understanding among all the peoples of the world has not occurred. And, of course, no one could argue that we have witnessed any degree of cultural homogenization of world populations. Instead, this rapid globalization of world economies is making the need for understanding the cultural dimension of our business enterprises increasingly *more* imperative, not less. Working, as many of us do today, with ultra highspeed technology in the world of e-commerce does not absolve us from having to understand the cultures (values and behaviors) of our customers, suppliers, or business partners. The cultural differences found in today's world are every bit as important in our cyber-businesses as they were a mere ten years ago when few people had even heard of the Internet.

During the nineteenth and much of the twentieth centuries, companies lived or died by the availability of physical resources, such as steel or plastics, which were used to manufacture their products. Commerce, as we have known it up until a few decades ago, was largely the exchange of material goods from producer to consumer. With the rapid globalization the world has experienced since the 1980s, however, a major shift has taken place away from physical commodities toward knowledge. In this new information age that is developing, it is people and the knowledge they possess that constitute the real competitive advantage. The organizations that will thrive in the twentieth century are those willing and able to mobilize, develop, and reward their key resources: people. They will need to develop what Robert Rosen refers to as "globally literate leaders, . . . who manage their own culture and the cultures of others" (2000, 24).

How well the United States will fare in this increasingly interdependent world in the decades to come is not altogether predictable. During the quarter of a century immediately following World War II, the United States enjoyed unprecedented and unparalleled economic success. Our postwar technologies gave rise to products that the world wanted, and we were very willing and able to supply everything from atomic energy and microelectronics to Levis and Big Macs. The United States, owing to its technology, managerial techniques, and investment capital, was in the enviable position of being the "only game in town." During this period our world market shares were large, and we enjoyed a healthy balance of payments. Then, in the early 1970s, the trade surpluses that we had enjoyed for so long disappeared, and we began to have trade deficits. Ironically, it was in 1976—our bicentennial year—that our trade accounts moved into a negative imbalance. The substantial trade deficit of over $9 billion in 1976 has risen dramatically since then.

Some have argued that this serious, negative trade imbalance is largely the result of unfair trade practices by some of our trading partners. However we might choose to explain it, the inescapable conclusion is that we are not selling our goods and services to the rest of the world as successfully as we did during the past. American businesses must realize that—despite what may have occurred in the past—the product will no longer sell itself. Since there are so many good products on the market today, the crucial factor in determining who makes the sale is not so much the intrinsic superiority of the product but rather the skill of the seller in understanding the dynamics of the transaction between oneself and the customer. A large part of that dynamic involves understanding the cultural differences and similarities operating in the global marketplace. Unfortunately, because of our relative success in the past, we are not particularly well equipped to meet the challenges of the international economic arena during the twenty-first century.

Part of the problem lies in the fact that many U.S. companies, particularly middle-sized ones, have not attempted to sustain sales and production by venturing into the international marketplace. Although there has been an increase during the 1980s in the number of U.S. firms that export, it remains that fewer than 1 percent of all U.S. companies are responsible for 80 percent of all U.S. exporting activities. Even though most U.S. corporations have competed successfully in domestic markets, with a unified language and business practices, they have not been very adept at coping with the wide range of different languages, customs, and cultural assumptions found in the international business arena. For many of the firms that do enter foreign markets, success has

---

One of the most eloquent statements of the need for international businesspeople to become better attuned to other languages and cultures was made by William Rugh, former U.S. ambassador to Yemen and the United Arab Emirates:

As the U.S. Ambassador to a wealthy country in the Persian Gulf for the past three years, I saw a constant stream of U.S. company representatives passing through our embassy on their way to try to sell their goods and services to local importers and local government officials. In an embarrassing number of cases, the businessman was woefully ignorant of even the basic rules of successful marketing in the Middle East. Seeing a number of lucrative opportunities snatched from us by savvy British or French or Japanese businessmen, who had taken the time to learn about the local culture and even some of the local language, I realized that some of my compatriots were very naive, and assumed that the sales pitch that worked in the United States would work anywhere abroad. Not necessarily. Some U.S. firms, which have been doing business in the region for a while, have learned the ropes, but many have not. (1995)

been inconsistent at best. Nowhere is this better illustrated than in the area of Americans living and working abroad.

Statistics on Americans returning from overseas working assignments before the end of their contracts vary widely throughout the international business literature. Estimates of attrition rates in the late 1970s ran as high as 65 to 85 percent for certain industries (Harris 1979, 49; Edwards 1978, 42). More recent figures, while not as high, still serve to illustrate how difficult it is for Americans to live and work successfully abroad. For example, Shari Caudron (1991, 27) cites premature returns of Americans living in Saudi Arabia to be as high as 68 percent; 36 percent in Japan; 27 percent in Brussels; and 18 percent in London, a city that one would expect most Americans to adjust to easily. Regardless of whether we are dealing with attrition rates of 68 percent or 18 percent, the costs are enormous. Considering that it costs a firm between three and five times an employee's base salary to keep that employee and his or her family in a foreign assignment (Greengard 1999, 106), the financial considerations alone can be staggering. These costs refer only to premature returns; there is no way of measuring the additional losses incurred by those firms whose personnel don't become such statistics. Those personnel who stay in their overseas assignments are frequently operating with decreased efficiency and, owing to their less than perfect adjustment to the foreign cultural environment, often cost their firms enormous losses in time, reputation, and successful contracts.

INTERNATIONAL COMPETENCY—A NATIONAL PROBLEM

The situation that has emerged in the 1990s is that as the world grows more interdependent, we Americans can no longer expect to solve all the world's problems by ourselves, nor is it possible to declare ourselves immune from them. If our nation is to continue to be a world leader, we must build deep into our national psyche the need for international competency—that is, a specialized knowledge of foreign cultures, including professional proficiency in languages, and an understanding of the major political, economic, and social variables affecting the conduct of international and intercultural affairs.

At the same time that we are faced with an ever-increasing need for international competency, the resources our nation is devoting to its development are declining. This problem is not limited to the area of business. It is, rather, a national problem that affects many aspects of American life, including our national security, diplomacy, scientific advancement, and international political relations, in addition to economics. Future generations of American businesspeople, however, must be drawn from the society at large, and it is this society, through its educational institutions, that has not in the past placed central importance on educating the general populace for international competence.

When compared with other countries, the United States does not stack up very well in terms of international or intercultural competence. A Gallup poll conducted for the National Geographic Society in the late 1980s revealed that Americans between the ages of eighteen and twenty four scored lower on geographic and cultural knowledge than did similarly aged young adults in the eight other industrialized nations in the study (Gallup, 1988). A Department of Education report in 1990 showed that one in six high school seniors in the United States thought that the Panama Canal shortened travel time between New York and London. The bad news continues. In a more recent study of 313 students at a major public university in the southwestern part of the United States, Raymond Eve, Bob Price, and Monika Counts (1994) found that only 43 percent were able to correctly identify Australia as the continent with coastlines on both the Pacific and Indian Oceans; only 42 percent correctly placed Libya in North Africa; and fewer than 50 percent knew that Portuguese was the primary language of Brazil. Moreover, the United States continues to be the only country in the world where it is possible to earn a college degree without taking any courses in a foreign language. Most American university students in fact graduate without any functional knowledge of a language other than English.

Given the relatively low priority that international competency has had in our educational institutions in recent years, it is not surprising that those Americans who are expected to function successfully in a multicultural environment are so poorly prepared for the task. If the international dimension is weak in our general education programs today, it is even weaker in our business school curricula. To illustrate, in the majority of M.B.A. programs in the United States, it is still possible to earn a degree without ever taking a single course in international business.

Although graduate schools in business have increased their international offerings over the past decade, courses on the cultural environment of international business have received relatively little attention. This basic neglect of cross-cultural issues in business education is generally reflected in the attitudes of the international business community. To illustrate, in a study of 127 U.S. firms with international operations, respondents showed very little concern for the cultural dimension of international business. When asked what should be included in the education of an international businessperson, respondents mentioned—almost without exception—only technical courses. In other words, very little interest was shown in language, culture, or history of one's foreign business partners (Reynolds and Rice, 1988, 56). As we enter the new millenium, however, evidence suggests that some companies are beginning to take these cultural considerations more seriously.

However we choose to measure it, Americans are poorly equipped to deal with the numerous challenges of our changing world. Whether we are talking about language competence, funding for international education, opportunities for foreign exchange, or simply the awareness of global knowledge, the inadequacies are real and potentially threatening to many areas of our national welfare, international business in particular. The

---

Whenever Westerners believe that other cultures have nothing worthwhile to offer, they are engaging in a type of cultural arrogance that can be self-defeating, as Professor Howard Perlmutter of the Wharton School of Business reminds us: "If you have a joint venture with a Japanese company, they'll send 24 people here to learn everything you know, and you'll send one person there to tell them everything you know. . . ." (Kupfer 1988, 58)

problem referred to in the literature as a national crisis has no easy solution. What is required initially is broad public awareness of the problem, followed by concerted actions on a number of fronts.

One way of helping to meet the challenge is by creating a dialogue between (1) people whose professions are directly and negatively affected by the problem and (2) cultural anthropologists, whose major objective is the comparative study of cultural systems. As a long-overdue corrective, this text focuses on how cultural variations can affect the conduct of international business.

2

Culture
and International Business
A Conceptual Approach

As mentioned in Chapter 1, anthropologists do more than simply accumulate and cat-alog information on the world's exotic and not so exotic cultures. Like other scientists, they attempt to generate theories about culture that apply to all human populations. Since it is impossible for any individual to master every cultural fact about every cul-ture in the world, a more theoretical approach can be instructive; that is, a number of general concepts about culture can be applied to a wide variety of cross-cultural situ-ations, regardless of whether one is dealing with Nigerians, Peruvians, or Appalachi-an coal miners.

In this chapter we explore what is meant—and what is not meant—by the term *culture*. In addition to defining this central anthropological concept, we also examine six important generalizations concerning the concept of culture and their significance for the U.S. businessperson operating in the world marketplace. Being equipped with such gen-eral concepts can facilitate the adjustment to an unfamiliar cultural environment.

CULTURE DEFINED

In everyday usage, the term *culture* refers to the finer things in life, such as the fine arts, literature, and philosophy. Under this very narrow definition of the term, the cultured person is one who prefers Handel to hard rock; can distinguish between the artistic styles of Monet and Manet; prefers pheasant under glass to grits and red-eye gravy and twelve-year-old scotch to beer; and spends his or her leisure time reading Kierkegaard rather than watching wrestling on television. For the anthropologist, however, the term *culture* has a much broader meaning that goes far beyond mere personal refinements. The only re-quirement for being cultured is to be human. Thus, all people have culture. The scantily clad Dani of New Guinea is as much a cultural animal as is Isaac Stern. For the anthropologist, cooking pots, spears, and mud huts are as legitimate items of culture as symphonies, oil paintings, and great works of literature.

The term *culture* has been defined in a variety of ways. Even anthropologists, who claim culture as their guiding conceptual principle, do not agree on a single definition of the term. In fact, A. L. Kroeber and C. Kluckhohn (1952) identified over 160 different definitions of culture. One of the earliest widely cited definitions, offered by Edward Tylor over a 125 years ago, defined *culture* as "that complex whole which includes knowledge, belief, art, morals, law, custom, and any other capabilities and habits acquired by man as a member of society" (1871, 1). More recently, Clyde Kluckhohn and W. H. Kelly have referred to culture as "all the historically created designs for living, explicit and implicit, rational, irrational, and nonrational, which exist at any given time as potential guides for the behavior of men" (1945, 97). M. J. Herskovits spoke of culture as being "the man made part of the environment" (1955, 305), and James Downs defined culture as being "a mental map which guides us in our relations to our surroundings and to other people" (1971, 35).

Running the risk of adding to the confusion, here is still another definition: *Culture is everything that people have, think, and do as members of their society.* The three verbs in this definition (*have, think*, and *do*) can help us identify the three major structural components of the concept of culture; that is, for a person to <u>have</u> something, some material object must be present. When people <u>think</u>, ideas, values, attitudes, and beliefs are present. When people <u>do</u>, they behave in certain socially prescribed ways. Thus, culture is made up of (1) material objects; (2) ideas, values, and attitudes; and (3) normative, or expected, patterns of behavior.

The final phrase of our working definition, "as members of their society," should serve as a reminder that culture is shared by at least two or more people. Real, live societies are of course always larger than that. In other words, there is no such thing as the

---

Anthropologist Hendrick Serrie has provided an excellent example of how an anthropological understanding of local cultural patterns in southern Mexico prevented the costly mistake of mass producing a solar cooker developed for this area (1986, xvi–xvii). Designed to reduce the use of firewood for cooking by encouraging the use of solar energy, these solar stoves, with the assistance of a four-foot parabolic reflector, produced levels of heat comparable to a wood fire. Although initial demonstrations of the cooker caught the interest of the local people, a number of cultural features militated against the widespread acceptance of this technological device. To illustrate, (1) the major part of the cooking in this part of Mexico is done early in the morning and in the early evenings, at those times when solar radiation is at its lowest level, and (2) although the solar stove was very effective for boiling beans and soup, it was inadequate for cooking tortillas, a basic staple in the local diet. Thus, for these and other cultural reasons, it was decided not to mass produce and market the solar cookers because, even though the cooker worked well *technically*, it made little sense *culturally*.

culture of a hermit. If a solitary individual thinks and behaves in a certain way, that thought or action is idiosyncratic, not cultural. For an idea, a thing, or a behavior to be considered cultural, it must be shared by some type of social group or society.

In addition to this working definition, a number of features of the concept of culture should be made explicit. In the remainder of this chapter, we briefly examine these features that hold true for all cultures, and discuss why they are valuable insights into the cultural environment of international business.

CULTURE IS LEARNED

Culture is transmitted through the process of learning and interacting with one's environment, rather than through the genetic process. Culture can be thought of as a storehouse of all the knowledge of a society. The child who is born into any society finds that the problems that confront all people have already been solved by those who have lived before. For example, material objects, methods for acquiring food, language, rules of government, forms of marriage, and systems of religion have already been discovered and are functioning within the culture when a child is born. If a male child is born into a small country village in Spain, for example, during his lifetime he will likely acquire his food by farming, pay allegiance to the Spanish government, enjoy bullfighting, and be a Catholic. If a male child is born into an East African herding society, in contrast, he will probably acquire his food from his cattle, obey the laws of his elders, spend his leisure time telling tribal folktales, and worship his ancestors as gods. Although these children will grow up to behave quite differently, one basic principle concerning culture is clear: Both children were born into an already existing culture. Each child has only to learn the various solutions to these basic human problems that his culture has set down for him. Once these solutions are learned, behavior becomes almost automatic. In other words, culture is passed on from one generation to another within a society. It is not inborn or instinctive.

If the power of cultural learning needs documentation, one only has to cite the cases of extremely isolated children. Today, there are a number of tragic yet well-documented instances of infants who have been shut away in closets or attics with only the barest minimum of human contact during their formative years. One such case was that of Anna, who at nearly six years of age was found tied to a chair in the attic of her grandfather's house in a condition that was barely human. According to Kingsley Davis, "She had no glimmering of speech, absolutely no ability to walk, no sense of gesture, not the least capacity to feed herself . . . and no comprehension of cleanliness" (1947, 434). At age eight and a half, after spending three years in a home for retarded children, Anna had made dramatic progress in developing human characteristics. She could bounce and catch a ball, she had become toilet trained, she could feed and dress herself, and she had developed a speech proficiency of about a normal two-year-old.

Since Anna had received virtually no socialization or meaningful human interaction during the first six years of her life, her early motor and mental retardation was clearly the direct result of this human deprivation. She had few, if any, opportunities to learn her culture. In the absence of such learning, infants cannot hope to develop into

> The learned nature of culture is dramatically illustrated by Amram Scheinfeld, who writes of an American-Chinese man:
>
> Fung Kwok Keung, born Joseph Rhinehart (of German-American stock), who, at the age of two, was adopted by a Chinese man on Long Island and three years later taken to China, where he was reared in a small town (Nam Hoy, near Canton) with the family of his foster father until he was 20. Returning then to New York (in 1928), he was so completely Chinese in all but appearance that he had to be given "Americanization" as well as English lessons to adapt him to his new life. A few years later, after the outbreak of World War II, he was drafted into the American army and sent to Italy. In many ways he was alien to the other American soldiers and tried continuously to be transferred to service in China, but army red tape held him fast in Italy until the war's end. Back again in New York, Rhinehart-Fung at this writing works as a compositor on a Chinese newspaper (an intricate job which few but Chinese could handle), and stills speaks English very imperfectly, with a Chinese accent. (1950, 505)

functioning humans. The significance of this tragic case demonstrates how little one's biological resources, when taken alone, can contribute to one's humanness.

Despite the enormous variations in the details of cultures throughout the world, all people acquire their culture through the same process: learning. It is sometimes easy to fall into the trap of thinking that since the Australian Bushman and the Central African Pygmy do not know what we know, they must be childlike, ignorant, and generally incapable of learning. These primitives, the argument goes, have not learned about calculus, Shakespeare, or the Los Angeles Dodgers because they are not as intelligent as we are. Yet no evidence whatsoever suggests even remotely that people in some cultures are less efficient learners than people in other cultures. What the comparative study of culture does tell us is that people in different cultures learn different cultural content—that is, different ideas, values, behavior patterns, and so on—and they learn that content every bit as efficiently as anyone else. For example, despite the inability of the average Kikuyu of East Africa to solve a problem by using differential equations, they would be able to recite exactly how they are related (step by step) to a network of hundreds of kinspeople. Kikuyu farmers have mastered what to us is a bewildering amount of kinship information because their culture places great emphasis on such knowledge if the rather complex Kikuyu marriage and kinship system is to work. The Bushman hunters in Namibia are at ease in determining which direction the wounded impala traveled when the herd they have been tracking split and went in two different directions. Such a problem for them is certainly no harder to solve than a typical verbal problem found on the S.A.T. exam: "A is to B as B is to?" And it is more relevant to their everyday survival. Hence, people from different cultures learn those things that contribute to adjusting to their particular environments.

This notion that culture is acquired through the process of learning has several important implications for the conduct of international business. First, such an understanding can lead to greater tolerance for cultural differences, a prerequisite for effective intercultural communication within a business setting. Second, the learned nature of culture

Even though these children have very different life styles from children in the United States, they acquire their culture through the same process—learning.

serves as a reminder that since we have mastered our own culture through the process of learning, it is possible (albeit more difficult) to learn to function in other cultures as well. Thus, cross-cultural expertise for Western businesspeople can be accomplished through effective training programs. Finally, the learned nature of culture leads us to the inescapable conclusion that foreign workforces, although perhaps lacking certain job-related skills at the present time, are perfectly capable of learning those skills in the future, provided they are exposed to culturally relevant training programs.

CULTURE INFLUENCES BIOLOGICAL PROCESSES

If we stop to consider it, the great majority of our conscious behavior is acquired through learning and interacting with other members of our culture. Even those responses to our purely biological needs (eating, coughing, defecating) are frequently influenced by our cultures. For example, all people share a biological need for food. Unless a minimum number of calories is consumed, starvation will occur; therefore, all people eat. But *what* we eat, *how often* and, *how much* we eat, *with whom* we eat, and *according to what set of rules* are all regulated, at least in part, by our culture.

Clyde Kluckhohn, an anthropologist who spent many years in Arizona and New Mexico studying the Navajo, provides us with a telling example of how culture affects biological processes:

I once knew a trader's wife in Arizona who took a somewhat devilish interest in producing a cultural reaction. Guests who came her way were often served delicious sandwiches filled with a meat that seemed to be neither chicken nor tuna fish yet was reminiscent of both. To queries she gave no reply until each had eaten his fill. She then explained that what they had eaten was not chicken, not tuna fish, but the rich, white flesh of freshly killed rattlesnakes. The response was instantaneous—vomiting, often violent vomiting. A biological process is caught into a cultural web. (1968, 25–26)

This is a dramatic illustration of how culture can influence biological processes. In fact, in this instance, the natural biological process of digestion was not only influenced but also was reversed. A learned part of our culture (the idea that rattlesnake meat is a repulsive thing to eat) actually triggered the sudden interruption of the normal digestive process. Clearly, there is nothing in rattlesnake meat that causes people to vomit, for those who have internalized the opposite idea—that rattlesnake meat should be eaten— have no such digestive tract reversals.

The effects of culturally produced ideas on our bodies and their natural processes take many different forms. For example, instances of the voluntary control of pain reflexes are found in a number of cultures throughout the world. Among the nineteenth-century Cheyenne nation, as part of the religious ceremony known as the Sun Dance, young men were taught that self-inflicted pain was a way to achieve supernatural visions. One popular method of self-torture was to remain suspended from the top of a high pole, supported only by leather thongs attached to wooden skewers inserted under the skin of the chest or back. The Cheyenne believed that by remaining in what must have been an excruciatingly painful position for long periods of time without showing signs of pain, the young men were able to communicate more directly with the deity. The ritual firewalkers from Fiji are similarly motivated to control pain reflexes voluntarily, for they believe that the capacity to not show pain brings people closer to those supernatural forces that control their lives. The ethnographic examples are too numerous to cite, but whether we are looking at Cheyenne men engaged in the Sun Dance ceremony, Fiji firewalkers, or U.S. women practicing the Lamaze (psychoprophylactic) method of childbirth, the principle is the same: People learn ideas from their cultures that when internalized can actually alter the experience of pain. In other words, a component of culture (that is, ideas) can channel or influence biologically based pain reflexes.

Those nontangible parts of culture, composed of ideas, values, beliefs, and so on, can have powerful effects on the human body. For anyone familiar with the pages of *National Geographic*, the variety of forms of bodily mutilation found throughout human populations is vast. People alter their bodies because their cultures teach them that to do so will make them more attractive, healthier, or more socially acceptable. For instance, women in the Padaung tribe in Burma elongate their necks by wearing large numbers of steel neck rings; Masai men and women in East Africa put increasingly larger pieces of wood through their earlobes, thereby creating loops in their ears; men in New Guinea put bones through their noses; traditional Chinese women had their feet tightly bound as young girls to retard the growth of their feet; Nubians in the Sudan scar their faces and bodies in intricate geometric designs; Pacific Islanders practice elaborate body tattooing; and the Kikuyu of Kenya circumcise both men and women as part of the rite of passage into adulthood. It has even been reported that a group of people living between Canada and Mexico engage in the somewhat barbaric practice of putting holes in their earlobes for the purpose of hanging pieces of jewelry from them. And they practice this type of bodily mutilation for the very same reason that people tattoo their bodies, scar their faces, or put bones through their noses—because their cultures teach them that it is the acceptable thing to do.

The effects that cultural ideas have on our bodies and our bodily processes are not always as benign as the piercing of ears. For example, many of the forms of bodily mutilation—such as circumcision, tattooing, and scarification—can have deleterious effects on one's health, such as the spread of infection. As reported by W. Cannon (1942), individuals whose cultures include witchcraft can be so thoroughly convinced that they are being bewitched that the resulting severe disturbances of bodily functioning end in death. In the United States it has been suggested that a possible explanation for the greater incidence of urinary tract infections among women is that, for purely social purposes, they avoid urinating more than do men, thereby causing greater stress on the bladder and the greater likelihood of infection. Moreover, the cultural idea of associating slimness with feminine attractiveness in the United States, when taken to excess, can lead to the life-threatening condition of anorexia.

The basic anthropological notion that culture channels biological processes can provide some important insights for the international businessperson when confronted with cross-cultural managerial or marketing problems. For example, in Bombay such a concept should be a reminder not to serve beef noodle soup in the company cafeteria, for to do so might cause a mass exodus to the infirmary. Or if we know that strongly held cultural beliefs in, for example, witchcraft can produce physiological maladies that can render the normally efficient worker dysfunctional, it would be reasonable for the company to have in its employ a local ritual specialist capable of counteracting the witchcraft. It is interesting to speculate if there would have been an infant formula controversy had Western manufacturers of this product understood the connection between low-level technology in third-world cultures (lack of unpolluted water, fuel supplies, and refrigeration) and the high mortality rates among those infants using the formula.

CULTURAL UNIVERSALS

All cultures of the world—despite many differences—face a number of common problems and share a number of common features, which we call cultural universals. Even the most casual perusal of an introductory textbook in cultural anthropology leads us to the inescapable conclusion that there are many societies with their own unique cultures. The determination of how many different cultures exist today depends largely on how one defines the problem, a definitional question on which there is hardly consensus among the world's anthropologists. We can get a rough approximation of world cultural variation by realizing that approximately 850 separate and distinct cultures (speaking mutually unintelligible languages) are on the continent of Africa alone. Rather than being

Here are two examples of how cultural ideas concerning beauty affect how women adorn themselves.

preoccupied with the precise number of cultures in the world at any one time, we should emphasize the significance of the variability; that is, the great number of differences between cultures illustrates how flexible and adaptable humans are in relation to other animals, for each culture has arrived at different solutions to the universal human problems facing all societies.

As we encounter the many different cultural patterns found throughout the world, there is a natural tendency to become overwhelmed by the magnitude of the differences and overlook the commonalities. Even anthropologists, when describing "their people," tend to emphasize the uniqueness of the culture and only infrequently look at the similarities between cultures. But *all* societies, if they are to survive, are confronted with fundamental universal needs that must be satisfied. When cultures develop ways of meeting these needs, general cultural patterns emerge. At a very concrete level, differences in the details of cultural patterns exist because different societies have developed different ways of meeting these universal societal needs. Yet at a higher level of abstraction, a number of commonalities exist because all cultures have worked out solutions to certain problems facing all human populations. Let's briefly examine the needs that all cultures must satisfy and the universal cultural patterns that emerge to satisfy these needs.

Economic Systems

One of the most obvious and immediate needs of a society is to meet the basic physiological requirements of its people. To stay alive, all humans need a certain minimal caloric intake, potable water, and, to varying degrees, protection from the elements in terms of clothing and shelter. No societies in the world have access to an infinite supply of such basic resources as food, water, clothing, and housing materials. Since these commodities are always in finite supply, each society must develop systematic ways of producing, distributing, and consuming these essential resources. Thus, each society must develop an *economic system*.

To illustrate this principle of cultural universals, we can look at one component of economic systems—namely, forms of distribution. Besides working out patterned ways of producing basic material goods (or procuring them from the immediate environment), all societies must ensure that these goods are distributed to all those members of the society whose very survival depends on receiving them. In the United States, most goods and services are distributed according to the capitalistic mode, based on the principle of "each according to his or her capacity to pay." In such socialist countries as the People's Republic of China, Albania, and Cuba, goods and services are distributed according to another quite different principle—that is, "each according to his or her need."

These two well-known systems of distribution hardly exhaust the range of possibilities found in the world. The Pygmies of Central Africa distribute goods by a system known as "silent barter," in which the trading partners, in an attempt to attain true reciprocity, avoid face-to-face contact during the exchange. The Bushmen of present-day

Namibia distribute the meat of an animal killed in the hunt according to the principle of kinship— each share of meat is determined by how one is related to the hunter. But whatever particular form the system of distribution might take, there are no societies—at least not for long—that have failed to work out and adhere to a well-understood and systematic pattern of distribution.

Marriage and Family Systems

For a society to continue over time, it is imperative that it work out systematic procedures for mating, child rearing, and education. If it fails to do this, it will die in a very short time. No society permits random mating, for all societies have worked out rules for determining who can marry whom, under what conditions, and according to what procedures. All societies, in other words, have patterned systems of *marriage*. And since human infants (as compared with the young of other species) have a particularly long period of dependency on adults, every society needs to work out systematic ways of meeting the needs of dependent children. If the basic needs of dependent children are not satisfied, they simply will not survive to adulthood; consequently, the very survival of the society is in jeopardy. Thus, we can say that all societies have patterns of child rearing and family institutions.

Educational Systems

Along with ensuring that the basic physical needs of the child are met, a society must see to it that the children learn the way of life of the society. Rather than expecting each new child to rediscover for himself or herself all the accumulated knowledge of the past, a society must have an organized way of passing on its cultural heritage from one generation to another. This universal societal need for cultural transmission gives rise to some form of *educational system* in every society.

Social Control Systems

If groups of people are to survive, they must develop some established ways of preserving social order; that is, all societies must develop mechanisms that will ensure that most of the people obey most of the laws most of the time. If this need is not met, people will violate each other's rights to such an extent that anarchy will prevail. Certainly, different societies meet this need for social order in different ways. In the United States, behavior control rests on a number of formal mechanisms, such as a written constitution; local, state, and federal laws; and an elaborate system of police, courts, and penal institutions, among other things. Many small-scale, technologically simple societies have less formal means of controlling the behavior of their members. Regardless of the specific methods used, one thing is certain: Every society has a system for coercing people to obey the social rules, and these are called *social control systems*.

Although the marriage practices in Africa and the United States differ in many ways, both practices are responses to the universal need to have an orderly system of mating and child rearing.

Supernatural Belief Systems

All societies have a certain degree of control over their social and physical environments. All people in a society can understand and predict a number of things. For example, a heavy object when dropped into a lake will sink to the bottom; if I have $5 and give you $2, I will have only $3 left; the sun always rises in the east and sets in the west. However, we cannot explain or predict with any degree of certainty many other things: Why does a child develop a fatal disease, but the child's playmate next door does not? Why do tornadoes destroy some houses and leave others unharmed? Why do safe drivers die in auto accidents and careless drivers do not? Such questions have no apparent answers, for they cannot be explained by our conventional systems of justice or rationality. Therefore, societies must develop *supernatural belief systems* for explaining these unexplainable occurrences. The way people explain the unexplainable is to rely on various types of supernatural explanations such as magic, religion, witchcraft, sorcery, and astrology.

Thus, despite the great variety in the details of cultural features found throughout the world, all cultures, because they must satisfy certain universal needs, have a number of traits in common. This basic anthropological principle, known as *cultural universals*, can be an important tool for helping international businesspeople more fully understand and appreciate culturally different business environments. Greater empathy for cultural differences—a necessary if not sufficient condition for increased knowledge—can be

attained if we can avoid concentrating solely on the apparent differences between cultures but appreciate their underlying commonalities as well. According to Richard Robinson,

> The successful international manager is one who sees and feels the similarity of structure of all societies. The same set of variables are seen to operate, although their relative weights may be very different. This capacity is far more important than possession of specific area expertise, which may be gained quite rapidly if one already has an ability to see similarities and ask the right questions—those that will provide the appropriate values or weights for the relevant variables. Such an individual can very quickly orient himself on the sociocultural map. (1983, 127)

In other words, we will be less likely to prejudge or be critical of different practices, ideas, or behavior patterns if we can appreciate the notion that they represent different solutions to the same basic human problems facing all cultures of the world, including our own.

CULTURAL CHANGE

All cultures experience continual change. Any anthropological account of the culture of any society is a type of snapshot view of one particular time. Should the ethnographer return several years after completing a cultural study, he or she would not find exactly the same situation, for no culture remains completely static year after year. Early twentieth-century anthropologists—particularly those of the structural/functional orientation—tended to de-emphasize cultural dynamics by suggesting that some societies were in a state of equilibrium in which the forces of change were negated by those of cultural conservatism. Although small-scale, technologically simple, preliterate societies tend to be more conservative (and thus change less rapidly) than modern, industrialized, highly complex societies, it is now generally accepted that, to some degree, change is a constant feature of all cultures.

Students of culture change recognize that cultural innovation (the introduction of new thoughts, norms, or material items) occurs as a result of both internal and external forces. Mechanisms of change that operate within a given culture are called *discovery* and *invention*. Despite the importance of discovery and invention, most innovations introduced into a culture are the result of borrowing from other cultures. This process is known as *cultural diffusion*, the spreading of cultural items from one culture to another. The importance of cultural borrowing can be better understood if viewed in terms of economy of effort: Borrowing someone else's invention or discovery is much easier than discovering or inventing it all over again. Anthropologists generally agree that as much as 90 percent of all things, ideas, and behavioral patterns found in any culture had their origins elsewhere. Individuals in every culture, limited by background and time, can get new ideas with far less effort if they borrow them. This statement holds true for our own culture as well as other cultures, a fact that Americans frequently tend to overlook.

Since so much cultural change is the result of diffusion, it deserves a closer examination. Keeping in mind that cultural diffusion varies considerably from situation to situation, we can identify certain regularities that will help us make some general statements that hold true for all cultures.

First, cultural diffusion is a *selective process*. Whenever two cultures come into contact, each does not accept everything indiscriminately from the other. If they did, the vast cultural differences that exist today would have long since disappeared. Rather, items will be borrowed from another culture only if they prove to be useful and/or compatible. For example, we would not expect to see the diffusion of swine husbandry from the United States to Saudi Arabia, the predominant Muslim population of which holds a strong dietary prohibition on pork. Similarly, polyandry (the practice of a woman having two or more legal husbands at a time) is not likely to be borrowed by the United States because of its obvious lack of fit with other features of mainstream American culture. Successful international marketing requires an intimate knowledge of the cultures found in foreign markets to determine if, how, and to what extent specific products are likely to become accepted by these foreign cultures.

According to a study by Everett Rogers (1971, 22–23), the rapidity with which an innovation is adopted—or, indeed, whether it will be adopted at all—is affected by the following five variables:

1. *Relative advantage*: the extent to which an innovation is thought to be superior to whatever it replaces
2. *Compatibility*: the extent to which an innovation is perceived to be congruous with the existing cultural values, attitudes, behavior patterns, and material objects

Culture historian Ralph Linton reminds us of the enormous amount of cultural borrowing that has taken place in order to produce the complex culture found in the United States:

> Our solid American citizen awakens in a bed built on a pattern which originated in the Near East but which was modified in Northern Europe before it was transmitted to America. He throws back covers made from cotton, domesticated in India, or linen, domesticated in the Near East, or wool from sheep, also domesticated in the Near East, or silk, the use of which was discovered in China. All of these materials have been spun and woven by processes invented in the Near East. He slips into his moccasins, invented by the Indians of the Eastern woodlands, and goes to the bathroom, whose fixtures are a mixture of European and American inventions, both of recent date. He takes off his pajamas, a garment invented in India, and washes with soap invented by the ancient Gauls. He then shaves, a masochistic rite which seems to have been derived from either Sumer or ancient Egypt.
>
> Returning to the bedroom, he removes his clothes from a chair of southern European type and proceeds to dress. He puts on garments whose form originally derived from the skin clothing of the nomads of the Asiatic steppes, puts on shoes made from skins tanned by a process invented in ancient Egypt and cut to a pattern derived from the classical civilizations of the Mediterranean, and ties around his neck a strip of bright-colored cloth which is a vestigial survival of the shoulder shawls worn by the seventeenth-century Croatians. Before going out for breakfast he glances through the window, made of glass invented in Egypt, and if it is raining puts on overshoes made of rubber discovered by the Central American Indians and takes an umbrella, invented in southeastern Asia. Upon his head he puts a hat made of felt, a material invented in the Asiatic steppes.
>
> On his way to breakfast he stops to buy a paper, paying for it with coins, an ancient Lydian invention. At the restaurant a whole new series of borrowed elements confronts him. His plate is made of a form of pottery invented in China. His knife is of steel, an alloy first made in southern India, his fork a medieval Italian invention, and his spoon a derivative of a Roman original. He begins breakfast with an orange, from the eastern Mediterranean, a canteloupe from Persia, or perhaps a piece of African watermelon. With this he has coffee, an Abyssinian plant, with cream and sugar. Both the domestication of cows and the idea of milking them originated in the Near East, while sugar was first made in India. After his fruit and first coffee he goes on to waffles, cakes made by a Scandinavian technique from wheat domesticated in Asia Minor. Over these he pours maple syrup, invented by the Indians of the Eastern woodlands. As a side dish he may have the egg of a species of bird domesticated in Indo-China, or thin strips of the flesh of an animal domesticated in Eastern Asia which have been salted and smoked by a process developed in northern Europe.
>
> When our friend has finished eating he settles back to smoke, an American Indian habit, consuming a plant domesticated in Brazil in either a pipe, derived from the Indians of Virginia, or a cigarette, derived from Mexico. If he is hardy enough he may even attempt a cigar, transmitted to us from the Antilles by way of Spain. While smoking he reads the news of the day, imprinted in characters invented by the ancient Semites upon a material invented in China by a process invented in Germany. As he absorbs the accounts of foreign troubles he will, if he is a good conservative citizen, thank a Hebrew deity in an Indo-European language that he is 100 percent American. (1936, 326–27).

3. *Complexity*: the ease with which an innovation can be understood and utilized
4. *Trialability*: the degree to which an innovation can be tested on a limited basis
5. *Observability*: the extent to which people in the society can see the positive benefits of the innovation

Put another way, an innovation is most likely to be diffused into a recipient culture if (1) it is seen to be superior to what already exists, (2) it is consistent with existing cultural patterns, (3) it is easily understood, (4) it can be tested on an experimental basis, and (5) its benefits are clearly visible to a relatively large number of people. These five variables should be considered by international business strategists when considering the introduction of new marketing or managerial concepts into a foreign culture.

Second, cultural borrowing is a two-way process. Early students of change believed that contact between "primitive" societies and "civilized" societies caused the former to accept traits from the latter. This position was based on the assumption that the "inferior" primitive societies had nothing to offer the "superior" civilized societies. Today, however, anthropologists would reject such a position, for it has been found time and again that cultural traits are diffused in both directions.

European contact with Native Americans is a case in point. Native Americans, to be certain, have accepted a great deal from Europeans, but diffusion in the other direction has been significant. For example, it has been estimated that those crops that make up nearly half of the world's food supply were originally domesticated by Native American (Driver 1961, 584). These include corn, beans, squash, sweet potatoes, and the so-called Irish potato. Native Americans have given the world such articles of clothing as woolen ponchos, parkas, and moccasins, not to mention American varieties of cotton, a material used widely throughout the world for making clothing. Even the multibillion-dollar pharmaceutical industry in the Western world continues to produce and market commercial drugs first discovered by Native Americans, including such painkillers as cocaine and novacaine, anesthetics, quinine, and laxatives.

Third, very infrequently are borrowed items ever transferred into the recipient culture in exactly their original form. Rather, new ideas, objects, or techniques are usually reinterpreted and reworked so that they can be integrated more effectively into the total configuration of the recipient culture. Lowell Holmes has offered an illuminating example of how the form of a particular innovation from Italy (pizza) has been modified after its incorporation into U.S. culture:

> Originally, this Italian pie was made with mozzarella or scamorza cheese, tomatoes, highly spiced sausage, oregano spice, and a crust made of flour, water, olive oil and yeast. Although this type of pizza is still found in most eastern cities, and in midwestern ones as well, in many cases the dish has been reinterpreted to meet midwestern taste preferences for bland food. Authentic Italian pizza in such states as Kansas, Missouri, Iowa, Nebraska, or the Dakotas is often considered too spicy; therefore, it is possible to purchase in restaurants or in supermarkets pizzas that are topped with American process cheese, have no oregano at all, and in place of spiced sausage, hamburger or even tuna fish rounds out the Americanized version. In many home recipes, the crust is made of biscuit mix. Although the Italians would hardly recognize it, it still carries the name pizza and has become extremely popular. (1971, 361–62)

Sometimes the reinterpretation process involves a change in function but not form. While conducting fieldwork in East Africa, I observed an example of how the function of an object from one culture can be changed upon adoption into a recipient culture. The Masai, not unlike some other ethnic groups in Kenya and Tanzania, practice the custom of piercing their earlobes and enlarging the hole by inserting increasingly larger pieces of wood until a loop of skin is formed. One group of Masai, rather than stretching out their earlobes with pieces of wood, used instead flashlight batteries obtained from the United States. Although the form of the batteries remained unchanged, the function was definitely reinterpreted.

Fourth, some cultural traits are more easily diffused than others. By and large, technological innovations are more likely to be borrowed than are social patterns or belief systems, largely because the usefulness of a particular technological trait can be recognized quickly. For example, a man who walks five miles each day to work quickly realizes that an automobile can get him to work faster and with far less effort. It is much more difficult, however, to convince a Muslim to become a Hindu or an American middle-class businessperson to become a socialist.

It is important for the international businessperson to understand that to some degree all cultures are constantly experiencing change. The three basic components of culture (things, ideas, and behavior patterns) can undergo additions, deletions, or modifications. Some components die out, new ones are accepted, and existing ones can be changed in some observable way. Although the pace of culture change varies from society to society, when viewing cultures over time, there is nothing as constant as change. This straightforward anthropological insight should remind the international businessperson of the following: (1) Any cultural environment today is not exactly the same as it was last year or will be one year hence; the cultural environment therefore needs constant monitoring. (2) Despite a considerable lack of fit between the culture of a U.S. corporation operating abroad and its overseas workforce, the very fact that cultures do change provides some measure of optimism that the cultural gap can eventually be closed.

Moreover, the notion of cultural diffusion has important implications for the conduct of international business. Whether one is attempting to create new markets abroad or instill new attitudes and behaviors in a local workforce, understanding that cultural diffusion is selective is imperative. To know with some degree of predictability which things, ideas, and behaviors are likely to be accepted by a particular culture, those critical variables affecting diffusion—such as relative advantage, compatibility, and observability—should be understood.

The concept that cultural diffusion is a two-way process should help international managers be more receptive to the idea that the corporate culture, as well as the local culture, may change. The local culture may in fact have a good deal to offer the corporate culture, provided the corporate culture is open to accepting these new cultural features.

An understanding that cultural diffusion frequently involves some modification of the item is an important idea for those interested in creating new product markets in other cultures. To illustrate, before a laundry detergent—normally packaged in a green box in

Most culture change occurs through a process of diffusion.

the United States—would be accepted in certain parts of West Africa, the color of the packaging would need to be changed because the color green is associated with death in certain West African cultures.

Also, the idea that some components of culture are more readily accepted than others into different cultural environments should at least provide some general guidelines for assessing what types of changes in the local culture are more likely to occur. By assessing what types of things, ideas, and behavior have been incorporated into a culture in recent years, strategic planners should better understand the relative ease or difficulty involved in initiating changes in consumer habits or workplace behavior.

So far we have examined how an understanding of the concept of culture change can facilitate the management of change that will inevitably occur in both the U.S. corporate culture operating abroad and the local indigenous culture. Such theoretical understanding, however, does not relieve the corporation of its ethical responsibilities for influencing change in the most humane and nondestructive fashion. The creation of new markets solely for the sake of increasing markets, with no concern for the effects of those products on the local populations, is absolutely indefensible. Likewise, an overly heavy-handed approach in coercing local workers to change their attitudes and behaviors is both unethical and is likely to be counterproductive as well. In short, any conceptual understanding about culture change carries with it the very strong imperative that it be applied in an ethical manner and with a genuine concern for the well-being of the people whose culture is being changed.

ETHNOCENTRISM

All cultures—to one degree or another—display ethnocentrism, which is perhaps the greatest single obstacle to understanding another culture. *Ethnocentrism*—literally "culture centered," is the tendency for people to evaluate a foreigner's behavior by the standards of their own culture and to believe that their own culture is superior to all others. Since our own culture is usually the only one we learn (or at least the first), we take our culture for granted, assuming that our behavior is correct and all others are wrong. The extent to which ethnocentrism pervades a culture is clearly seen in our history textbooks. Consider, for example, the historic event of the Holy Wars between the Christians and the Muslims during the Middle Ages. In our textbook accounts of the wars, we refer to the Christians as crusaders and the Muslims as religious fanatics. Yet if we read the Islamic accounts of the wars, the terms *crusaders* and *fanatics* would be reversed.

A similarly poignant illustration of ethnocentric interpretations of the same historic events became apparent to me when I was doing fieldwork among the Kikuyu of Kenya and read approximately sixty years of colonial reports from the Kenya National Archives. The British District Commissioners, when describing any Kikuyu involved in the so-called Mau Mau rebellion of the 1950s, consistently used the term *terrorist*. However, when Kikuyu informants were asked about their lives during the 1950s, they would respond proudly that they were *freedom fighters*. Quite obviously, the connotations of these two terms are radically different. In this instance, both the British officials and the Kikuyu were seeing these tragic historical events from their own narrow cultural perspective.

No society has a monopoly on ethnocentrism, for it is found in all societies. Every society with its own distinct culture has the tendency to refer to themselves as "us" and everyone else as "them." People come to feel that they are the center of the world, and everyone and everything revolves around them. For example, there are a number of non-Western societies whose name for themselves means "man" or "people," the implication being that all outsiders are somewhat less than human. The ancient Chinese felt that unless a person spoke Chinese and observed Chinese customs, he or she was a barbarian. The Masai of East Africa have long felt that their god had given them all the cattle in the world. Whenever they encountered non-Masai with cattle, they felt perfectly justified in taking them back, thinking they must have been acquired illegally.

Sometimes our own ethnocentrism can startle us when we find ourselves in a different cultural setting. A particularly revealing episode occurred when an American vis-

---

Sharon Ruhley tells a rather humorous story of ethnocentrism:

Two U.S. tourists in Germany . . . were traveling on a public bus when one of them sneezed. A German turned around and said, sympathetically, "Gesundheit." The U.S. tourist commented, "How nice that he speaks English." If the German understood the comment, he may have had reason to question the tourist's intellect. (1982, 29)

ited a Japanese classroom for the first time. On the wall of the classroom was a brightly colored map of the world. But something was wrong: directly in the center of the map (where he had expected to see the United States) was Japan. To his surprise, the Japanese did not view the United States as the center of the world.

A fundamental assumption of ethnocentric people is that their way of doing things is right, proper, and normal and those ways practiced by culturally different people are wrong and inferior. Such a blanket condemnation of cultural differences prevents us from seeing that other people view our customs as equally strange and irrational. For example, people in the United States think of themselves as being particularly conscious of cleanliness. As a nation we probably spend more money per capita on a whole host of commercial products designed to make ourselves and our environments clean, hygienic, and odor free. Yet a number of practices found in the United States strike people in other parts of the world as deplorably unclean. To illustrate, whereas most Americans are repulsed by an Indonesian who blows his nose onto the street, the Indonesian is repulsed by the American who blows his nose in a handkerchief and then carries it around for the rest of the day in his pocket; the Japanese consider the American practice of sitting in a bathtub full of dirty, soapy water to be at best an ineffective way of bathing and at worst a disgusting practice; and East Africans think that Americans have no sense of hygiene because they defecate in rooms (the bathroom) that are frequently located adjacent to that part of the house where food is prepared (the kitchen).

All people in all societies are ethnocentric to some degree regardless of how accepting or open minded they might claim to be. Our ethnocentrism should not be a source of embarrassment for it is a natural by-product of growing up in our society. In fact, ethnocentrism may serve the positive function of enhancing group solidarity by discouraging assimilation into another culture and legitimizing the existing cultural group. On the

---

A particularly revealing illustration of how some Western customs can strike non-Westerners as offensive has been reported by E. Royston Pike in his discussion of kissing:

What's so strange about a kiss? Surely kissing is one of the most natural things in the world, so natural indeed that we might almost ask, what are lips for if not for kissing? But this is what we think, and a whole lot of people think very differently. To them kissing is not at all natural. It is not something that everybody does, or would like to do. On the contrary, it is a deplorable habit, unnatural, unhygienic, bordering on the nasty and even definitely repulsive.

When we come to look into the matter, we shall find that there is a geographical distribution of kissing; and if some enterprising ethnologist were to prepare a "map of kissing" it would show a surprisingly large amount of blank space. Most of the so-called primitive races of mankind, such as the New Zealanders (Maoris), the Australian aborigines, the Papuans, Tahitians, and other South Sea Islanders, and the Esquimaux of the frozen north, were ignorant of kissing until they were taught the technique by the white men. . . . The Chinese have been wont to consider kissing as vulgar and all too suggestive of cannibalism. . . . (1967, 11–12)

other hand, ethnocentrism can contribute to prejudice, contempt for outsiders, and intergroup conflict. Although it is a deeply ingrained attitude found in every society, it is important that we become aware of it so that it will not hinder us in learning about other cultures. Awareness of our own ethnocentrism will never eliminate it but will enable us to minimize its negative effects. It is vital for businesspeople to refrain from comparing our way of life with those of our international business partners. Instead, we should seek to understand other people in the context of their unique historical, social, and cultural backgrounds.

CULTURES ARE INTEGRATED WHOLES

Cultures should be thought of as integrated wholes—that is, cultures are coherent and logical systems, the parts of which to a degree are interrelated. Upon confronting an unfamiliar cultural trait, a usual response is to try to imagine how such a trait would fit into one's own culture; that is, we look at it ethnocentrically, or from our own cultural perspective. All too frequently we view an unfamiliar cultural item as simply a pathological version of one found in our own culture. We reason that if the foreign cultural item is different and unfamiliar, it must be deviant, strange, weird, irrational, and consequently inferior to its counterpart in our own culture. This ethnocentric interpretation, with its unfortunate consequences, is the result of pulling the item from its proper cultural context and viewing it from the perspective of another culture. It is also the result of the individual's inability to see the foreign culture as an integrated system.

When we say that a culture is integrated, it is an organized system in which particular components may be related to other components, not just a random assortment of customs. If we can view cultures as integrated systems, we can begin to see how particular culture traits fit into the integrated whole and consequently how they tend to make sense within that context. Equipped with such an understanding, international businesspeople should be in a better position to cope with the "strange" customs encountered in the international business arena.

Perhaps a specific example will help clarify this notion of integrated culture. Most Americans have difficulty identifying with the marital practice of polygyny (a man having two or more wives at the same time). In addition to general misgivings about polygyny, a number of compelling reasons militate against its inclusion in the American cultural system. In other words, other parts of U.S. culture not only fail to support polygyny but also actually conflict with it. First, if a man attempts to have more than one wife at a time, he runs the risk of finding himself behind bars because polygyny conflicts directly with our legal system. Moreover, the practice is counterproductive in a society based on a cash economy— for the more wives a man has, the more money he needs to support them. As a corollary, more wives mean more children, who require more visits to the pediatrician, Barbie dolls, hockey sticks, bicycles, swimming lessons, frozen pizzas, and eventually college tuition—all of which put additional strains on family income. In short, little in the American cultural configuration would lend support to the practice of polygyny.

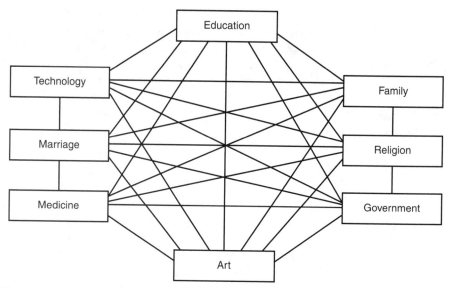

The various parts of a culture are all interrelated, to some degree,.

However, if we view polygyny within its proper cultural context, we find that it is not only *not* immoral, illegal, or irrational but also is probably the most logical marital form that could be adopted. An ethnographic example of a polygynous society is clearly required. Although literally hundreds of cultures could be used to illustrate the point, I have selected the traditional Kikuyu of East Africa because they are the people with whom I lived for thirteen months.

For the Kikuyu, as is the case for many other peoples of the world, polygyny is the ideal marital form. Unlike American culture, the Kikuyu cultural configuration contains a number of traits that tend to support polygyny and make it a viable marital alternative. First, the traditional Kikuyu economy is based on subsistence agriculture, which as practiced in fertile Kikuyuland is a relatively efficient means of livelihood. A single Kikuyu farmer can produce sufficient food for himself and several others. But the more hands contributing to the family farm, the better off economically the whole family would be. Thus, viewed from an economic perspective, it makes sense for the Kikuyu man to want more than one wife because the acquisition of new wives and children enhances the economic well-being of the household.

Second, the basic social unit of the Kikuyu is the patrilineage, a corporate group of male kinspeople ranging up to ten generations in depth, the members of which live together on lineage-controlled land. Since all lineage members want to see the lineage grow and prosper, considerable pressure is put on the Kikuyu to contribute male offspring, to ensure the group's continued growth. What better way is there to increase one's chances of having male offspring than by maximizing the number of wives?

Third, the Kikuyu system of social status is based on the size of one's household, not on the household's material wealth. Simply put, prominent men are those with the greatest number of wives and children. Moreover, Kikuyu women also lend support to the practice of polygyny, for it is not at all unusual for Kikuyu wives to encourage their husbands to take additional wives to enhance the status of the household. Like their American counterparts, no Kikuyu woman wants to be married to a "nobody."

Fourth, polygyny as a marital form tends to be encouraged by the Kikuyu religion, one of the fundamental features of which is the belief in ancestral gods. When a prominent male Kikuyu dies, he is not buried and forgotten but is actually elevated to the status of deity and becomes an object of worship for the living members of his family. If his family consists of a single wife and child, he cannot expect to have much of a religious following. However, the larger his family (wives and children), the greater the number of people worshiping him.

Presenting a number of other explanations of why polygyny fits into the Kikuyu system would be possible. The important point, however, is that any cultural item—be it a learned behavioral response, an idea, or an object—must be viewed as a component of the total cultural system in which it is found. When items are wrenched from their proper cultural context and viewed from the perspective of another culture (that is, ethnocentrically), meanings and functions become distorted, and the true nature of the item is at best imperfectly understood. But when we view a cultural item from within its proper or original cultural context, we have a much better chance of seeing how it logically fits into the integrated cultural system of which it is a part. By so doing, we obtain a fuller understanding of how the culture functions.

The notion of integrated culture helps us to better understand why culturally different people think and behave the way they do. However, we should avoid taking the concept too literally. To assume that all cultures are perfectly integrated, we would have to conclude that every idea or behavior is both absolutely rational and morally defensible, provided that it performs a function for the well-being of the society. However, believing in the general validity of the integrated nature of culture does not require that we view all cultures as morally equivalent; that is, not all cultural practices are equally worthy of tolerance and respect. Some practices (such as the genocide perpetuated by Stalin, Hitler, or the Serbs in Bosnia) are morally indefensible within *any* cultural context. To be certain, cultural anthropologists have sometimes been overly nonjudgmental about the customs of people they study. But, as Richard Barrett has suggested, "The occasional tendency for anthropologists to treat other cultures with excessive approbation to the extent that they sometimes idealize them, is less cause for concern than the possibility that they will misrepresent other societies by viewing them through the prism of their own culture" (1991, 8).

If cultures are in fact coherent systems, with their constituent parts interrelated with one another, it follows logically that a change in one part of the system is likely to produce concomitant changes in other parts of the system. The introduction of a single technological innovation may set off a whole series of related changes. In other words, culture changes beget other culture changes.

To illustrate, one has only to look at the far-reaching effects on U.S. culture of a single technological innovation, which became widespread in the early 1950s—the TV set. This one single technological addition to our material culture has had profound consequences on the nonmaterial aspects of our culture, including our political, educational, and religious systems, to mention only three. For example, political campaigning for the presidency in 1948 and earlier had been conducted largely from the back end of a railroad car on "whistle-stop" tours. By 1960, the year of the first televised presidential debates, television had brought the ideas, positions, speaking styles, and physical appearances of the candidates directly into the living rooms of the majority of voters. Today, political candidates, because of the power of television, need to be as attentive to makeup, clothing, and nonverbal gestures as they are to the substantive issues of the campaign. In formal education, one of the many consequences of the widespread use of television has been to lower the age at which children develop reading readiness, a direct result of such programs as *Sesame Street*. In terms of evangelical religion, we must ask ourselves if there would even be an Oral Roberts University had it not been for television. Television has been described by various social commentators as both a blessing and a curse. Yet however we might feel about its pluses and minuses, we can hardly deny that it has contributed to profound changes in many other parts of the U.S. cultural system. The reason for these changes is that cultures tend to be integrated systems with a number of interconnected parts so that a change in one part of the culture is likely to bring about changes in other parts.

A particularly dramatic illustration of linked changes has been offered by Lauriston Sharp (1952) in his study of an aboriginal people in Australia, the Yir Yoront. Sharp shows how the introduction of steel axes to these stone-aged people by well-meaning but shortsighted missionaries altered significantly the relationship among family members and trading partners and eventually led to the disintegration of Yir Yoront culture.

To understand how this happened, we must first understand the function of the stone axes that the steel axes replaced. First, since only men owned stone axes, women and children had to borrow them according to regular patterns of kinship interaction. This system of borrowing served to establish and maintain a well-defined system of sex, status, and role inequality. Second, since the stones used in making the stone axes were not available locally, Yir Yoront males had to obtain them by means of an elaborate trading network with neighbors located 400 miles to the south. These exchanges took place at large ceremonial gatherings, at which Yir Yoront met with other aboriginal peoples.

When the steel axes (which were clearly technologically superior to the stone axes) were dispensed by the missionaries, most of the traditional forms of social intercourse were disrupted. Kinship, age, and sex roles became confused because the existence of steel axes eliminated the necessity of going through traditional channels to borrow axes; traditional trading networks were abandoned, as were many of the aboriginal ceremonies where the trading took place; there was a loss of clearly defined authority patterns; and since the new steel axes had no origin myth or mythical ancestors associated with them, people became suspicious about all the various creation myths.

In short, the introduction of a seemingly harmless innovation can lead to complex cultural repercussions.

The notion of integrated culture has several important implications for international businesspeople. First, when we understand that the parts of a culture are interrelated, we will be less likely to view foreign cultures ethnocentrically. Rather than wrenching a foreign cultural item from its original context and viewing it in terms of how well it fits into our own culture, we will be reminded to view it from within its proper cultural context. In other words, any cultural feature must be understood in terms of that culture. Thus, we can begin to see how all cultures tend to be logical and coherent systems. Such an approach leads us to the inescapable conclusion that no cultures are inherently better or worse than any other, only different. This view of cultures as integrated wholes is not a value-laden philosophical rationalization for any type of behavior, however bizarre, destructive, or inhumane. Instead, such a culturally relativistic approach allows us to understand more fully why a particular cultural item is found in a society, even if it violates our sense of personal morality.

An understanding of the interconnectedness of the parts of culture can also help explain the nature of cultural change. When systems are integrated, changing only one part of the system is impossible. Such an understanding would be critical for responsible international businesspeople interested in expanding their markets into areas where their products (and perhaps ideas and behavior patterns associated with these products) are unknown. Some seemingly harmless commercial products could have profoundly disruptive effects on the very fabric of the society. By knowing the nature of the interconnectedness of the parts of a particular culture, the prudent, humane, and ultimately successful international businessperson will be able to predict the deleterious effects of a product in that cultural environment.

CONCLUSION

Through the comparative study of a wide range of cultures throughout the world, cultural anthropologists have developed the general concept of culture and an understanding of those basic traits and processes shared by all specific cultures. We have explored some of these cultural generalizations in an effort to provide a deeper appreciation of the cultural environment of international business. In addition to the various definitions of culture, we have examined some of the basic characteristics that all cultures share: (1) the learned nature of culture, (2) how culture influences biological processes, (3) cultural universals, (4) the ubiquity of culture change, (5) ethnocentrism, and (6) the integrated nature of culture. It is assumed that an awareness of the concept of culture (what culture is and how it functions) is a necessary yet not sufficient prerequisite for an understanding of any particular culture.

Whenever dealing with any concept or generalization, such as the concept of culture, it is important to avoid viewing it in an overly rigid or concrete way. To arrive at statements that hold true for all cultures, anthropologists are operating at a relatively high level of abstraction. Since these generalizations are constructed from literally thousands of cultures in the world, there will be times when generalizations do not always jibe perfectly with reality. In no way does that fact invalidate the usefulness of the concept. The generalizations regarding culture discussed throughout this chapter should be viewed as heuristic in nature, rather than as exact representations of reality. They are generally valid descriptions of what happens most of the time. But even when discrepancies appear, the concept is still useful as a stimulant to further investigation.

When moving to the level of a specific culture, it is equally important to avoid overly rigid thinking. Anthropological statements about a particular culture are generalizations about what most of the people do and think most of the time. Although cultural norms exert a strong influence on behavior, they are hardly ironclad propositions that can be used to predict with precision how people will respond in any given situation. Each culture must strike a balance between individual self-interests and the needs of the total society. Without denying the strong influence that culture has on behavior, people are nevertheless endowed with free will. To one degree or another, individuals are free to go against their cultural norms, even though most do not. It is indeed the rare person in any society who complies totally with the social rules. As Barrett points out, "There is always a tendency to evade or stretch the meaning of the rules or to otherwise minimize their consequences" (1991, 75). As a result, cultural anthropologists make the distinction between *ideal* behavior (what society says people should do) and *actual* behavior (what people in fact do).

The consequences of this fact are that in any given culture it is likely that individual variations in thought and action can be observed. To illustrate the nature and extent of this diversity, let's look at a familiar scene from our own culture, a high school classroom. In any given classroom, even the most untrained observer will notice students behaving somewhat differently. As the teacher is lecturing, one male student may be flirting with the girl two rows over, another may be doodling, a third student may be working on her unfinished homework for another class, and a fourth may actually be listening intently to extract some meaning from the lecture. Yet despite these individual variations, the students are nevertheless responding in generally similar ways. All remain seated; all are silent; all refrain from doing anything that would seriously interrupt the lecturer. Although the boy continues to flirt, he is not singing out loud or doing a handstand. The observable variations in behavior, in other words, are contained within socially acceptable limits. One of the tasks of the anthropologist—or any other cultural observer—is to determine where the normative limits are. It is the description of these variations in behaviors within limits that constitutes the patterns of any specific culture.

Finally, cultures are complex networks of features, some of which change rapidly and others are much more resistant to change. Thus, when encountering another culture, some features will appear quite like one's own cultural features, whereas others will seem exotic and bizarre. Robert Collins, who has written widely on cultural differences between Japan and the United States, describes how difficult it is to sort out the levels of cultural difference between these two countries:

The initial Level on a Westerner's perception scale clearly indicates a "difference" of great significance. The Japanese speak a language unlike any other human tongue. To compound things, they write the language in symbols that reason alone cannot decipher. . . . Level Two is represented by the sudden awareness that the Japanese are not different at all. Not at all. They ride in elevators, have a dynamic industrial/trade/financial system, own great chunks of the United States, and serve corn flakes at the Hotel Okura. Level Three is the "hey, wait a minute" stage. The Japanese come to all the meetings, smile politely, nod in agreement with everything said, but do the opposite of what's expected. And they do it all together. They really are different. But are they? Level Four understanding recognizes the strong group dynamics, common education and training, and the general sense of loyalty to the family. . . . Nothing is fundamentally different. Level Five can blow one's mind, however. Bank presidents skipping through the streets dressed as dragons at festival time; single ladies placing garlands of flowers around huge, and remarkably graphic, stone phallic symbols; Ministry of Finance officials rearranging their bedrooms so as to sleep in a "lucky" direction; there is something different in the air. And so on. Some Westerners, the old Japan hands, have gotten as far as Levels 37 or 38. (1987, 14–15)

CROSS-CULTURAL SCENARIOS

Read the following cross-cultural scenarios. In each mini-case study, a basic cultural conflict occurs between the actors involved. Try to identify the source of the conflict and suggest how it could have been avoided or minimized. Then see how well your analyses compare to the explanations in Appendix A.

2-1   Sam Lucas, a construction supervisor for an international engineering firm, had the reputation of being tough but fair minded. He was a very forceful, confrontive individual who always spoke his mind. He never hesitated to call on the carpet any worker whom he felt was performing poorly. Even though during his six years with the company Sam had never worked outside of the United States, he was chosen to supervise construction on a new hotel project, in Jidda, Saudi Arabia, primarily because of his outstanding work record. On this project, Sam supervised the work of about a dozen Americans and nearly 100 Saudi laborers. It was not long before Sam realized that the Saudi laborers, to his way of thinking, were nowhere as reliable as the workers he had supervised in the United States. He was becoming increasingly annoyed at the seeming lack of competence of the local workforce. Following the leadership style that held him in such good stead at home, he would reprimand any worker who was not doing his job properly, and he would make certain that he did it publicly so that it would serve as an object lesson to all the other workers. He was convinced that he was doing the right thing and was being fair, for after all, he reprimanded both Americans and Saudis alike. He was troubled, however, by the fact that the problems seemed to be growing worse and more numerous.

What advice might you give Sam?

2-2   George Burgess was a chief engineer for a machinery manufacturer based in St. Louis. His company had recently signed a contract with one of its largest customers in Japan to upgrade the equipment and retrain mechanics to maintain the equipment more effectively. As part of the contract, the Japanese company sent all ten of their mechanics to St. Louis for a three-month retraining course under George's supervision. Although George had never lived or worked abroad, he was looking forward to the challenge of working with the group of Japanese mechanics, for he had been told that they were all fluent in English and tireless workers. The first several weeks of the training went along quite smoothly, but soon George became increasingly annoyed with the constant demands they were making on his personal time. They would seek him out after the regularly scheduled sessions were over, for additional information. They sought his advice on how to occupy their leisure time. Several even asked him to help settle a disagreement that developed between them. Feeling frustrated by all these demands on his time, George told his Japanese trainees that he preferred not to mix business with pleasure. Within a matter of days, the group requested another instructor.

What was the principle operating here?

2-3   Bernice Caplan, purchaser for women's apparel for a major U.S. department store, had just taken over the overseas accounts. Excited and anxious to make a good impression on her European counterparts, Bernice worked long, hard hours to provide information needed to close purchasing contracts in a timely manner. Stefan, one of her Dutch associates in Amsterdam, sent an urgent message on May 1, requiring information before the close of day on 6/5.

Although she thought it odd for the message to be marked URGENT for information needed over a month away, Bernice squeezed the request into her already busy schedule. She was pleased when she had whipped together the information and was able to fax it by May 10, three full weeks before the deadline. Pleased with herself, she placed a telephone call to Stefan to make sure that he had received the fax and was met with an angry, hostile response. The department store not only lost the order at the agreed-upon cost, but the Dutch office asked that Bernice be removed from their account.

Where did Bernice go wrong?

2-4   Bob Mitchell, a retired military attaché with considerable experience in the Middle East, was hired by a large U.S. computer software company to represent it in a number of Persian Gulf countries. Having received an introduction from a mutual acquaintance, Bob arranged to meet with Mr. Saade, a wealthy Lebanese industrialist, to discuss the prospects of a joint venture between their companies. Having spent many years in the Middle East, Bob knew that they would have to engage in considerable small talk before they would get down to business. They talked about the weather, Bob's flight from New York, and their golf games. Then Saade inquired about the health of Bob's elderly father. Without missing a beat, Bob responded that his father was doing fine, but that the last time he saw his father at the nursing home several months ago he had lost a little weight. From that point on, Saade's demeanor changed abruptly from warm and gracious to cool and aloof. Though the rest of the meeting was cordial enough, the meeting only lasted another two hours, and Bob was never invited back for further discussions on the joint venture.

What went wrong?

2-5   A U.S. fertilizer manufacturer headquartered in Minneapolis decided to venture into the vast potential of third-world markets. The company sent a team of agricultural researchers into an East African country to test soils, weather conditions, and topographical conditions in order to develop locally effective fertilizers. Once the research and manufacturing of these fertilizer products had been completed, one of the initial marketing strategies was to distribute, free of charge, 100-pound bags of the fertilizer to selected areas of rural farmers. It was thought that those using the free fertilizer would be so impressed with the dramatic increase in crop productivity that they would spread the word to their friends, relatives, and neighbors.

Teams of salespeople went from hut to hut in those designated areas, offering each male head of household a free bag of fertilizer along with an explanation of its capacity to increase crop output. Although each head of household was very polite, they all turned down the offer of free fertilizer. The marketing staff concluded that these local people were either uninterested in helping themselves grow more food and eat better or so ignorant that they couldn't understand the benefits of the new product.

Why was this an ethnocentric conclusion?

CHAPTER 3

Communicating across Cultures

Language

Business organizations, like other social systems, require effective communication in order to operate efficiently and meet their objectives. International business organizations require effective communication at a number of levels. The firm must communicate with its workforce, customers, suppliers, and host-government officials. Effective communication among people from the same culture is often difficult. But when attempting to communicate with people who do not speak English—and who have different ideas, attitudes, assumptions, perceptions, and ways of doing things—one's chances for miscommunication increase enormously.

Communication takes place in two ways: (1) through language (using words that have mutually understood meanings and are linked together into sentences according to consistently followed rules) and (2) through nonverbal communication, or what Edward Hall (1959) refers to as the "silent language." In Chapters 3 and 4, we examine the nature of communication in international business and how communication problems can develop when people communicate, or attempt to communicate, across cultures. In this chapter we focus on language, and in Chapter 4 we look at the nonverbal dimension of communication.

THE NEED FOR LINGUISTIC PROFICIENCY IN INTERNATIONAL BUSINESS

If the success of the international businessperson is to be maximized, there is no substitute for an intimate acquaintance with both the language and the culture of those with whom one is conducting business. In fact, because of the close relationship between language and culture, it is virtually impossible not to learn about one while studying the other. The argument in favor of foreign-language competence for international businesspeople seems so blatantly obvious that to have to recount it here causes twinges of embarrassment. Yet the very fact that so many Westerners enter the international business arena without competence in a second language should help us overcome that embarrassment.

Most of the explanations offered for not learning to speak another language appear transparent and designed to justify past complacency and/or ethnocentrism. For example, we frequently hear that U.S. firms doing business abroad need not train their overseas personnel in a second language because English is rapidly becoming the international language of business. After generations of assuming that our goods and services were so desirable that the rest of the world would come to us, we now find ourselves in a highly competitive world marketplace with greater linguistic parity. English is now just one of the major languages of world trade and the mother tongue of only 5 percent of the world's population.

A host of other arguments have also been advanced to justify a monolinguistic approach to international business. For example, it has been suggested that Western businesspeople can avoid the time and energy needed to learn a second language by hiring in-country nationals who are well grounded in the local language and culture. Others have argued that a second language is not practical, since most international businesspeople do not remain in the host country for more than a year or two. Moreover, it has even been suggested that becoming proficient in a second language could actually hinder one's career advancement, since that individual, spending most of his or her time out of the home country, would be away from the organization's political mainstream (Terpstra 1978, 21).

Despite these and other arguments (or perhaps post facto rationalizations), the simple fact remains that a fundamental precondition of any successful international business enterprise is effective communication. Whether dealing with international sales, management, or negotiations, the Western businessperson who must rely on translators is at a marked disadvantage. International business, like any business, must be grounded in trust and mutual respect. What better way to gain that trust and respect than by taking the time and energy to learn someone else's language? In terms of international marketing and negotiations, Theodore Huebener reminds us that

> a knowledge of a customer's language has a distinct sales value. This is particularly true in Latin countries, where business conferences are conducted in a leisurely and unhurried way, in a highly social atmosphere. The American businessman who can speak the foreign tongue fluently and who can make intelligent comments on the art and literature of the country will gain not only the business but also the respect of the person he is dealing with. (1961, 46)

Thus, proficiency in a second language enables the international businessperson to understand the communication patterns within their proper cultural context, as well as increase general rapport with foreign business counterparts.

This in itself should be ample justification for Western businesspeople to have second-language competence, but we can add three other compelling reasons as well. First, as Benjamin Lee Whorf (1956, 212–14) has suggested, the only way to really understand the *worldview* (a system of categories for organizing the world) of another culture is through its language. Second, the experience of learning a second language is beneficial in the learning of third and fourth languages, so that the time spent today learning Span-

Even though English is a major *lingua franca* of international business, some American and British companies are beginning to realize that it pays to learn foreign languages. For example, in 1983, Jaguar, the British automobile manufacturer, started an in-house language center for the study of German. According to the *Economist* (1987), Jaguar sales in West Germany the following year jumped a dramatic 60 percent against stiff competition from its local competitors, Mercedes and BMW.

ish will facilitate the learning of Chinese or Arabic in the future. Third, learning another language (and culture) is the best way to gain a fuller appreciation of one's own language (and culture). With all these cogent arguments in favor of second-language proficiency, one cannot help noticing the flagrant lack of attention foreign-language competence has been given by Western business establishments.

With business becoming increasingly international, the role of language is becoming more important. American firms that in the past had exclusively domestic operations are now struggling with international correspondence, letters of credit, and customs regulations in a number of different languages; multinational firms, which have had long histories of operating across linguistic boundaries, are having to add new languages to their repertoires. Some U.S. firms have taken the challenge of coping with other languages more seriously than others. Those U.S. firms that continue to work with their monolingual provincialism do so at a rather high risk to their own corporate health and longevity. Paul Aron, a high-level international businessman with Daiwa Securities America, perhaps put it most directly when he said, "American companies put little premium on language—and see how they're doing overseas" (Machan 1988, 140).

Yet even for those firms that take seriously the multilinguistic environment of international business, many hazards lie along the way. The literature is filled with examples of problems U.S. firms have had in their international advertising campaigns because of sloppy translations. One such example was reported by Jonathan Slater:

> An American ink manufacturer attempted to sell bottled ink in Mexico while its metal outdoor signs told customers that they could "avoid embarrassment" (from leaks and stains) by using its brand of ink. The embarrassment, it seems, was all the ink company's. The Spanish word used to convey the meaning of "embarrassed" was "embarazar," which means "to become pregnant." Many people thought the company was selling a contraceptive device. (1984, 20)

In other instances of imprecise translations, U.S. firms have advertised cigarettes with low "asphalt" (instead of tar), computer "underwear" (instead of software), and "wet sheep" (instead of hydraulic rams). As amusing as these examples may seem, such translation errors have cost U.S. firms millions of dollars in losses over the years, not to mention the damage done to their credibility and reputations.

It is important to keep in mind that U.S. firms do not have a monopoly on linguistic faux pas. Even when people *think* they know English, they frequently convey messages they don't particularly intend.

*If you want to communicate effectively in international business,
there is no substitute for the hard work it takes to learn a language.*

- A sign in a Romanian hotel informing the English-speaking guests that the elevator was not working read, "The lift is being fixed. For the next few days we regret that you will be unbearable" (Besner 1982, 53).
- A sign in the window of a Paris dress shop said, "Come inside and have a fit" (Besner 1982, 53).
- Reporting to his firm's headquarters, an African representative of an electronics firm referred to the "throat-cutting competition" when in fact he meant "cut-throat competition" (Salmans 1979, 46).
- A notice in a Moscow tourist hotel stated, "If this is your first visit to the U.S.S.R., you are welcome to it" (Besner 1982, 53).

In all these examples, it is clear that the translators knew the language, but they still sent unintended messages. Even though they knew the meanings of all the words used and the grammatical rules for putting them together, communication was nevertheless short-circuited.

Not only do businesses face formidable problems when translating from one language into another, but confusion can also occur between two groups that ostensibly speak the same language. We often hear this comment: "Fortunately, we are being transferred by the company to London, so we won't have a language problem." It is true that they will not have to master a totally new language, complete with grammar, vocabulary, and sound system. But it is equally true that there are a number of significant differences between British and American English that can lead to confusion and misunderstandings. In some cases, the same word can have two very different meanings on either side of the Atlantic. The U.S. businessman in London will be in for quite a jolt when his British counterpart, in a genuine attempt to pay a compliment, refers to the American's wife as "homely," for in the United States the word means "plain" or "ugly" but in the United Kingdom it means "warm" and "friendly." Another such misunderstanding actually occurred at a meeting of representatives from a U.S. firm and a British firm. According to Sandra Salmans, things were proceeding smoothly

> until one of the . . . [British] executives suggested "tabling" a key issue. To his amazement, the Americans reacted with outrage. The reason, as he learned shortly, was that while in the UK "tabling" an item means giving it a prominent place on the agenda, in the U.S. it means deferring it indefinitely. (1979, 45)

And just imagine the look on the American businessman's face when his female British counterpart asks him for a "rubber" (an eraser) or invites him to "knock her up" (stop by her house).

More frequently, two different words refer to the same thing. To illustrate, the British live in "flats," not apartments; they "queue" up rather than line up; and they wear "plimsoles" rather than sneakers. When the American steps into a British automobile, most parts of the vehicle have different names: To the British the trunk is the "boot"; the hood is the "bonnet"; the windshield is the "windscreen"; the horn is the "hooter"; and the vehicle runs on "petrol," not gasoline.

LINGUISTIC DIVERSITY

Perhaps the most significant feature of being human is the ability to build and manipulate language and other symbolic codes. Other animal species communicate in a variety of ways: by means of nonlinguistic calls, body movements, gestures, olfactory stimuli, and other instinctive or genetically based mechanisms. Some nonhuman species, like certain great apes, have a limited capacity to learn symbolic codes (for example, American Sign Language), but they are unable to develop a language of their own. It is this ability to symbolize through language that is the hallmark of humanity. Language allows humans to transcend many of their biological limitations by building cultural models and transmitting them from generation to generation.

But what do we mean by language? A *language* (a universal found in all cultures of the world) is a symbolic code of communication consisting of a set of sounds (phonemes) with understood meanings and a set of rules (grammar) for constructing messages. The meanings attached to any word by a language are totally arbitrary. For example, the word *cat* has no connection whatsoever to that animal the English language refers to as cat. The word *cat* does not look like a cat, sound like a cat, or have any particular physical connection to a cat. Somewhere during the development of the English language, someone decided that the word *cat* would refer to that particular type of four-legged animal, whereas other languages symbolized the exact same animal by using totally different words. Language, then, consists of a series of arbitrary symbols with meanings that, like other aspects of culture, must be learned and that, when put together according to certain grammatical rules, can convey complex messages.

Since languages are arbitrary symbolic systems, it is not surprising that there is enormous linguistic diversity on the face of Earth. There does not appear to be universal agreement about how many languages there are in the world. Estimates range from several thousand to as many as 10,000. It seems reasonable to suggest 3,000 as a credible estimate. Even though exact numbers are not available, it is generally recognized that there are more than 1,000 languages among Native Americans, about 750 in sub-Saharan Africa, over 150 on the subcontinent of India, and in excess of 750 on the single island of New Guinea. However, these estimates should be kept in their proper perspective. As Kenneth Katzner has suggested,

> A single statistic tells a great deal: of the several thousand languages of the world, fewer than 100 are spoken by over 95 percent of the earth's population. One language, Chinese, accounts for 20 percent all by itself, and if we add English, Spanish, Russian, and Hindi, the figure rises to about 45 percent. German, Japanese, Arabic, Bengali, Portuguese, French and Italian bring the figure to 60 percent. . . . When we realize that the last five percent speak thousands of different languages, it is clear that the great majority of these languages are spoken by tiny numbers of people. . . . (1975, viii–ix)

There are several reasons for this vagueness in the number of discrete languages in the world. First, there is a question of whether to include in the total number all those languages that are dying out or have already died out. Second, certain remote areas of the world (such as New Guinea and parts of Brazil) have not been the subject of intensive descriptive linguistic study; consequently, very little is known of the linguistic mosaics in these areas. Third, and by far the most problematic factor, is that linguists fail to agree on where to draw linguistic boundaries. Mutual unintelligibility is frequently used as the criterion for distinguishing between language groups: If people can understand one another, they speak the same language; if they can't, they don't. Yet, as is all too obvious, this criterion is hardly ironclad because there are varying degrees of intelligibility. Despite the fact that we cannot determine with absolute certainty the precise number of languages in the world today, the fact remains that the range of linguistic modes throughout the world is vast (see Table 3-1). And despite the claims by some U.S. businesspeople that English is widely used in international business, this enormous linguistic diversity in the world must be of concern to any U.S. businessperson attempting to compete in an increasingly interdependent marketplace.

The typical American divides the great variety of cultures found in the world today into two categories: advanced civilizations like his or her own and so-called primitive cultures, which are frequently based on small-scale agriculture or hunting-gathering and have simple systems of technology. In keeping with this bipolar thinking, it is popularly held that technologically simple societies have equally uncomplex or unsophisticated languages. In other words, we frequently think that primitive people have primitive languages. Yet anthropological linguists tell us that this is not the case, for technologically simple people are no less capable of expressing a wide variety of abstract ideas than are people with high levels of technology.

To illustrate this point, consider the Navajo language spoken by Native Americans living in Arizona and New Mexico. When compared with English, the Navajo language is no

TABLE 3-1   MAJOR LANGUAGES OF THE WORLD

Language	Primary Country	Number of First-Language Speakers (in millions)
1. Mandarin	China	885
2. Spanish	Spain	332
3. English	UK/USA	322
4. Bengali	Bangladesh	189
5. Hindi	India	182
6. Portuguese	Portugal	170
7. Russian	Russia	170
8. Japanese	Japan	125
9. German	Germany	98
10. Wu	China	77

Source: Ethnologue, website site of the Summer Institute of Linguistics, 1999 (http:www.sil.org).

less efficient in terms of expressing abstract ideas. All we can say is that the two linguistic systems are different. It is true that Navajo does not have certain grammatical distinctions commonly found in English, as Ralph Beals, Harry Hoijer, and Alan Beals have noted:

> The Navajo noun has the same form in both the singular and the plural—there are no plural noun endings (such as the -s of books or the -en of oxen) in Navajo. Similarly, the third-person pronoun of Navajo is singular or plural and nondistinctive in gender: it can be translated he, she, it, or they, depending on the context. Finally, we find no adjectives in Navajo. The function performed by the English adjective is in Navajo performed by the verb. (1977, 513)

Yet in another area of structure, the Navajo language is considerably more precise than English. As Peter Farb reminds us, it is impossible for a Navajo speaker simply to say, "I am going" (1968, 56). Rather, considerably more information will be built into the verb form. For example, the verb stem would indicate whether the person is going on foot or by horseback, wagon, boat, or airplane. If the Navajo speaker is in fact going on horseback, she or he then must choose another verb form that will specify if the horse will walk, trot, gallop, or run. Moreover, the verb form chosen also will indicate if the speaker is "preparing to go," "going now," "almost at one's destination," or a number of other options. To be certain, the English speaker can convey the same information, but to do so would require a vast quantity of words. The Navajo language can provide an enormous amount of information by the proper verb form.

The central point is this: despite the fact that the Navajo and English languages are very different, we can hardly conclude that one is any more efficient than the other at expressing a wide variety of abstract ideas. All cultural groups have symbolic systems that are, by and large, equally efficient at sending and receiving verbal messages. Such an understanding on the part of the international businessperson should serve as an important reminder that English is not inherently superior to the language of those with whom one is doing business and whose language one is learning.

Even though the English and Navajo languages have very different structures, these Navajo speakers can express abstract ideas every bit as effectively as native English speakers.

LANGUAGE AND CULTURE

A fundamental tenet of anthropological linguistics is that there is a close relationship between language and culture. It is generally held that it is impossible to understand a culture without taking into account its language; and it is equally impossible to understand a language outside of its cultural context. Yet despite the close connection between language and culture, we should not think of the relationship as being complete or absolute. Some societies, for example, share common cultural traditions but speak mutually unintelligible languages. On the other hand, societies with quite different cultures may speak mutually intelligible languages. Nevertheless, culture influences language and language influences culture in a number of ways.

The Influence of Culture on Language

Perhaps the most obvious relationship between language and culture is seen in vocabulary. The vocabularies of all languages are elaborated in the direction of what is considered adaptively important in that culture. In industrialized societies, the vocabularies contain large numbers of words that reflect complex technologies and occupational specialization. The average speaker of standard American English knows hundreds of technological terms, such as *carburetor, microchip*, and *bulldozer*, as well as a myriad of terms designating occupational specialities, such as *accountant, philosopher, teacher, clerk*, and *thoracic surgeon*, because technology and professions are focal concerns in U.S.

culture. Thus, standard American English enables Americans to adapt most effectively to their environment by providing a conceptual lexicon most suited to U.S. culture.

It is equally true for nonindustrialized societies that those aspects of environment and culture that are of special importance will be reflected in the vocabulary. The Koga of southern India have seven different words for *bamboo*, an important natural resource in their tropical environment, yet have not a single word for *snow* (Plog and Bates 1980, 209). The pastoral Nuer of the Sudan, whose everyday lives revolve around their cattle, have words in their language that enable them to distinguish between hundreds of types of cows, based on color, markings, and configuration of horns. This elaborate vocabulary is an indication of the central economic and social role that cattle play in their society (Hickerson 1980, 112). The Inuit complex classification of types of snow is a classic example of the close connection between language and culture. Whereas the typical New Yorker has a single word for *snow*, the Inuit have a large number of words, each designating a different type of snow, such as drifting snow, softly falling snow, and so on. Even though the New Yorker can express the same ideas with a number of modifiers, the Inuit view snow as categorically different substances because their very survival requires a precise knowledge of snow conditions. Whether we are looking at the Koga, the Nuer, or the Inuit language, the point remains the same: In all languages, points of cultural emphasis are directly reflected in the size and specialization of the vocabularies. In other words, a language will contain a greater number of terms, more synonyms, and more fine distinctions when referring to features of cultural emphasis.

Although it is frequently more difficult to find points of cultural emphasis in large, highly differentiated societies, one area of cultural emphasis in the United States is sports. To illustrate, Nancy Hickerson (1980, 118) reminds us that standard American English contains a number of colloquialisms that stem from the popular sport of baseball:

1. He made a grandstand play.
2. She threw me a curve.
3. She fielded my questions well.
4. You're way off base.
5. You're batting 1,000 (500, zero) so far.
6. What are the ground rules?
7. I want to touch all the bases.
8. He went to bat for me.
9. He has two strikes against him.
10. That's way out in left field.
11. He drives me up the wall.
12. He's a team player (a clutch player).
13. She's an oddball (screwball, foul ball).
14. It's just a ballpark estimate.

The Influence of Language on Culture

We have just seen how languages tend to reflect cultural emphases. On the other side of the linguistic coin, however, some linguists have posited that language may actually influence certain aspects of culture. Language, they suggest, establishes the categories on which our perceptions of the world are organized. According to this theory, language is more than a system of communication that enables people to send and receive messages with relative ease. Language also establishes categories in our minds that force us to distinguish those things we consider similar from those things we consider different. And since every language is unique, the linguistic categories of one language will never be identical to the categories of any other. Consequently, speakers of any two languages will not perceive reality in exactly the same way. Edward Sapir was one of the first linguists to explain how language tends to influence our perceptions:

> The fact of the matter is that the real world is to a large extent unconsciously built up on the language habits of the group. No two languages are ever sufficiently similar to be considered as representing the same social reality. The worlds in which different societies live are distinct worlds, not merely the same world with different labels attached. (1929, 214)

Along with the amateur linguist Benjamin Lee Whorf, Sapir developed what has been referred to as the *Sapir–Whorf hypothesis*. This hypothesis, dealing with the relationship between language and culture, states that language is not merely a mechanism for communicating ideas but is the shaper of ideas. There is no general agreement among scholars concerning the validity of the Sapir–Whorf hypothesis. Although it has been shown that in some languages some correspondence does exist between grammatical categories and cultural themes, linguistic determinism is not an established fact. For example, the gender distinction made in English is *not* indicative of the relative importance of gender in other parts of the culture. Yet some tests of the hypothesis have suggested that language indeed can influence perceptions or worldview.

One of the more ingenious attempts at testing the Sapir–Whorf hypothesis was devised by anthropologist Joseph Casagrande (1960) of the Southwest Project in Comparative Psycholinguistics. The study used a sample of over 100 Navajo children divided into two groups: those who spoke only Navajo and those who spoke both Navajo and English. Since the two groups were similar in all other major sociocultural variables (education, family income, religion, and so on) except language, it was assumed that whatever differences in perception emerged among the two groups could be attributed to the variable of language.

Having a thorough knowledge of the Navajo language, Casagrande understood that Navajo speakers, when referring to an object, are led by their linguistic categories to choose among a number of different verbs, depending on the shape of the object. That is, when asking to be given a particular object, a Navajo speaker will use one verb form if the object is long, thin, and flexible (like a rope) and another if the object is long, thin, and rigid (like a stick). This feature of the Navajo language led Casagrande to hypothesize that Navajo-speaking children would be more likely to sort or discriminate according to shape than English-speaking children, who would be more likely to sort according to other criteria such as size or color. To test the hypothesis, the children from both groups were shown two objects (a yellow stick and a blue rope) and then asked to tell which of these objects was most like a third object (a yellow rope). In other words, all the children were asked to tell whether the yellow rope was more like the yellow stick or the blue rope. As the hypothesis had predicted, Casagrande found that those children who spoke only Navajo were more likely to sort according to shape (blue rope and yellow rope), whereas those who were bilingual more often sorted according to color.

Thus, the Sapir–Whorf hypothesis (the structure of a language can significantly influence perception and categorization) seems to have been supported by this series of experiments. Although it is considerably easier to demonstrate the cultural influence on language, the Sapir–Whorf hypothesis continues to remind us that the relationship can also flow in the other direction.

The implications of the Sapir–Whorf hypothesis for the international businessperson are obvious. The hypothesis states that linguistically different people not only communicate differently but also think and perceive the world differently. Thus, by learning the local language, the international businessperson will acquire a vehicle of communication as well as a better understanding of why people think and behave as they do.

Language Mirrors Values

Besides reflecting its worldview, a language also reveals a culture's basic value structure. For example, the extent to which a culture values the individual, as compared to the group, is often reflected in its language or linguistic style. The value placed on the individual is deeply rooted in the American psyche. Most Americans start from the cultural assumption that the individual is supreme and not only can but should shape his or her own destiny. That individualism is highly valued in the United States can be seen throughout its culture, from the love of the automobile as the preferred mode of transportation to a judicial system that fiercely protects the individual rights of the accused. Even when dealing with children, Americans try to provide them with a bedroom of their own, respect their individual right to privacy, and attempt to instill in them a sense of self-reliance and independence by encouraging them to solve their own problems. (For a more thorough discussion of this basic value difference, see Chapter 5.)

Owing to the close interrelatedness of language and culture, values (such as individualism in the United States) are reflected in standard American English. One such indicator of how our language reflects individualism is the number of words found in any American English dictionary that are compounded with the word *self.* To illustrate, one is likely to find in any standard English dictionary no fewer than 150 such words, including *self-absorbed, self-appointed, self-centered, self-confident,* and *self-supporting.* The list of English terms related to the individual is significantly larger than one found in a culture that places greater emphasis on corporate or group relationships.

In the United States, individual happiness is the highest good; in such group-oriented cultures as Japan, people strive for the good of the larger group such as the family, the community, or the whole society. Rather than stressing individual happiness, the Japanese are more concerned with justice (for group members) and righteousness (by group members). In Japan the "we" always comes before the "I"; the group is always more predominant than the individual. As John Condon reminds us, "If Descartes had been Japanese, he would have said, 'We think, therefore we are'" (1984, 9).

An important structural distinction found in Japanese society is between *uchi* (the in-group) and *soto* (the out-group), or the difference between "us" and "them." This basic social distinction is reflected in the Japanese language. For example, whether a person is "one of us" or "one of them" will determine which conversational greeting will be used, either *Ohayo gozaimasu*, which is customarily used with close members of your in-group, or *Konnichiwa*, which is more routinely used to greet those outside one's inner circle. O. Mizutani (1979) has conducted an interesting experiment outside the Imperial Palace in Tokyo, which is a favorite place for jogging. Dressed like a jogger, he greeted everyone he passed, both other joggers like himself and nonjoggers, and noted their response. Interestingly, 95 percent of the joggers greeted him with *Ohayo gozaimasu* (the term reserved for in-group members), while only 42 percent of the nonjoggers used such a phrase. He concluded that the joggers, to a much greater degree than the nonjoggers, considered him to be an in-group member because he, too, was a jogger.

Group members in Japan don't want to stand out or assert their individuality because, according to the Japanese proverb, "The nail that sticks up gets hammered down." In Japan the emphasis is on "fitting in," harmonizing, and avoiding open disagreement within the group. People in the United States express their individualism in exactly the opposite way by citing their proverb "The squeaky wheel gets the grease." If Japanese must disagree, it is usually done gently and very indirectly by using such passive expressions as "It is said that . . ." or "Some people think that . . . ." This type of linguistic construction enables one to express an opinion without having to be responsible for it in the event that others in the group might disagree. In a study of speech patterns among Japanese and American students, R. Shimonishi (1977) found that the Japanese students used the passive voice significantly more than did their American counterparts.

How language is used in Japan and the United States both reflects and reinforces the value of group consciousness in Japan and individualism in the United States. The goal of communication in Japan is to achieve consensus and promote harmony, whereas in the United States it is to demonstrate one's eloquence. Whereas language in Japan tends to be cooperative, polite, and conciliatory, language in the United States is often competitive, adversarial, confrontational, and aimed at making a point. The Japanese go to considerable length to avoid controversial issues that might be disruptive; Americans seem to thrive on controversy, debate, argumentation, and provocation, as is evidenced by the use of the expression "Just for the sake of argument." Moreover, the Japanese play down individual eloquence in favor of being good listeners, a vital skill if group consensus is to be achieved. Americans are not particularly effective listeners because they are too busy mentally preparing their personal responses rather than paying close attention to what is being said. Thus, all these linguistic contrasts between Japan and the United States express their fundamentally different approaches to the cultural values of "groupness" and individualism.

EXPLICIT VERSUS IMPLICIT COMMUNICATION

Cultures also vary in terms of how explicitly they send and receive verbal messages. In the United States, for example, effective verbal communication is expected to be explicit, direct, and unambiguous. Good communicators are supposed to say what they mean as precisely and straightforwardly as possible. Speech patterns in some other cultures are considerably more ambiguous, inexact, and implicit. Basil Bernstein's (1964) distinction between elaborated and restricted codes provides a conceptual framework that allows us to better understand the differences between these two fundamentally different types of speech patterns. *Restricted codes* use shortened words, phrases, and sentences and rely heavily on hidden, implicit, contextual cues such as nonverbal behavior, social context, and the nature of interpersonal relationships. Restricted codes are a form of shorthand communication that does not rely on verbal elaboration or explication. *Elaborated codes*, on the other hand, emphasize elaborate verbal amplification and place little importance on nonverbal or other contextual cues.

Bernstein's notion of restricted and elaborated codes is quite similar to Edward Hall's conceptualization of high-context cultures and low-context cultures:

> A high-context (HC) communication or message is one in which most of the information is either in the physical context or internalized in the person, while very little is in the coded, explicit, transmitted part of the message. A low-context (LC) communication is just the opposite; i.e., the mass of the message is vested in the explicit code. (1976, 79)

To combine these two schemes of Bernstein and Hall, high-context cultures, relying heavily on restricted codes and contextual cues, demonstrate inexact, implicit, and indirect communication patterns. In contrast, low-context cultures, relying on elaborated verbal messages, demonstrate precise, explicit, and straightforward communication patterns.

Like so many other bipolar typologies found in the social science literature, the notions of restricted versus elaborated codes or high-context versus low-context cultures are not either-or categories. Relatively restricted or elaborated codes can be found in any speech community, although one or the other mode is likely to predominate. Whereas the United States is not the best example of a low-context culture, it is clearly near the low-context end of the continuum. Based on the writings of Edward Hall (1976) and L. Robert Kohls (1978), it is possible to place twelve nationalities on a high- versus low-context continuum:

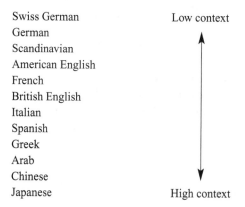

As would be predicted, low-context cultures, relying on elaborated verbal codes, demonstrate high value and positive attitudes toward words. The Western world (northern Europe and the United States, specifically) has had a long tradition of rhetoric, a tradition that places central importance on the delivery of verbal messages. According to William Gudykunst and Y. Y. Kim, "A primary function of speech in this tradition is to express one's ideas and thoughts as clearly, logically, and persuasively as possible, so the speaker can be fully recognized for his or her individuality in influencing others" (1984, 140). In contrast, in such high-context cultures as Japan and China, verbal messages, although important, are only a part of the total communication context. It is not that words are unimportant in Eastern cultures, but rather that the words are inseparably interrelated to social relationships, politics, and morality. Given this more holistic approach to communication, its purpose in many Eastern cultures is not to enhance the speaker's individuality through the articulation of words but to promote harmony and social integration. In such societies one is expected to be sensitive to subtle contextual cues and to not assume that critical information will always be verbalized. To illustrate, a U.S. corporate manager would most likely ask a subordinate directly for the budgetary reports that she needed as soon as possible. In a less explicit culture, however, the same message might be conveyed nonverbally by raising her eyebrow while glancing at him during a meeting at which budgetary reports were being discussed. Thus, whereas Western cultures place a great deal of power in words, many Asian cultures show a certain mistrust or skepticism of words or at least have a keen awareness of the limitation of words alone.

This cautious approach can be seen in the general suppression of negative verbal messages. As a result, politeness and the desire to avoid embarrassment often take precedence over the truth. This approach, at least in part, explains why Eastern cultures have so many nonverbal ways of saying "no" without directly or unambiguously uttering the word. This practice has caused considerable misunderstanding when Americans try to communicate with Japanese. To illustrate, the Japanese in everyday conversation frequently use the word *hai* (*yes*) to convey that they understand what is being said, not necessarily agreement.

When negotiating with Asians, it is important to understand that yes is not always an affirmative response. Before taking yes for an answer, one must ascertain if in fact it was merely a polite response that really meant no. Asian businesspeople, for example, are

---

Chinese scholar Robert Kapp describes the indirect style of communicating found among the Chinese, which can affect business negotiations between U.S. and Chinese businesspeople:

The indirection that permeates Chinese speech even in English translation can be particularly disconcerting to Americans. "Perhaps" and "maybe" are cultural stock-in-trade. "Maybe I will come with you" usually means "I'm coming." "Perhaps it is too far for you to walk" means "There's no way I'll let you walk." When something is "inconvenient," it most likely is impossible. But more than verbal indirection is at work here. The absence of a categorical statement implies that "perhaps" some room for discussion remains; and, in any case, a subsequent reversal will not represent a clear backing-down. Despite the firm signal that conditional speech often implies, negotiation is never totally foreclosed and dignity is maintained, at the expense of American patience. (1983, 20–21)

not likely to say no directly to a proposal but rather will reply in ways that are synonymous with no. To illustrate, Christopher Engholm suggests a number of ways that Asians say no without coming right out and saying it (1991, 115–16). In response to a Westerner's question "Has my proposal been accepted?" an Asian businessperson is likely to reply in a number of different ways:

> *The conditional "yes"*: "If everything proceeds as planned, the proposal will be approved."
> *The counterquestion*: "Have you submitted a copy of your proposal to the Ministry of Electronics?"
> *The question is criticized*: "Your question is difficult to answer."
> *The question is refused*: "We cannot answer this question at this time."
> *The tangential reply*: "Will you be staying longer than you originally planned?"
> *The "yes, but . . ." reply*: "Yes, approval looks likely, but . . . ." The meaning of "but" could mean "it might not be approved."
> *The answer is delayed*: "You will know shortly."

Implicit and explicit styles of communications often lead to misunderstandings and miscommunications. Many Americans view a person who is being indirect as tricky, deceptive, and of questionable integrity. At best, Westerners consider indirect communication to be a waste of their time. On the other hand, those from implicit cultures see the explicit communication styles of Americans to be rude, coarse, and insensitive. Since Americans, who need to be told all the relevant information, are less accustomed to reading implicit cues, they are often seen as insensitive or a bit slow on the uptake. They

Japanese people tend to be much less direct in their discourse than are North Americans.

often lack the contextual (background) information and the observational skills to read between the lines.

In these same high-context societies that rely on relatively restricted codes, it is not unusual to leave sentences unfinished or to tolerate intermittent periods of silence. Whereas most Westerners try to make their point as quickly and straightforwardly as possible, many Eastern cultures value silence as a major element of their rhetorical styles. Silence allows Japanese communicators, for example, to gain a better feel for their partners, and for this reason, they are not reluctant to let long silences develop. The radically different meaning of silence in Japan as compared with the West is well described by Helmut Morsbach:

> These silences are frequently misunderstood by Westerners, who tend to interpret them as noncomprehension, and therefore try to shorten the silence by explaining their point once again, or by moving on to the next topic. Well meaning attempts to make the Japanese partner(s) "speak up" often tend to cause silent frustration and resentment since, from the Japanese viewpoint, the Westerners are often seen as being the culprits who should rather be taught how to "shut up." (1982, 310)

Simply put, in certain Asian societies, rhetorical ambiguity results from restricted codes, and successful communication depends on a sensitivity to the nonverbal context. Other speech communities, such as certain Arabic cultures, are equally imprecise but for exactly the opposite reason; that is, they engage in overassertion, exaggeration, and repetition. The Arabic language is filled with forms of verbal exaggeration. For example, certain common ending words are meant to be emphasized; frequently certain pronouns will be repeated in order to fully dramatize the message; highly graphic metaphors and similes are common; and an Arabic speaker often uses a long list of adjectives to modify a single noun for the sake of emphasizing the point.

This propensity for verbal overkill was the subject of research conducted by E. T. Prothro (1955), who rated groups of Arabs and Americans on a continuum of under-

---

In addition to the level of explicitness, another aspect of linguistic style deals with pace and turn taking between speakers. As Christopher Engholm and Diana Rowland remind us, these differences in timing can cause problems:

> Brazilians frequently have two people talking at once in a conversation, with almost no pauses. Americans sometimes have brief pauses between speakers and sometimes have a little overlay of speakers. If you are speaking with people from a culture that has many verbal overlays, such as the Brazilians, you may have to be more assertive if you want to participate in the conversation. . . . If you are speaking with people from a culture with more verbal pauses, you may have to learn to pause more often to make sure others get a chance to speak. When talking with a Japanese, it is typical for Americans to wait just long enough to become uncomfortable and then begin speaking again. The Japanese person, however, has remained silent to show respect for the speaker or the comment, and by the time he feels it is appropriate to say something, the American is already speaking again. The result is that we end up monopolizing conversations. (1996, 81–82)

statement and overstatement. This study concluded that Arabs were considerably more likely to overstate the case than were Americans. What would be an assertive statement to an American might appear to be weak and equivocating to an Arab. Even though verbal threats are commonplace in the Arabic language, they tend to function more as a psychological catharsis than as an accurate description of the speaker's real intentions. It should be kept in mind that this rhetorical feature of linguistic overassertion is just another form of verbal ambiguity or inexactness because it fails to send direct, precise messages.

LANGUAGE AND SOCIAL CONTEXT

The understanding of linguistic differences in international business can be further complicated by the fact that people frequently speak several different languages or different forms of the same language, *depending on the social situation.* Bilingualism (or multilingualism) is the most obvious form of situational language use, for a person may speak one language at home, another language at work, and still another language in the marketplace. But people who speak only one language also switch styles of language. For example, the expressions college students use when speaking to one another in the dormitory are noticeably different than the forms of expression they use when they are conversing with their ministers, grandparents, or professors. Levels of formality between speakers, relative status, and sex and age of the speakers can frequently determine what is said and how it is said. As Peter Farb has put it, "Between the grammar of my language and its expression in audible speech lies the filter of the social system in which I live" (1974, 43).

Depending on who is addressing him, a man could be referred to as "Dr. Allen," "Richard," "Dick," "Sir," "Sweetheart," "Doc," or "Fella," among others. It is not likely that his wife or mother would address him as "Dr. Allen," nor is it likely that the nurses at the hospital would refer to him as "Dick" or "Fella." Moreover, the same person may use different terms of address in different social situations. His wife may address him as "Dick" at the dinner table, "Sweetheart" while making love, and "Richard" if they are engaged in an argument.

It has been shown (Brown and Ford 1961) that in the United States people are addressed by either (FN) first name (Richard) or by (TLN) title and last name (Dr. Allen), depending on the level of formality and relative social status between the speakers. In the American English context, there are only three possible combinations of address between two people: (1) reciprocal use of TLN, as in the exchange "Hello, Professor Davis"; "Good evening, Mrs. Bolton"; (2) reciprocal use of FN, as in the exchange "What's happening, Jack?"; "Not much, Norm"; and (3) nonreciprocal use of TLN and FN, as in the exchange "Good morning, Dr. Graves"; "Hello, Ricky." The first two exchanges—both reciprocal—imply relatively equal status between the speakers. The first situation indicates a formal, nonintimate relationship, whereas the second situation indicates an informal, more intimate relationship. Unlike the first two cases, the third case (TLN/FN) is indicative of marked status inequality, either differences in age (children and adults) or differences in rank within an organization (teacher and student; executive and secretary; surgeon and nurse).

In the Javanese language, every speech situation (not just terms of address) requires the speaker to make choices that reflect the relative social status of the person being addressed. Before a word is uttered, the speaker must choose one of three basic linguistic styles: the plain, the fancy, and the elegant. In addition, the Javanese speaker can use special terms known as *honorifics*, which enable the speaker to express minute gradations of social respect within each of these three styles. As Farb has noted, "He has no choice but to inform his listener exactly what he thinks of him—because the style he selects reveals whether he considers the listener worthy of low speech, the middle-ground fancy speech, or elegant speech, with or without honorifics" (1974, 44).

Not only is social status reflected in speech patterns, but linguistic differences can be frequently observed in the same speech community between men and women. Sometimes the distinctions between the sexes are reflected in vocabulary. In some languages these vocabulary differences are not simply a matter of relative frequency of usage; rather, there are pairs of words (doublets) carrying the same meanings, one word being a male word and one word being a female word. To illustrate, among the Island Carib of the West Indies, women use the word *kuyu* for rain, and men use the word *kunobu*; many more doublet nouns are found in this language (Hickerson 1980, 91). In Koasati, a native language of southwestern Louisiana, differences appear in certain indicative and imperative verb forms, depending on the sex of the speaker. Koasati men say *lakawho's* to mean "lift it," whereas Koasati

The form of language that this teenager might use with his/her peers is very different from that used with his/her minister.

women would use the word *lakawhol* (Haas 1964, 228). Thus, in this case, grammatical forms are chosen to match the gender of the speaker rather than the referent.

Gender differences can also be seen in more subtle areas of language, such as intonation, loudness, assertiveness, and style. For example, according to Chevis Kramer (1974), women in the United States speak less forcefully than men, as evidenced by their more frequent use of qualifiers (for example, "It may just be my opinion, but . . .") or the practice of following a declarative statement with such questions as "Isn't it?" or "Wouldn't you agree?" Moreover, according to Julia Wood (1994), men and women in the United States have very different communication styles, a phenomenon found in many other cultures as well. To illustrate, Wood found that American women talk for the purpose of building and supplementing rapport with others, whereas men use talk to assert themselves; women use self-disclosure as a way of learning about others, whereas men tend to avoid self-disclosure; women's discourse strives for equality in social relationships, whereas men's discourse attempts to establish status and power; women will often match experiences with others for the sake of showing understanding and empathy ("I know how you feel"), whereas men match experiences for the sake of gaining attention ("I can top that"); finally, women show their support by expressing their understanding; whereas men show their support by giving advice or wanting to solve a problem.

Variations in language usage according to age appear to be even more widespread than those based on sex. One particularly commonplace occurrence is "baby talk," a specialized form of language used to communicate with children. In the English language, we sometimes hear adults use such terms as *night-night* ("good night"), *choo-choo* ("train"), or *woof-woof* ("dog"). Although English baby talk is quite unsystematic (to the extent that it is used inconsistently), other languages, such as Comanche, have a very well-defined and consistently used form of baby talk. According to Joseph B. Casagrande (1948), the Comanche use about forty words and phrases covering general topics of communication such as *nana* ("it might hurt") and *koko* (referring to candy, cookies, or between-meal snacks). Interestingly enough, these Comanche words share a key feature with the baby talk found in most other parts of the world: They use simple sounds in a repetitive fashion. Regardless of where we might find it, the relatively widespread oc-

---

Sometimes U.S. businesspeople can get themselves into hot water by assuming that foreigners are unable to understand English. C. Barnum and N. Wolniansky (1989, 53) tell of a representative of a U.S. aircraft manufacturer riding into Cairo from the airport with his American colleague and an Egyptian chauffeur. As the two Americans chatted, one made a somewhat disparaging remark about Egyptians' ability to handle the aircraft they were purchasing from the American firm. Unfortunately, the Egyptian chauffeur's understanding of English was much better than the American had thought. The chauffeur relayed the contents of this remark to a colleague, who contacted the minister of defense, who in turn contacted the U.S. ambassador. Within forty eight hours, the insensitive businessman had been deported from Egypt.

currence of baby talk serves to remind us that variations of a language can depend on the age of the speaker or the age of the person being addressed.

SOME ADDITIONAL COMPLICATING FACTORS

To function effectively in any language community, it is necessary to know not only the formal structure of the language (vocabulary and grammar, for example) but also how it is used in different social situations. We have seen that what is said and how it is said can vary depending on the sex, age, or relative social status of the speakers. In other words, to understand linguistic communication in an international business context, it is necessary to understand the social context in which the communication is taking place, or as the anthropological linguist would put it, the ethnography of speaking.

To further complicate the learning of another language, most languages, for a variety of cultural reasons, employ certain nonstandard forms such as slang, euphemisms, proverbs, verbal dueling, and humor, and all have various conversational taboos.

Slang

Slang has been defined as "very informal usage in vocabulary and idiom that is characteristically more metaphorical, playful, elliptical, vivid, and ephemeral than ordinary language" (Stein 1979, 1235). This definition should not lead us to conclude that slang is the language of the common people. Instead, slang should be viewed as the speech of those who consider themselves to be part of a particular subgroup within the wider linguistic community. In certain northern U.S. cities, blacks use such slang terms as *hawks* ("strong winds"), *oreo* ("a person who is black on the outside but white on the inside"), and *bad* ("good"). Jazz musicians, computer buffs, teenagers, prostitutes, psychologists, and truck drivers are just several subgroups within the United States that have their own slang. The importance of slang, whether we are referring to the speech of black New Yorkers or that of truck drivers, is that it helps determine who is a member of an in-group and who is not.

Businesspeople, too, have their own slang, which they use within their own in-groups. Such expressions as "dead in the water" (*inoperative*), "take no prisoners" (*harsh*), "red tape" (*complicated procedures*), and "bottom line" (*net profit*), among many others, are used daily by American businesspeople. These examples of slang present two important problems for the person trying to learn a second language. First, slang increases the possible variations of expressions in any given speech community. Second, since many slang words are used for only several years before disappearing or becoming incorporated into the standard form of the language, keeping up with current slang trends is difficult.

Euphemisms

Behavioral and verbal taboos exist in all known societies; that is, certain categories of words should be avoided in normal, polite parlance. In many but certainly not all cases, the prohibited words are associated with sexual relations and everyday bodily functions

> When communicating across cultures, it is best to avoid using jargon, slang, or eu-
> phemisms. Terence Brake, Danielle Walker, and Thomas Walker remind us (in a hy-
> pothetical discussion between an American and his potential business partner from
> India) that, although they might seem innocuous, these irregular forms of the En-
> glish language can cause problems:
>
> > "I've been reviewing the materials you gave me, Mr. Neuru. You have a real cash cow
> > here. Excellent."
> > First of all, is Mr. Neuru going to have any idea what a "cash cow" is? And if Mr. Neuru is
> > a Hindu, isn't it possible he might take offense to the use of "cow" in this context? (1995, 174)

such as menstruating, urinating, and defecating. Whatever words may be deemed to be
taboo by a language, it is a fairly arbitrary process, for a word prohibited in one speech
community may be perfectly acceptable in another. Taboo words are dealt with through
the use of *euphemisms*—that is, by substituting a bland, vague, or indirect expression for
one thought to be too direct, harsh, or blunt. In the English language, for example, the
subject of death is so unpleasant that we have developed an entire system of euphemisms
to avoid dealing with the subject in a direct way. People don't die, they "pass away."
Those in charge of burials are no longer undertakers but are now "funeral directors."
Corpses are not buried in graves, but rather the "dearly departed" are "interred" in "memo-
rial parks." And hearses, which clearly are single-purpose vehicles, are now euphemisti-
cally called "coaches."

Even though the English language has more than its share of euphemisms, this
practice of substituting vague words for more precise ones can be found to some degree
in all languages. Again, the existence of taboo words and euphemisms presents yet another obstacle to second-language learning for the international businessperson. The
learner must become familiar with the prevailing value system of the particular speech
community in order to understand which topics can legitimately be dealt with in a direct
and straightforward manner. Without such an understanding, knowing when to use a
bland expression and when not to will be impossible.

Proverbs

Another nonstandard form of language that must be mastered is the general category of *proverbs, aphorisms*, and *maxims*. These wise sayings, regardless of where they
might be found, have certain things in common with one another: (1) They deal with the
essential truths as defined by the culture; (2) they are usually expressed simply and con-
cretely, though often metaphorically; (3) they advise and instruct how people should
comport themselves. The English language is filled with pithy proverbial expressions
(for example, Burton Stevenson's *The Home Book of Proverbs, Maxims and Familiar
Phrases*, 1948, contains 2,666 pages of English proverbs) that are widely understood if
not always used on a regular basis:

The early bird catches the worm.
All that glitters is not gold.
He who hesitates is lost.
A penny saved is a penny earned.
Too many cooks spoil the broth.
It is wise to risk no more than one can afford to lose.
Early to bed, early to rise, makes a man healthy, wealthy, and wise.

Proverbs are found in all languages and are related to other forms of folk literature, such as riddles, fables, and myths. A cross-cultural examination of proverbs reveals that the same basic idea can appear in two widely divergent and unrelated languages. For example, the biblical injunction "An eye for an eye, a tooth for a tooth" can be found in the Nandi (East African) proverb "A goat's hide buys a goat's hide and a gourd a gourd." Many similarities in the style and substance of proverbs can also be identified in geographically contiguous speech communities. The proverb "A bird in the hand is worth two in the bush" originated in Latin but can be found today in the Romanian, Spanish, Portuguese, German, and Icelandic languages.

Since proverbs tend to be recited in the present tense, people tend to think of them as being universally applicable, as relevant guides for living today as they have been in the past and will continue to be in the future. Different societies rely on proverbs to varying degrees as guides for present behavior. An important part of mastering a second language is understanding both the meanings of proverbs and how seriously they are taken as prescriptions for behavior.

Verbal Dueling

In certain speech communities and under specified conditions, people are encouraged to engage in *verbal dueling* (competitive communication), in which the speakers are more concerned with asserting their dominance than with imparting information. One particularly well-documented example of verbal dueling from our own society is an institutionalized form of an insult contest played by urban black adolescent males—"playing the dozens." This form of verbal dueling begins when one player insults a member of the opponent's family, in most cases his mother. Although the person whose family member has been disparaged can choose not to play, in most cases he will retort with a counterinsult of his own. These insulting verbal thrusts and parries will continue until the participants get bored or someone emerges victorious, with both participants being incited by an attentive audience.

A similar type of verbal dueling is played by Turkish male adolescents. The objective of the Turkish version is to call into question a young man's virility, thereby forcing him into a subordinate role. Even societies that have reputations for being particularly peaceful in nature, such as the Inuit, engage in verbal dueling. It is not surprising to find verbal dueling in nonaggressive societies, for its serves as an effective mechanism for diffusing personal enmity by the use of words rather than weapons.

In some cases verbal dueling can be carried out at a national level. According to Ehud Ya'ari and Ira Friedman (1991), all three of the major players in the 1991 Gulf War (Iraq, Kuwait, and Saudi Arabia) used an archaic rhetorical art form to exchange insults over the airwaves. This traditional form of verbal dueling, known as *hija*, dates back to biblical times when warriors (such as Goliath) would loudly ridicule their opponents while boasting of their own prowess. This ancient literary tradition of "cursing in verse" was based on the notion that one could gain a supernatural advantage by insulting one's adversaries in rhyme. The *hija* form of verbal dueling—which has its own format, meters, and rhyming patterns—begins with boastful self-praise and then proceeds to vitriolic insults. Immediately after the Iraqi invasion of Kuwait in August 1990, the Saudi, Iraqi, and Kuwaiti television stations broadcasted hours of uninterrupted *hija* poetry, praising themselves while berating the opposition. The content of the dueling poets was scathing. To illustrate, because the allied forces included some women, the Iraqi *hija* poets ridiculed the Saudis for hiding behind the skirts of women, a direct and unequivocal insult to their virility. On the other side, Saudi *hija* poets composed brutal verses that accused Saddam Hussein of attacking his neighbors at night, of being ungrateful for the help given him in his earlier efforts against the Iranians, and, the ultimate insult, of being a Jew.

All these forms of verbal dueling—be they found in a Philadelphia ghetto, a Turkish village, the Alaskan tundra, or the Middle East—are examples of nonstandard forms of language use that must be understood if the second-language learner is to appreciate fully the subtleties of the communication patterns in the international marketplace.

Humor

Humor is another aspect of language that tends to confuse the new language learner. No known cultures lack humor, but what is perceived as being funny varies enormously from one culture to another. In some cultures, like the British and American, humor is used in business meetings, and business presentations often start with a humorous antidote. In other cultures, however, business is considered no joking matter. It is not unusual at international business conferences, particularly in Asia, to hear the interpreter say, "The American is now telling a joke. When he finishes, the polite thing to do is to laugh." Often jokes are told in an international business context when in fact it is inappropriate to use humor in such situations. But, even if humor is appropriate, the meaning of the joke or humorous story is frequently lost because it doesn't translate well from one culture to another.

Jokes are difficult to understand because they contain a good deal of information about the culture of the joke teller. To "get" the joke, the listener must understand these pieces of cultural information and how they are combined to make something funny. The long-standing joke in the United States about lawyers is a case in point. "Why do lawyers not have to worry about sharks when they vacation at the beach?" The answer: "Professional courtesy." To appreciate the humor, the listener would have to know several pieces of cultural information about the United States: (1) Sharks have been known to attack

Americans while swimming; (2) lawyers in the United States have the reputation of preying on people; and (3) members of some professions in the United States give special considerations to other members of their profession. Assuming that the listener does understand these culture-specific pieces of information, he or she still needs to appreciate the idea that humor is found in ridiculing an entire profession of people. Asians, however, with their strong traditions of Buddhism and Confucianism, place a high value on politeness and face-saving for others and would find little to laugh about in this type of sarcasm or parody.

Humor tends to be so culture specific that it is usually a good entrée into understanding the culture of the teller of the joke. In other words, jokes tell you a good deal about what is valued in a particular culture. To illustrate, there is a contemporary joke in the United States about the attractive young woman who asks the old man, "Would you like supersex?" His response, "I think I'll take the soup," reflects the generally negative stereotypes that most Americans have concerning the elderly: They have no interest in sex, are hard of hearing, or are so mentally diminished that they cannot distinguish between soup and sex. Americans like to joke about getting old, but people from many parts of Asia, Africa, and South America have the highest regard for the elderly. Thus, such an attempt at humor would not only be not funny, but it also would be offensive.

Conversational Taboos

Communicating in a business context, whether we are managing, selling, or negotiating, requires a certain amount of small talk before the business at hand actually takes place. All linguistic communities have certain topics of conversation, *conversational taboos*, that are considered inappropriate in either polite society or in a business context. When Americans deal with one another for the first time, the small-talk conversation usually starts off with topics that are fairly innocuous, such as the weather, sports, or some noncontroversial aspects of the physical environment. Such topics as religion or politics are usually scrupulously avoided because they are likely to be contentious. Other topics are avoided because they are considered to be too personal and thus off limits, particularly in initial meetings. These include such topics as health, the health of family members, how much one earns, the cost of personal possessions, and such personal data such as age, weight, or sexual preference.

Just as with other aspects of culture, what is an appropriate topic of conversation varies from one group to another. Some cultures, such as German and Iranian, do not share our American taboos on discussing politics; in fact, they often think of Americans as being intellectual lightweights for avoiding such topics. In many parts of the world that place a high value on group and family (such as South America), inquiries about the well-being of a family member is considered quite appropriate. People from a number of cultures do not appreciate discussing topics that may be historically embarrassing, such as World War II for the Germans and Japanese, or illegal immigration into the United States for Mexican businesspeople. Because of the enormous cultural variation on taboo topics, the best advice to follow is (1) do your homework beforehand and (2) take your cue from the other person by allowing him or her to initiate the discussion.

CONCLUSION

It has been estimated conservatively that there are some 3,000 mutually unintelligible languages in the world today. Some of them have hundreds of millions of speakers, whereas some have only hundreds. Yet despite the diversity in the size of different linguistic communities, no languages are inherently more efficient at expressing a wide range of ideas than others. Thus, there is no reason for English-speaking businesspeople to harbor a linguistic superiority complex.

Learning a language requires time, hard work, and dedication on the part of the learner and a sense of commitment on the part of the employer. Even after one masters the vocabulary, grammar, and syntax of a second language, engaging in verbal miscommunication is still possible, even likely. First, it is frequently impossible to translate some ideas from one language into another without a loss of some meaning. Second, some languages rely more on the explicit spoken word, whereas others rely more on the use of nonverbal cues and communication context. Third, people frequently speak different forms of the same language, depending on the social situation in which the communication takes place. Finally, to further complicate communication, all languages, to some extent, use nonstandard forms such as slang and euphemisms.

Yet despite the formidable task that learning a second language is for most Americans, many good reasons justify the effort:

- Learning the host language builds rapport and sets the proper tone for doing business abroad.
- Learning a second language facilitates learning other languages.
- To provide the best possible medical care for oneself and one's family, communicating clearly the nature of a medical problem to local medical personnel who do not speak English is vital.
- With the increasing threat of terrorism against U.S. citizens, a knowledge of the local language might prevent involvement, injury, or death.
- Learning the local language can play a major role in adjusting to culture shock because efficient communication can (1) minimize the frustrations, misunderstandings, and aggravations that face the linguistic outsider and (2) provide a sense of safety, mastery, and self-assurance.

In addition to all these cogent reasons, perhaps the best reason for learning a second language is that it enables the learner to get "inside" another culture. Communicating effectively—so essential to the conduct of business affairs—involves more than a proficiency in sending and receiving messages. Effective communication requires an understanding of how people think, feel, and behave. In short, it involves knowing something about the cultural values, attitudes, and patterns of behavior, and one of the best ways to gain cultural awareness is through a culture's language.

CROSS-CULTURAL SCENARIOS

Read the following cross-cultural scenarios. In each mini-case study, a basic cultural conflict occurs between the actors involved. Try to identify the source of the conflict and suggest how it could have been avoided or minimized. Then see how well your analyses compare to the explanations in Appendix A.

3-1   Wayne Calder, a recent Harvard M.B.A. and one of his organization's most innovative planners, was assigned to the Paris office for a two-year period. Wayne was particularly excited about the transfer because he could now draw on the French he had taken while in school. Knowing that his proficiency in the French language would be an excellent entrée into French society, Wayne was looking forward to getting to know his French colleagues on a personal level. During the first week in Paris, an opportunity to socialize presented itself. While waiting for a planning meeting with top executives to begin, Wayne introduced himself to Monsieur LeBec. They shook hands and exchanged some pleasantries, and then Wayne told LeBec how excited his family was to be in France. Wayne then asked LeBec if he had any children. LeBec replied that he had two daughters and a son. But when Wayne asked other questions about LeBec's family, his French colleague became quite distant and uncommunicative.

What did Wayne do wrong?

3-2   Bill Nugent, an international real estate developer from Dallas, had made a 2:30 P.M. appointment with Mr. Abdullah, a high-ranking government official in Riyadh, Saudi Arabia. From the beginning things did not go well for Bill. First, he was kept waiting until nearly 3:45 before he was ushered into Abdullah's office. When he finally did get in, several other men were also in the room. Even though Bill wanted to get down to business with Abdullah, he was reluctant to get too specific because he considered much of what they needed to discuss sensitive and private. To add to Bill's sense of frustration, Abdullah seemed more interested in engaging in meaningless small talk rather than dealing with the substantive issues concerning their business.

How might you help Bill deal with his frustration?

3-3   After graduating fourth in his class from a highly ranked engineering school, Eric Anderson took a job with an international construction company that had major contracts throughout the world. As a child, Eric had traveled widely with his parents and had never lost his interest in other cultures and other parts of the world. After a six-month orientation in the home office in California, Eric was excited about his assignment as a consulting engineer on a new multimillion-dollar government office building in a West African country. For the first several months, Eric worked with a team of people planning the project before the actual construction began. Since Eric had shown a high aptitude for learning foreign languages in college, he was seen as the most "international" of all the American engineers on the project and was asked by the project manager to enroll in a full-time language course so that he would be able to communicate directly with the local construction workers and supervisors.

The intensive language training went reasonably well for the first several weeks, but after the first month Eric's interest in the course declined considerably. After six weeks, despite the fact that the instructor had nothing but praise for Eric's progress, Eric became increasingly discouraged with the language training and eventually asked to be transferred to another project.

Why did Eric become so dissatisfied?

3-4   A large Baltimore manufacturer of cabinet hardware had been working for months to locate a suitable distributor for its products in Europe. Finally invited to present a demonstration to a reputable distributing company in Frankfurt, it sent one of its most promising young executives, Fred Wagner, to make the presentation. Fred not only spoke fluent German but also felt a special interest in this assignment because his paternal grandparents had immigrated to the United States from the Frankfurt area during the 1920s. When Fred arrived at the conference room where he would be making his presentation, he shook hands firmly, greeted everyone with a friendly *Guten Tag,* and even remembered to bow the head slightly as is the German custom. Fred, a very effective speaker and past president of the Baltimore Toastmasters Club, prefaced his presentation with a few humorous anecdotes to set a relaxed and receptive atmosphere. However, he felt that his presentation was not very well received by the company executives. In fact, his instincts were correct; the German company chose not to distribute Fred's hardware products.

What went wrong?

3-5   Betty Carpenter, president of a cosmetics firm headquartered in Chicago, was interested in expanding its European markets. After attending a four-day trade show in London, she decided to spend several days in Paris, talking to some potential distributors of their more popular product lines. She figured that the three years of college French she had taken while an undergraduate at Radcliffe would hold her in good stead with her business contacts in Paris. Upon arrival she felt quite confident with her proficiency in French, in getting from the airport and checking into her hotel. The next morning she met with Monsieur DuBois, vice president of a large French department store chain. Although their initial conversation went quite well, when the subject turned to business, Betty felt that she was not communicating very effectively with DuBois. He seemed to be getting mildly annoyed and showed little interest in continuing the discussions.

What was Betty's problem?

Communicating across Cultures
The Nonverbal Dimension

Successful communication in the international business environment requires not only an understanding of language but also the nonverbal aspects of communication that are part of any speech community. *Nonverbal communication* has been referred to as *meta-communication, paralinguistics, second-order messages*, the *silent language*, and the *hidden dimension of communication*, among other terms. As important as language is to the sending and receiving of messages, nonverbal communication is equally important because it helps us interpret the linguistic messages being sent. Nonverbal cues frequently indicate whether verbal messages are serious, threatening, jocular, and so on. In addition, nonverbal communication is responsible in its own right for the majority of messages sent and received as part of the human communication process. In fact, it has been suggested on a number of occasions that only about 30 percent of communication between two people in the same speech community is verbal in nature. In a cross-cultural situation (as is likely in international business), when people are not from the same speech community, they will rely even more heavily on nonverbal cues.

THE NATURE OF NONVERBAL COMMUNICATION

Nonverbal communication functions in several important ways in regulating human interaction. It is an effective way of (1) sending messages about our feelings and emotional states, (2) elaborating on our verbal messages, and (3) governing the timing and turn taking between communicators. Even though some nonverbal cues function in similar ways in many cultures, considerable differences in nonverbal patterns can result in breakdowns in communication in a cross-cultural context. The literature is filled with scenarios of how a misreading of nonverbal cues leads directly to cross-cultural friction. The need to master the nonverbal repertoire of another culture—in addition to gaining linguistic competence—increases the challenge of working successfully in an international business setting. Yet, as has been suggested by P. Collett (1971), people who know the nonverbal cues of another culture will be better liked by members of that culture, and by implication, will have a greater chance for successful interaction.

In much the same way that languages are arbitrary systems of communication, nonverbal aspects also display a certain arbitrariness, to the extent that there is a wide range of alternative ways of expressing ideas and emotions nonverbally. The enormous range of nonverbal expressions found throughout the world clearly demonstrates two broad categories of differences: (1) the same nonverbal cue that carries with it very different meanings in different cultures and (2) different nonverbal cues that carry the same meaning in different cultures.

Often the same gesture has different, or even opposite, meanings. Hissing, for example, used as a somewhat rude way of indicating disapproval of a speaker in U.S. society, is used as a normal way to ask for silence in certain Spanish-speaking countries and as a way of applauding among the Basuto of South Africa. In U.S. society, protruding one's tongue is an unmistakable gesture of mocking contempt, whereas in southern China it is an expression of embarrassment over a faux pas (LaBarre 1947, 57). The hand gesture of inserting the thumb between the index and third fingers is a sign for good luck in Portugal but an invitation to have sex in Germany. The hand gesture of putting one's index finger to the temple communicates "He is smart" in the United States but also means just the opposite—"He is stupid"—in certain Western European cultures.

In contrast, the same message can be sent in various cultures by very different nonverbal cues. To illustrate, in the United States and most Western European societies, the nonverbal cue for affirmation (that is, signifying yes or agreement) is nodding the head up and down. Despite contentions by early twentieth-century psychologists that such a nonverbal gesture is natural or instinctive to all humans, we now know that affirmation is in fact communicated nonverbally in a variety of different ways. For example, affirmation is signaled among the Semang of Malaya by thrusting the head forward sharply, in Ethiopia by throwing the head back, among the Dyaks of Borneo by raising the eyebrows, among the Ainu of northern Japan by bringing both hands to the chest and then gracefully waving them downward with palms up, and by rocking the head from shoulder to shoulder among the Bengali servants of Calcutta (Jensen 1982, 264–65).

The last decade has witnessed a dramatic increase in research on the general topic of nonverbal communication. Like any new field of study, what constitutes the subject matter of nonverbal communication has not always met with widespread agreement. Classifications of nonverbal behavior vary from the threefold scheme of A. M. Eisenberg and R. R. Smith (1971) to the typology of John Condon and Fathi Yousef (1975, 123–24), which includes twenty four categories. Despite the many alternative ways of categorizing the domain of nonverbal communication, the following topics are found widely in the literature:

- Facial expressions (smiles, frowns)
- Hand gestures
- Walking (gait)
- Posture

- Space usage (proxemics)
- Touching
- Eye contact
- Olfaction (scents or smells such as perfume)
- Color symbolism
- Artifacts (jewelry, fly whisks, lapel pins)
- Clothing
- Hairstyles
- Cosmetics
- Time symbolism
- Graphic symbols
- Silence

A thorough discussion of all these aspects of nonverbal communication would take us beyond the scope of this book. However, to convey the importance of nonverbal communication in an international business context, we will examine some of the more obvious domains in some detail. This discussion will be limited to those nonverbal phenomena that most significantly affect interpersonal communication, including posture, gestures, touching, facial expressions, eye contact, and the use of space. Before such a discussion, however, it is imperative that we first understand some of the potential pitfalls of studying nonverbal communication in the international business environment.

First, there is the potential hazard of overgeneralization. We frequently hear references made to such geographical areas as the Middle East, Latin America, or sub-Saharan Africa, yet these are hardly appropriate units of analysis for observing patterns of nonverbal communication. In sub-Saharan Africa alone, there are over forty independent nation-states and more than 800 different linguistic communities that speak mutually unintelligible languages. Yet we cannot count on uniformity even within a single speech community, for even here there are likely to be internal variations in nonverbal communication patterns, depending on such variables as class, education, occupation, and religion. For example, many of Edward Hall's insightful conclusions on Arab nonverbal communication (discussed subsequently) are based on the observations of middle- and upper-class males, largely students and businesspeople. Arab females would not very likely conform to the same patterns of nonverbal communication as the Arab males that Hall describes. Thus, it is advisable to exercise some caution when generalizing even within a single culture or speech community.

A second potential obstacle is the unwarranted assumption that within any given speech community all nonverbal cues are of equal importance. Some nonverbal patterns may be rarely used and imperfectly understood, whereas others are more widely used and universally understood.

A third possible pitfall lies in overemphasizing the differences between cultures in terms of their nonverbal communication patterns. Although in this chapter we focus on the great variety of nonverbal patterns found throughout the world, many nonverbal similarities also exist between different speech communities. The problem, of course, for the international businessperson is to distinguish between them.

Finally, we should avoid thinking that the consequences of misunderstanding nonverbal cues are always catastrophic. To be certain, misreading some nonverbal cues can lead to the misinterpretation of social meanings, which in turn can result in serious breakdowns in communication and the generation of hostility. Many other nonverbal cues, on the other hand, have no such dire consequences but only cause minor irritations, even amusement. Misreading *all* nonverbal cues is not a grave matter, but the greater knowledge we have of the nonverbal cues found in the international business environment, the greater will be our chances of successful communication and the achievement of our personal and professional objectives.

Having mentioned these methodological caveats, let's now briefly examine some of the more salient areas of nonverbal communication. The following discussion of such subdivisions as posture, gestures, and proxemics (space usage) should not suggest that these points are isolated or unrelated to one another. Used here solely for purposes of presentation, this approach should not be interpreted as denying or overlooking the very real connections between these aspects of nonverbal communication found in any speech community.

BODY POSTURE

The way that people hold their bodies frequently communicates information about their social status, religious practices, feelings of submissiveness, desires to maintain social distance, and sexual intentions, to mention only several areas. When communicating, people tend to orient their bodies toward others by assuming a certain stance or posture. A person may stand over another person, kneel, or "turn a cold shoulder"; in each case, something different would be communicated by the body posture. Postural cues constitute very effective signs of a person's inner state, as well as his or her behavioral expectations of others.

It has been suggested that the human body is capable of assuming approximately 1,000 different body postures (Hewes 1955, 231). Of course, which body position any given culture chooses to emphasize will be learned by the same process by which other aspects of culture are internalized. To illustrate this point, let's look at differences in body posture that people assume when relaxing. People in the United States, for example, are sitters, whereas people in some rural parts of Mexico are squatters. This basic cultural difference has actually been used by the U.S. Border Patrol to identify illegal aliens. According to Larry A. Samovar and Richard E. Porter (1991, 192), by flying surveillance planes at low altitudes over migrant worker camps in southern California, the Border Patrol can tell which groups of campers are squatting and which are sitting, the implication being that the squatters are the illegal aliens.

When people are interacting in a cross-cultural environment, sharp differences can be seen in terms of what postures are taken and what meanings they convey. For example, in the United States we stand up to show respect; in certain Polynesian cultures, people sit down. We frequently lean back in our chairs and put our feet on our desks to convey a relaxed, informal attitude, but the Swiss and Germans would think such posture rude. For many people, squatting is the most normal position for relaxing, yet for the typical American it seems improper, "uncivilized," or at least not terribly sophisticated.

Sometimes we can inadvertently choose a body posture that will have disastrous results. Condon and Yousef describe such a case:

The British professor of poetry relaxed during his lecture at Ain Shams University in Cairo. So carried away was he in explicating a poem that he leaned back in his chair and so revealed the sole of his foot to an astonished class. To make such a gesture in a Moslem society is the worst kind of insult. The Cairo newspapers the next day carried banner headlines about the student demonstration which resulted, and they denounced British arrogance and demanded that the professor be sent home. (1975, 122)

Perhaps one of the most visible and dramatic nonverbal messages sent by posture or body stance is that of submissiveness. Generally, submissiveness is conveyed by making oneself appear smaller, by cringing, crouching, cowering, or groveling. The idea behind this posture is that the individual is so weak, small, and nonthreatening that he or she is hardly worth attacking. In its most extreme form, we can see prisoners of war crouching before their captors in a squatting position, heads lowered, with their bodies curled up. In its mildest form, we can notice a subordinate person bending ever so slightly at the waist (bowing) in the direction of the superordinate person. This form of bowing is a very subtle and temporary lowering of the body in deference to the higher-status person.

The degree to which a bowing or lowering of the body is emphasized varies from one culture to another. In many cultures today, the full bow or other dramatic lowering of the body is generally reserved for formal occasions such as greeting a head of state or monarch or as part of certain religious ceremonies. For example, British commoners standing before the queen or being honored by royalty in a ceremony of knighthood would be expected to bow, curtsey, or kneel. As part of their religious practices, some Christians kneel, Catholics genuflect, and Muslims kowtow, an extreme form of body lowering in which the forehead is brought to the ground. Although bowing as a worldwide phenomenon has been on the decrease in recent decades, it has survived in German culture and exists to an even greater degree in modern Japan. In the United States, however, bowing or any type of submissive body posture is particularly irritating, for it tends to connote undue formality, aristocracy, and a nonverbal denial of egalitarianism.

Nowhere is bowing more important to the process of communication today than in Japanese society. As an indication of how pervasive bowing is in present-day Japan, Helmut Morsbach reports that "some female department store employees have the sole function of bowing to customers at department store escalators" and that many Japanese "bow repeatedly to invisible partners at the other end of a telephone line" (1982, 307). Bowing initiates interaction between two Japanese, it enhances and embellishes many parts of the ensuing conversation, and it is used to signal the end of a conversation. Although Westerners, in a very general sense, understand the meaning attached to bowing, appropriate bowing in Japan is an intricate and complex process. Reciprocal bowing is determined largely by rank. In fact, the depth of their bows reveals the relative social status of two communicators (the deeper the bow, the lower the status). When bowing deeply,

Bowing is an important mode of nonverbal communication in Japan.

it is conventional to lean slightly to the right to avoid bumping heads. The person of lower status is expected to initiate the bow, and the person of higher status determines when the bow is completed. People of equivalent status are expected to bow at the same depth while starting and finishing at the same time. And as H. Befu relates, this synchronization is an important feature:

> The matter of synchrony, in fact perfect synchrony, is absolutely essential to bowing. Whenever an American tries to bow to me, I often feel extremely awkward and uncomfortable because I simply cannot synchronize bowing with him or her. . . . Bowing occurs in a flash of a second, before you have time to think. And both parties must know precisely when to start bowing, how deep, how long to stay in the bowed position, and when to bring their heads up. (1979, 118)

How we position ourselves when communicating with another person is also culturally variable. To turn one's back on someone is a clear nonverbal indicator in the United States (and in many other societies as well) of an unwillingness to converse at all. But the degree to which two people are expected to face one another in normal conversation is not the same in all cultures. Even though two white, middle-class Americans have no difficulty conversing while walking next to each other with an occasional turn of the head, Edward Hall found it to be a major problem when attempting to walk and talk in this fashion with an Arab friend (1966, 160–61). While they walked, the Arab stopped to face Hall each time he spoke. Since many Arabic cultures insist on a high degree of eye contact when conversing, conversants must be facing one another directly. Hall soon discovered that to talk while walking side by side without maintaining intense eye contact was considered rude by the Arab's standards. This example illustrates not only how body stance or position communicates different messages but also how two domains of nonverbal communication—body position and gaze—are intimately interconnected.

HAND GESTURES

Until very recently, the importance of hand gestures has been largely unnoticed. Nonverbal communication in general and hand gestures in particular have long been considered a trivial aspect of communication, especially in the Western world. Since we are told that language (the capacity to use words to symbolize) is the hallmark of our humanity, we tend to consider all other forms of communication as pedantic and unimportant. But human communication is greatly enriched by the nonverbal component; the very meaning of words can in fact change, depending on the accompanying hand gestures. Randall Harrison (1974, 135) offers an illustration from the English language. The words "Just let me say . . ." when used with the gesture of the hand up, palm facing the addressee, are likely to mean "Wait, let me say. . . ." These same words with the gesture of the hand out, palm facing downward, would most likely imply "Let me tell you how it really is. . . ." Finally, to utter these words with the hand out, palm facing upward, would mean "It seems to me. . . ." Thus, these three different palm orientations can provide three quite different meanings to the same words. Obviously, words are nearly indispensible for the communication of facts, but without hand gestures the human communication process would be mechanical and less capable of subtle nuances.

The use of fingers, hands, and arms for purposes of communicating varies considerably from one culture to another. Some cultures (for example, those located in southern Europe and the Middle East) employ a wide variety of gestures frequently and with considerable force and purposefulness. The half-jocular notion that Italians would be unable to express themselves if their hands were tied behind their backs is more than a vulgar stereotype. Based on research conducted on Italian and Jewish immigrants in New York City, David Efron (1941) found that Italians used broad, full-arm gestures with relative frequency. At the other extreme, some indigenous Indian groups in Bolivia use hand gestures very sparingly because the cool highland climate requires them to keep their hands under shawls or blankets (Jensen 1982, 266). Still other cultures, like our own and those found in northern Europe, illustrating a middle position, tend to be more reserved in their use of gestures. These cultures place a higher value on verbal messages and no doubt consider excessive gesturing to be overly emotional, nonrational, and socially unsophisticated.

Unlike verbal communication, which is usually well documented in structure and meaning, the nonverbal aspects of communication in most language communities are very infrequently described; when they are, those descriptions are usually superficial and incomplete. One of the rare exceptions is the study conducted by Desmond Morris and colleagues (1979) of twenty major gestures found in Western Europe. Data were collected from forty localities, using twenty five languages, in twenty five different countries. A sizable number of these gestures, used and understood widely in contemporary Europe, are also used and understood in the United States. There is, for example, general consensus in both the United States and Western Europe about the meaning of crossed fingers (good luck), the contemptuous nose thumb, and the sexually insulting forearm jerk. Given our strong European heritage, many European gestures have survived the Atlantic crossing. Yet despite these similarities on both sides of the Atlantic, far more gestures that have little or no meaning in the United States are used commonly in Europe. Morris and his associates cite the following hand gestures, which are widely used in Europe but have little meaning to the average American:

> The *eyelid pull* (the forefinger is placed below one eye, pulling the skin downward and thereby tugging on the lower eyelid)—meaning "I am alert" or "Be alert" in Spain, France, Italy, and Greece.
>
> The *chin stroke* (the thumb and forefinger, placed on each cheek bone, are gently stroked down to the chin)—meaning "thin and ill" in the southern Mediterranean area.
>
> The *earlobe pull* or *flick* (the earlobe is tugged or flicked with the thumb and forefinger of the hand on the same side of the body)—a sign of effeminacy found predominantly in Italy, meaning "I think you are so effeminate that you should be wearing an earring."
>
> The *nose tap* (the forefinger in a vertical position taps the side of the nose)—meaning "Keep it a secret."

One source of confusion when trying to understand hand gestures in other cultures is that different cultures can use quite different gestures to signify the same idea. Morris (1977, 41–42) illustrates this notion by looking at how men in different parts of the world signal their appreciation of a physically attractive woman:

> The *cheek stroke* (Greece, Italy, and Spain)—the gesturer places his forefinger and thumb on his cheekbone and strokes them gently toward the chin.
>
> The *cheek screw* (Italy, Sardinia)—the forefinger is pressed into the cheek and rotated.
>
> The *breast curve* (found in a wide range of cultures)—hands simulate the curve of the female breast.
>
> The *waist curve* (common in English-speaking countries)—the hands sweep down to make the curvacious outline of the female trunk.
>
> The *eye touch* (South America, Italy)—a straight forefinger is placed on the lower eyelid and pulled down slightly.
>
> The *two-handed telescope* (Brazil)—the hands are curled one in front of the other as the man looks through them in telescope style.
>
> The *moustache twist* (Italy)—the thumb and forefinger twist an imaginary moustache.
>
> The *hand on heart* (South America)—the right hand is placed over the heart, signifying a "heart throb."
>
> The *fingertip kiss* (France)—the fingertips are kissed and then spread out in the direction of the woman.
>
> The *air kiss* (English-speaking countries)—a man kisses the air in the direction of the woman.
>
> The *cheek pinch* (Sicily)—a man pinches his own cheek.
>
> The *breast cup* (Europe in general)—both hands make a cupping movement in the air, simulating the squeezing of the woman's breast.

By researching the ethnographic literature, we could no doubt identify many other hand gestures found in different cultures to signify female attractiveness. However, the

This hand gesture has different meanings in different culutres. Beware! Don't use this gesture in parts of South America. It doesn't mean "OK."

major point has been made: since the human hand is such a precision instrument, and since communication patterns are so arbitrary, a vast array of alternative hand gestures can convey any given idea.

Cross-cultural misunderstandings can also occur when a single hand gesture has a number of different meanings in different parts of the world. For example, most people in the United States know that to signify that something is OK or good one raises one's hand and makes a circle with the thumb and forefinger. However, this same hand gesture means "zero" or "worthless" to the French, "money" to the Japanese, "male homosexual" in Malta, and a general sexual insult in parts of South America. Another example—and one that had some serious diplomatic repercussions—is the clasped-hands-over-the-head gesture made famous by Soviet Premier Khrushchev on his visit to the United States in the 1960s. Interpreted by Americans as an arrogant gesture used by victorious prizefighters, it was used by Khrushchev as a gesture of international friendship.

Those in high office are not immune from sending unintentional messages nonverbally when traveling abroad. As his limousine passed a group of protestors in Canberra, Australia, President George Bush early in 1992 held up his first two fingers with the back of his hand toward the protestors. Thinking that he was giving the nonverbal gesture meaning "victory," he failed to realize that in Australia that same hand gesture is equivalent to holding up the middle finger in the United States.

FACIAL EXPRESSIONS

The face, perhaps the single most important part of the body for channeling nonverbal communication, is particularly rich in its potential for communicating emotional states. Next to speech, the face is the "primary source of giving information" (Knapp 1972, 68–69). Although in English, and in most other languages as well, only a handful of words refer to specific facial expressions (for example, *smile, frown, grimace, squint*); human facial muscles, however, are so complex that approximately 1,000 different facial expressions are possible (Ekman, Friesen, and Ellsworth 1972, 1). The face is in fact so central to the process of communication that we speak of "face-to-face" communication, and English speakers to some extent, and Japanese to a far greater degree, speak of "losing face" in certain unfortunate situations.

There is little question about the importance of the face as a source of nonverbal communication. The face is capable of conveying emotional, attitudinal, and factual information in short periods of time. In addition, the question of facial expressions has been central to the nature–nurture debate surrounding all nonverbal communication. Unlike every other form of nonverbal communication—which tends to be largely culture bound—a substantial body of literature claims that some facial expressions may be innate human traits, regardless of cultural context. Charles Darwin (1872) was the first to propose the notion of certain universal facial expressions, an idea also supported by F. H. Allport (1924) and Paul Ekman, Wallace V. Friesen, and Phoebe Ellsworth (1972). All these researchers have attempted to demonstrate that certain emotions are expressed by the same facial expressions in widely diverse cultures, including isolated, preliterate cultures having no contact with the Western world. Some researchers have traveled the globe in search of remote tribal groups that have facial expressions identical to our own. For example, I. Eibl-Eibesfeldt (1971) contends that all people give a rapid "eyebrow flash" when greeting someone (the eyebrows are instantaneously raised and then lowered). Although this research is not exhaustive, the wide global distribution of this particular facial movement strongly suggests that the behavior is inborn. Moreover, children who were born blind and deaf exhibit the normal repertoire of facial expressions, which would tend to eliminate the possible explanation that the expressions were acquired through the process of learning (Eibl-Eibesfeldt 1972).

The nature–nurture question has not been settled, and others contend that facial expressions are culture bound. R. L. Birdwhistell (1963) advances the position that facial expressions do not have universal meanings but are instead the result of cultural, not biological, inheritance. To substantiate this position, one has only to examine the variations in smiling behavior throughout the world. Weston LaBarre (1947, 52) distinguishes between two well-described cultures in the southwest Pacific—the Papuans, known for their wide use of smiling, and the Dobus, where "dourness reigned." Geoffrey Gorer (1935, 10) reports that in certain parts of Africa laughter and smiling are used to express surprise, wonder, and embarrassment, not amusement or happiness. Morsbach (1982, 307) suggests that, although a sign of joy in Japan, smiling can also be used to hide displeasure, sorrow, or anger and the trained observer should be able to distinguish between these two types of smiling. J. V. Jensen (1982, 265) contends that in some Asian cultures smiling is a sign of weakness, and it is for this reason that teachers avoid smiling in class lest they lose control over their students. Thus, it would appear that, despite the fact that all people smile, the meanings attached to this particular facial expression vary widely.

In some parts of the world, it is considered highly desirable to maintain an expressionless face. Nowhere is this ideal more widely adhered to than in Japan, which no doubt accounts for the contention by many Westerners that the Japanese are "inscrutable." According to Morsbach,

> Self-control, thought of as highly desirable in Japan, demands that a man of virtue will not show a negative emotion in his face when shocked or upset by sudden bad news; and if successful, is lauded as *tiazen jijaku to shite* (perfectly calm and collected), or *mayu hitotsu ugokasazu ni* (without even moving an eyebrow). . . . The idea of an expressionless face in situations of great anxiety was strongly emphasized in the *bushido* (way of the warrior) which was the guideline for samurai and the ideal of many others. (1982, 308)

This ideal of masking one's emotions is well supported by research conducted by K. Shimoda, M. Argyle, and R. Bitti (1978). English, Italian, and Japanese judges were asked to read or "decode" the nonverbal facial expressions of performers from these three cultural groups. All three sets of judges had the least accuracy reading the facial expressions of the Japanese performers, a result explained by the lack of negative facial expressions.

It is not necessary here to decide which side in this nature–nurture debate is most correct; reality exists somewhere in between these two polarized positions. In other words, no facial expressions are either totally innate or totally acquired by learning. A more reasonable interpretation of the data would be that, although certain facial expressions may be universal, specific cultural norms may influence how, when, and why they are used. For example, the stimulus that elicits a particular facial expression may differ from culture to culture: In the United States, the sight of a rat running through one's kitchen might elicit fear and/or disgust; in another culture, where rodents are routinely eaten, such a sight might provoke pure joy and delight.

Another factor that tends to produce cultural differences is that facial expressions are filtered through one's culturally learned display rules. Our culture teaches us what we should feel and how we should show it. It might be appropriate to intensify a felt emo-

---

Smiles don't always indicate happiness. Christopher Engholm relates a personal experience that illustrates the meaning of a smile in China:

> One morning, standing in front of our hotel in Korla, a desert town in the Xinjiand province of China, a United Nations consultant and I saw a tractor-wagon, loaded with masonry rock, hit a ditch and dump its contents upon its driver. . . . Our hotel concierge ran over to examine the situation and gave us the lowdown with a toothy smile: "He dead for sure. Hit his head very hard, I think." We stood there horrified at his seeming indifference, until we remembered that his smile was a shield to protect us—the honored foreign guests—from being disturbed by the event. (1991, 134)

tion because it is socially expected, such as a display of exaggerated pleasure over receiving a Christmas present that was not particularly attractive or desirable. On other occasions, it might be socially appropriate to deintensify, or de-emphasize, an emotion, such as repressing one's delight over winning a large pot in a poker game. In some situations, a culture requires one emotion to mask another, as exemplified by the runner-up in a beauty contest who is expected to suppress her own disappointment by showing happiness for the winner. Or looked at from an intercultural perspective, Morsbach (1982, 307) reminds us that the Japanese often mask their sorrow or anger by laughing and smiling. Thus, these socially learned display rules of intensification, deintensification, and masking can modify facial expressions from one cultural context to another. If in fact cultural learning can affect how and to what extent messages are sent by facial expressions, it behooves international businesspeople to become familiar with this critical aspect of nonverbal communication.

GAZE

All cultures use gaze (eye contact) as a very important mechanism of communicating nonverbally. J. Heron refers to gaze as "the most fundamental primary mode of interpersonal encounter," for it is where two pairs of eyes come together "that people actually meet (in the strict sense)" (1970, 244). Unlike other forms of nonverbal communication, the gaze is particularly salient because it is so noticeable. As P. C. Ellsworth notes,

> For a behavior that involves no noise and little movement, it has a remarkable capacity to draw attention to itself even at a distance. . . . People often use a direct gaze to attract another person's attention in situations where noise or gesticulation are inappropriate. The fact that we expect others to be responsive to our gaze is illustrated by our exasperation when dealing with people who have learned immunity to the effects of a stare, such as waiters. (1975, 5–6)

The communicative function of the eyes has not escaped the nonsocial scientists, for as Ralph Waldo Emerson wrote, "One of the most wonderful things in nature is a glance of the eye; it transends speech; it is the bodily symbol of identity" (cited in Champness 1970, 309). The eyes are in fact such a powerful force for interpersonal interaction that it is impossible not to communicate through visual behavior; that is, if we maintain eye contact with someone, we are communicating just as much as if we avoid eye contact.

Although some aspects of eye communication are partially controlled by physiology, such as pupil dilation, much of the meaning attached to gaze and gaze avoidance is culturally determined. Like many other forms of learned behavior, gaze can be affected by early childhood socialization, as exemplified by Japanese infants who are carried on their mothers' backs and thus have little contact with the mothers' faces. In later life, cultures tend to be extremely efficient at instilling certain values concerning gaze or its avoidance. Yet whenever it may be internalized, how, when, and to what extent people in different parts of the world use gaze as a communication mechanism vary widely.

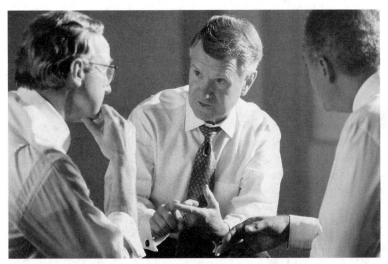

In some societies the direct intense gaze is a sign of attentiveness and respect while in others it is threatening and hostile.

One of the best scientifically controlled studies of eye contact in a number of different cultures was conducted by O. M. Watson (1970) among foreign-exchange students in the United States. Pairs of students were invited into a laboratory and asked to talk on any subject in their native language while being observed from a one-way screen. Watson found that the highest levels of gaze were recorded for Arabs and people from Latin America, and the lowest levels were found among Indians and northern Europeans. These findings lend credence to the earlier statement made by Edward Hall that "Arabs look each other in the eye when talking with an intensity that makes most Americans highly uncomfortable" (1966, 161). In addition, Watson found that, within any given group, gaze did not vary according to overseas cultural experience, such as length of time in the United States. This is a good indicator that gaze patterns are fairly rigidly fixed early in life and are relatively unaffected by adult experiences.

There are a number of cultures in which gaze tends to be more important than it is among middle-class Americans. For example, in Greece it is customary to look at people in public places, a practice that would make the typical resident of Kansas quite uncomfortable. In North Africa the Taureg place considerable emphasis on gaze because the other channels of nonverbal communication, such as hands and arms, are covered with clothing. In such cultures a lesser degree of eye contact (such as might be found in the United States) can be viewed as impolite, inattentive, insincere, and aloof.

On the other hand, many societies teach their children to avoid direct eye contact in general or in specific social situations. Michael Argyle and Mark Cook (1976, 29) report that among the Wituto and Bororo Indians of South America both parties in a conversation must avoid direct eye contact by looking at some external object while talking. In Japan, rather than looking a person straight in the eyes, one should focus the gaze somewhat lower, around the region of the Adam's apple (Morsbach 1982, 308). The Navajo define eye contact so negatively that they have as part of their folklore a mythical monster named He-Who-Kills-With-His-Eyes who serves to teach Navajo youngsters that to stare can actually kill another person. In many parts of sub-Saharan Africa, direct eye contact must be avoided when addressing a higher-status person. When we interact in an international business context with people from such cultures, we must realize that our insistence on maintaining a relatively high level of gaze could be interpreted as threatening, disrespectful, haughty, or insulting.

Just as there are considerable verbal differences between the English spoken in England and in the United States, there are also differences in certain nonverbal aspects of communication, such as the use of eyes to send and receive messages. Charles Mitchell tells of an American businesswoman who had developed a good working relationship (over the telephone) with a British colleague working in London:

> All went well until the American traveled to London to meet face-to-face with her British colleague to sign a research and development contract. The first meeting did not go well. "There was something that did not seem right," she says, "Throughout the presentation none of the Brits, not even the guy I had developed a phone relationship with, would look us in the eye. It was like they were hiding something. After a lot of internal discussion, we decided to sign the contract, but many of us still felt uneasy. . . . It almost ruined the relationship and sunk the deal." (2000, 5)

Rules for eye contact in public places also vary from one culture to another. In France, for example, it is quite acceptable for a man to stare blatantly at a woman on the street. In fact, according to Flora Davis, "Some French women complain that they feel uncomfortable on American streets—as if they had suddenly become invisible" (1971, 68). This is understandable because public eye behavior in the United States is considerably more restricted than in France or in other parts of the world. In the United States, staring openly at someone in a public place is considered rude and an infringement on his or her privacy. Instead, Americans practice what Erving Goffman (1963) refers to as "civil inattention," a very subtle practice whereby people give others just enough eye contact to acknowledge their presence but at the next moment withdraw that eye contact so they are not singled out as an object of particular curiosity. When two people are walking toward each other, civil inattention permits eye contact up to approximately eight feet before the eyes are cast downward as they pass, or as Goffman puts it, "a kind of dimming of lights" (1963, 84). Like so many other aspects of nonverbal behavior, civil inattention is such a subtle social ritual that most middle-class Americans are barely aware of it. Nevertheless, it remains an important nonverbal behavior that regulates interaction in the United States.

PROXEMICS

How people use personal space in their interactions with others is another "silent language" that must be understood to achieve clear communication within an international business setting. This area of nonverbal communication is known as the study of *prox-*

According to anthropologist Conrad Kottak,

> The world's cultures have strikingly different opinions about matters of personal space. When Americans talk, walk, and dance, they maintain a certain distance from others—their personal space. Brazilians, who maintain less physical distance, interpret this as a sign of coldness. When conversing with an American, the Brazilian characteristically moves in as the American "instinctively" retreats. In these body movements, neither Brazilian nor American is trying consciously to be especially friendly or unfriendly. Each is merely executing a program written on the self by years of exposure to a particular cultural tradition. Because of different cultural conceptions of proper social space, cocktail parties in such international meeting places as the United Nations can resemble an elaborate insect mating ritual, as diplomats from different cultures advance, withdraw, and sidestep. (1987, 210)

emics, a term introduced by anthropologist Edward Hall, most notably in his book *The Hidden Dimension* (1966). Although other researchers have developed similar concepts to Hall's notion of personal space (Sommer 1959; Kuethe 1962; Little 1965), his observations and theories are not only clearly presented but also rich in cross-cultural insights. Hall's major contribution to our understanding of intercultural communication has been to demonstrate that people follow predictable cultural patterns when establishing distance between themselves and others. How close a person gets to another in normal conversation depends on the nature of the social interaction, but in all cases the specific magnitude of the distance is dictated by *cultural* norms.

An important part of Edward Hall's (1966) typology of proxemics is his delineation of four categories of distance based on his observations of middle-class Americans:

1. *Intimate distance*: ranging from body contact to eighteen inches, a distance used for lovemaking, comforting, and protecting, at which olfactory and thermal sensations are at their highest.
2. *Personal distance*: from eighteen inches to four feet, depending on the closeness of the relationship. At this distancing mode people have an invisible "space bubble" separating themselves from others.
3. *Social distance*: from four to twelve feet, a distance used by acquaintances and strangers in business meetings and classrooms.
4. *Public distance*: from twelve to twenty five feet, at which the recognition of others is not mandatory and the subtle shades of meaning of voice, gesture, and facial expression are lost.

Although the specific distances described apply to middle-class Americans, all cultures have accustomed their people to feel comfortable at a specific distance. What is appropriate distance for one cultural group might appear to be "crowding" to another or "standoffish" to a third. For example, operating within Edward Hall's (1966) category of personal space, most middle-class Americans choose for normal conversations a distance of approximately twenty inches, with minor variations depending on sex and level of intimacy. For certain cultural groups in South America and the Caribbean, the normal conversational distance is in the range of fourteen to fifteen inches. And for certain cul-

Arabs and Westerners have different definitions of how closely people should stand to one another in normal conversation.

tures in the Middle East, that distance is as small as nine to ten inches. These appreciable differences should make it painfully obvious just how important an understanding of proxemic variables is to effective intercultural communication. To stand twenty inches from a Saudi Arabian, although normal for an American, communicates reserve, unfriendliness, and a sense of superiority. Yet when the Saudi moves closer, to establish what for him or her is a more comfortable conversational distance, the typical American interprets it as pushy or aggressive. Because of these culturally produced perceptions of space, Americans, when conversing with South Americans or Middle Easterners, may find themselves continually backpedaling in an attempt to maintain their twenty-inch distance as their foreign acquaintances continue to move closer. Although both conversants are simply trying to establish the normal conversational distance as determined by their cultural upbringing, considerable misunderstandings can occur.

Proxemic patterns are so important for cross-cultural communication largely because they represent such a subtle and frequently overlooked form of nonverbal communication. Each culture develops its own set of rules and uses of space, which like other aspects of culture are learned, but learned in an unconscious manner. It would be hard to find anyone in the United States who could testify that while growing up his or her adult role models explicitly taught him or her to maintain a conversational distance of twenty inches. Nevertheless, according to the findings of Edward Hall and others, middle-class

Americans have learned what "proper" distance is, and they have learned it with remarkable consistency.

Although Hall's (1966) descriptions of cultural differences in space usage are anecdotal, other, more empirically based research has come to essentially the same conclusions. O. M. Watson and T. D. Graves (1966), testing Hall's theories in a comparative study of American and Arab students, found that the Arab students not only stood closer to one another than did the Americans but also talked more loudly, touched each other more often, maintained a higher degree of eye contact, and faced each other more directly. In another study, K. B. Little (1968) used doll figures as a simulated measure of personal space among five cultural groups: Americans, Swedes, Scots, Greeks, and southern Italians. As Hall's theories predicted, the southern European cultures chose social schemes reflecting less interpersonal distances than northern European and American cultures. Later empirical research by Watson (1970) concluded that South Americans, Asians, and people from the subcontinent of India normally choose spatial distances that are midway between Arabs and northern Europeans. Finally, J. C. Baxter (1970), observing 859 pairs of people in a New York City zoo, found that Mexicans stood appreciably closer to one another than did white Americans, and black Americans stood farther apart than the other two groups.

An awareness of proxemics has important implications for the conduct of international business. How different cultural groups use their office space, for example, can lead to breakdowns in communications between business partners. Whereas many Americans are accustomed to having a desk between themselves and their business partners, many South Americans see a desk as an unnecessary barrier and may try to crowd into the American's personal space. At the other extreme, Germans, who see their personal space as an extension of their egos, tend to be very protective of it. Unlike Americans, who generally close their office doors only for private conferences, Germans are likely to keep their office doors closed all the time because to do otherwise is considered to be exceedingly unbusinesslike. Moreover, Germans become uncomfortable when someone moves his or her office chair closer to adjust the social situation. This cultural norm, at least in part, explains why Germans prefer heavy office furniture: people cannot rearrange the chairs and possibly intrude on their personal space. In fact, Edward Hall reports that "a German newspaper editor who had moved to the United States had his visitor's chair bolted to the floor 'at the proper distance' because he couldn't tolerate the American habit of adjusting the chair to the situation" (1966, 137–38). Regardless of whether we encounter a preference for open doors or closed doors, or flexible or inflexible office arrangements, these things are likely to have different meanings in different cultures, which can influence the nature of the international business relationship.

BODILY CONTACT (TOUCHING)

Touching is perhaps the most personal form of nonverbal communication, and yet paradoxically it is one that most people are reluctant to discuss. For the first several months of life, touching is by far the most intense channel of communication, particularly between mother and child. In fact, as Ashley Montagu (1972, 93) so dramatically points out, tactile communication is so important in infants that its deprivation can have devastating, even lethal, effects.

Humans touch in a variety of ways and for a variety of purposes. But of all the logical possibilities, each culture retains a limited number of forms of touching. For example, Argyle (1975, 287) suggests that in Western cultures the following types of touching are commonly found:

Patting (head, back)	Holding (hand, arm, knee)
Slapping (face, hand, bottom)	Guiding (hand, arm)
Punching (face, chest)	Embracing (shoulder, body)
Pinching (cheek)	Linking (arms)
Stroking (hair, face, upper body, knee)	Laying-on (hands)
Shaking (hands)	Kicking (bottom)
Kissing (mouth, cheek, breast, hand, foot)	Grooming (hair, face)
Licking (face)	Tickling (anywhere)

Cultures outside of the West may use some or all of these forms of touch, and they may use others as well. Each culture has a well-defined system of meanings for different forms of touching for various parts of the body. Each culture also defines who can touch whom, on what parts of the body, and under what set of social circumstances. In the United States, it is perfectly acceptable for two adult men to communicate friendliness and goodwill by shaking hands. But if these same two men held hands while walking down the street, they would be communicating a very different message—and one that is less congruent with conventional standards.

While conducting anthropological field research in central Kenya during the 1970s, I became particularly aware of how meanings conveyed through touch can vary across cultures. Even before going to Kenya, I had known through ethnographic readings that Kikuyu men routinely held hands with their close personal friends. After several months of living and working with the Kikuyu, I was walking through a village in Kiambu District with a local headman who had become a key informant

According to Conrad P. Kottak (1987, 210), one of the most obvious cultural differences between Brazil and the United States involves physical contact—kissing, hugging, touching in general. Middle-class Brazilian children—both boys and girls—are taught to kiss (on the cheek, twice or three times, coming and going) every adult relative they ever see. Given the size of Brazilian extended families, this can mean hundreds of people. Girls continue kissing throughout their lives. Males go on kissing their female relatives and friends. Until they are adolescents, boys also kiss adult male relatives. Thereafter, Brazilian men greet each other with hearty handshakes and the traditional male hug (*abraco*). These embraces are tighter and last longer the closer the relationship.

In certain parts of the world, this friendly gesture of touching someone with the left hand is considered a serious insult.

and a close personal acquaintance. As we walked side by side, my friend took my hand in his. Within less than thirty seconds, my palm was perspiring all over his. Despite the fact that I knew cognitively that this was a perfectly legitimate Kikuyu gesture of friendship, my own cultural values (that is, that "real men" don't hold hands) were so ingrained that it was impossible for me not to communicate to my friend that I was very uncomfortable. This personal incident illustrates (1) how the meaning of touching can vary from one culture to another, (2) how our own cultures can socialize us so thoroughly that we have little or no control over our reactions (for example, perspiring), and (3) how such differences in touching behavior can lead to cross-cultural misunderstandings.

Some cultures are high-touch cultures, and others are low-touch cultures. A number of studies (Montagu 1972; Sheflen 1972; Mehrabian 1981) have suggested that Mediterranean cultures, Arabs, Jews, and eastern Europeans are high-touch cultures, whereas the English, Germans, northern Europeans, and many Asian cultures are low-touch cultures. Striking differences between high-touch and low-touch societies can be observed in certain public situations. For example, in crowded areas such as subways, white Londoners are likely to assume an overrigid posture, studiously avoiding eye contact and in no way acknowledging the presence of other passengers. The same type of behavior is seen on subways in New York City, Washington, D. C., or San Francisco. The

French, in contrast, have no apparent difficulty with touching total strangers in the Paris metro, as Montagu describes:

> Here the passengers will lean and press against others, if not with complete abandon, at least without feeling the necessity either to ignore or apologize to the other against whom they may be leaning or pressing. Often the leaning and lurching will give rise to good-natured laughter and joking, and there will be no attempt to avoid looking at the other passengers. (1972, 304)

Some forms of touching routinely found in England or the United States are viewed as most inappropriate in other parts of the world. Consider, for example, the practice of social (or ballroom) dancing as practiced in the United States, whereby two adults of the opposite sex move about the dance floor in time with the music while holding each other in a semiembrace. It is common in such dancing for the front of their bodies to be in constant contact—and they do this in public. Despite the close physical touching involved in this type of dancing (a form of bodily contact not unlike that assumed in sexual intercourse), our society has defined it as almost totally asexual. Although ballroom dancing can involve high levels of intimacy, it is equally possible that there is no sexual content whatsoever. Many adult men in the United States have danced in this fashion with their mothers, their sisters, or the wives of their ministers at church socials without anyone raising an eyebrow. Yet many non-American cultures view this type of dancing as the height of promiscuity and bad taste. It is interesting to note that many of those non-Americans for whom our dancing is a source of embarrassment are the very people we consider to be promiscuous, sex-crazed savages because their women do not cover their breasts.

Although it is generally valid to speak of high-touch versus low-touch cultures, be careful not to overgeneralize. One empirical study conducted by Robert Shuter (1977),

---

The different meanings connected with certain types of touching can lead to serious miscommunications in international business. Sergey Frank cites one such case of a cross-cultural misunderstanding that occurred between a northern European businessman and a southern European businessman as they were walking to a restaurant to celebrate after reaching final agreement on the terms of a joint venture between their two companies. According to Frank,

> When the Southern partner made an attempt to link arms as they set off to the restaurant, his Northern partner misread the signal and panicked. What's this man's problem? Touching in public? The gentleman from the North had visions of a scandal in the newspaper back home, even to the extent of homosexual implications, and rather clumsily spurned the gesture. His surprised partner immediately took offense, the once-positive climate deteriorated, and the meal went miserably. And even though the follow-up negotiations were eventually concluded, they were unnecessarily bogged down by the climatic misunderstandings that could easily have been avoided through a better mutual understanding of culture and etiquette. (1992, 51)

which examined touching behavior among Germans, Italians, and Americans, found that some of these national stereotypes did not hold true for both males and females. For example, Shuter found that although German and American men were less tactile than Italian men, they were more tactile than Italian women. These findings are important because they serve as a critical reminder not to think in monolithic terms when trying to determine cultural characteristics. Touching behavior, in other words, can vary in any given culture according to a number of factors such as sex, age, or relative status, to mention only several key variables. Instead of relying solely on overly simplified stereotypes, it would be more advisable to sharpen one's skills of observation of what touching means in a wide variety of contexts.

CONCLUSION

The United States is a highly literate society that tends to emphasize the verbal channel of expression. Most Americans, if forced to think about it at all, see the spoken word as the primary carrier of meaning. They are much less likely to give much credence to the nonverbal aspects of communication. As important as language is to facilitating intercultural communication within an international business setting, it is only a first step to intercultural understanding. Of equal importance is the nonverbal dimension, which we all rely on but only vaguely recognize. Now that we have examined six of the more common modes of nonverbal communication in some detail, it would be instructive to look at some of the more salient features of nonverbal communication in general.

1. Like its verbal counterpart, nonverbal communication is largely a learned, or culturally transmitted, phenomenon. Although some convincing evidence shows that certain limited aspects of nonverbal communication are universal (for example, the expression of emotions through smiles, frowns, or eyebrow flashes), the great majority of nonverbal cues, and the meanings attached to them, vary from culture to culture.
2. The comparatively new field of nonverbal communication studies has not been able to describe comprehensive systems of nonverbal communication for a single speech community as linguists have done for language; that is, although linguists have demonstrated the logic and consistency of many linguistic structures through the careful descriptions of grammar and syntax, nonverbal communication studies have yet to reveal the systematic nature of any speech community's "silent language." In other words, we do not have, at least yet, a grammar specifying the rules for constructing nonverbal messages. Nor are nonverbal dictionaries available that might provide, in reference book fashion, the meaning of a particular nonverbal cue.
3. Unlike spoken language, many nonverbal cues are sent and received despite our best intentions to do otherwise. Whereas language is every bit as effective for masking our true feelings as it is for expressing them, much of nonverbal communication is beyond our purposeful control. We can smile when we are unhappy, and to that extent we can purposefully control some nonverbal cues, but we cannot control our blushing when embarrassed, perspiring when nervous, or pupil dilation when frightened.
4. Since some nonverbal communication is beyond the individual's control, finding a noticeable lack of fit between a person's words and the nonverbal messages he or she might

send is not at all uncommon. For example, in response to the question "How are you?" a person might respond "Fine," while sending a number of nonverbal messages (such as sullen tone of voice, downcast eyes, and a frown) that totally contradict the upbeat verbal response. Research (Burgoon, Buller, and Woodall 1989, 9–10) indicates that when a discrepancy occurs between the verbal and the nonverbal, the observer will most likely believe the nonverbal.

5. To a much greater degree than with language, nonverbal behavior is by and large unconscious. We send nonverbal messages spontaneously without giving much, if any, thought about what hand gestures we are choosing to punctuate our words, how far we are from someone else's mouth in normal communication, or how long we maintain eye contact. Since so much of our nonverbal behavior is operating in the unconscious realm, seeking clarification of a misunderstood nonverbal cue becomes nearly impossible. Although we can ask someone to repeat a sentence, we would be quite unlikely to ask someone to explain what he or she meant by a half smile, a particular posture, or a sudden movement of the head.

6. Based on past research, strong evidence indicates that women are better able to read nonverbal cues than are men. J. A. Hall (1978), reviewing fifty two gender-related studies, found that 75 percent showed a significant female advantage. Robert Rosenthal and colleagues (1979, 80–84), using the PONS (Profile of Nonverbal Sensitivity) test, found an even greater female advantage than the earlier studies.

Although much has been made of the distinction between language on the one hand and nonverbal communication on the other, the two forms of communication are in fact inextricably interconnected. To learn just the spoken language and to ignore the nonverbal behavior would be as inadequate a response to cross-cultural communication as doing just the opposite. An understanding of both modes is necessary to reveal the full meaning of an intercultural event. Being able to read facial expressions, postures, hand gestures, gaze, and space usage, among others, increases our sensitivity to the intricacies of cross-cultural communication so necessary for success in the international business arena. To really know another culture, we must first learn the language, and then we must be able to hear the silent messages and read the invisible words.

CROSS-CULTURAL SCENARIOS

Read the following cross-cultural scenarios. In each mini-case study, a basic cultural conflict occurs between the actors involved. Try to identify the source of the conflict and suggest how it could have been avoided or minimized. Then see how well your analyses compare to the explanations in Appendix A.

4-1 After completing an M. B. A. in international business and working for a Boston bank for several years, Don Bynum was assigned for several weeks as a troubleshooter in the Rome office. To facilitate his adjustment to the Italian banking system and to assist with translation, the branch manager had assigned Don to work with Maria Fellini, a bilingual employee of the bank. Maria, like Don, was single and in her early thirties, and she lived with her widowed mother. In response to a comment Don had made about the joys of Italian cuisine, Maria invited Don to her mother's home for dinner. The dinner went well, and Don felt fortunate to have had a chance to be entertained in an Italian home. Several days later, Don felt somewhat embarrassed because he had forgotten to bring Maria's mother a gift the evening he had gone to dinner. Several days before returning to the United States, he made a special trip back to Maria's house to deliver personally a large bouquet of chrysanthemums to Maria's mother as a token of his appreciation for her hospitality. Maria answered the door, greeted Don, and took the flowers into the kitchen. But when she took Don into the living room to say goodbye to her mother, no mention was made of the flowers. Don felt that perhaps he had done something inappropriate.

What went wrong?

4-2   Construction superintendent Justin Clark had just been transferred to Saudi Arabia to supervise the building of new state-of-the-art oil rigs for the Saudi government. The long-term assignment was to last for four years, so Justin's family accompanied him. Due to the cultural differences regarding the freedom of women in Saudi Arabia, his wife, Lorna, was experiencing some difficulty in adjusting to her new home. Upon moving into their rented house, they discovered several things that needed repair. The landlord, very happy to have rented the house on such a long-term lease, was very prompt in responding to their request for repairs. However, when he arrived, Justin was not home, and the landlord entered without speaking or acknowledging Lorna's presence. The repairs proceeded under the landlord's supervision. Lorna was insulted and felt that the landlord's behavior was rude and disrespectful. Since she was the one home at the time, she thought the landlord should have discussed the repairs with her.

Why did the landlord ignore Lorna?

4-3   In what was considered a "hostile takeover," a U.S. corporation purchased a regional wine-producing vineyard in Limoges, France, in a strategic maneuver to enter the European market. Frank Joseph, a human resource specialist, was sent to Limoges to smooth the ruffled feathers of the vineyard's workers. Along with videos and propaganda on the merits of working for a Fortune 500 corporation, Frank also brought to Limoges a number of company logo items. In what was intended as a goodwill gesture, he presented the workers with T-shirts, ball caps, ink pens, and coffee cups to take home to their families. Over the next several weeks, Frank never saw any of the company's logo items being worn or used by the workers. Instead, the workers were uncommunicative toward him and at times even hostile.

Why was Frank treated in this manner?

4-4   Aware of the enormous interest the Japanese have in the game of golf, a U.S. sports equipment manufacturer decided to explore the possibilities of a joint venture with a Japanese firm. Three representatives from each firm met in San Francisco to work out the details of the proposed venture. After the six men were introduced to one another, they were seated at opposite sides of a large conference table. In an attempt to show the Japanese their sincerity for getting down to the task at hand, the Americans took off their jackets and rolled up their sleeves. Then one of the Americans said to his counterpart across the table, "Since we are going to be working together for the next several days, we better get to know each other. My name is Harry. What's your name?" The joint venture never did take place.

What went wrong?

4-5   Randy Hightower, recently appointed to manage his firm's office in Singapore, was anxious to do well in his first overseas assignment. Shortly after his arrival, he called his first staff meeting, to outline the objectives for the coming fiscal year. He had already met with his staff individually and was feeling quite confident about the prospects for having a good first year. Toward the end of the staff meeting, Randy, in his characteristic upbeat fashion, told his employees that he looked forward to working with them and that he anticipated that this would be their best year ever. To emphasize his optimism for the coming year, Randy punctuated his verbal remarks by slapping his fist against his palm. The reaction was instantaneous: Most people laughed, giggled, or looked embarrassed. Unfortunately, he felt that the point of his dramatic climax was lost amid the laughter.

How might you explain the cause for the hilarious outburst?

5

Contrasting Cultural Values

It is not unusual for anthropologists to speak of people from different cultures as having different sets of assumptions or different value systems. A *value system* represents what is expected or hoped for in a society, not necessarily what actually occurs. Values deal with what is required or forbidden, what is judged to be good or bad or right or wrong. Thus, in any given society, values represent the standards by which behavior is evaluated, not necessarily the actual behavior.

If communication between people from different cultures is to be successful, each party must understand the cultural assumptions—or cultural starting points—of the other. Unfortunately, our own values, the result of cultural conditioning, are so much a part of our consciousness that we frequently fail to acknowledge their existence and consequently fail to understand that they may not be shared by people from other cultures. When that occurs, cross-cultural cues can be missed, communication becomes short-circuited, and hostilities can be generated.

To maximize our chances for successfully understanding the cultural environment of international business, it is imperative that we examine cultural values—theirs as well as our own. It is necessary to recognize the cultural influences on our own thinking and how they conform to or contrast with those of culturally different people. Before we can conclude that the Calcutta street vendor is repulsively smelly, we must first realize how much emphasis U.S. culture places on eliminating odors of *all* types. Before concluding that the Peruvian carpenter is either too lazy or too stupid to be on time, we must first come to grips with the importance Americans place on the *exact* reckoning of time. In short, before we can begin to understand other cultures, we must first understand how our own culture influences our thinking and behaviors.

Any attempt to analyze American values is bound to be a tricky business at best. Part of the difficulty stems from the inherent bias of analyzing one's own culture. Since we are all influenced to some degree by the experiences of our own culture, any attempt to describe that culture will inevitably be distorted. Equally vexing is the enormity of the task. Whenever we make descriptive statements about the nature of American culture, we are implying that other (non-American) cultures possess the opposite traits. For example, to say that people in the United States place a high value on the individual is to imply that other cultures—Tanzanians, for example—place a higher value on the group. Such comparative statements presuppose that we are dealing with two unified, monolithic cultures: the United States and Tanzania. In actual fact, the many cultures of the world cannot be sorted out into neat and tidy categories. Many of the non-American peoples that we tend to contrast with our own are linguistically and culturally heterogeneous. For example, in the East African country of Tanzania, approximately 120 mutually unintelligible languages are spoken. It must be assumed that this level of linguistic heterogeneity brings with it an equal level of cultural variability as well.

Similarly, it may be argued whether it is legitimate to speak of *the* American culture. Despite the often heard claims that the United States is a great "melting pot," many subcultural groups, particularly in major urban areas, have retained a good deal of their ethnic distinctiveness. There are, for example, appreciable numbers of Latinos in Los Angeles, Arabs in Detroit, Japanese in Seattle, Chinese in San Francisco, and Italian Americans in Boston, New York, and Baltimore. In fact, over 60 percent of the people living in Miami do not speak English as their first language. Approximately 20 million foreign-born people live in the United States, and over 31 million (roughly 14 percent) do not speak English as their primary language. As an indication of this considerable diversity, the United States is a country in which both the late Mother Teresa (a nun who ministered to the needs of the poor in India) and Madonna (the sexually explicit "bad" girl of popular music) appear on the same list of "most admired women." Moreover, it is not unusual to observe at a Haitian street festival in New York City a Chinese woman eating a slice of pizza in front of a green grocery run by a Korean family. Owing to this cultural complexity, it might be more reasonable to think of the United States as less of a "melting pot" and more of a "salad bowl," whereby the individual subcultures retain their own identity and integrity.

While acknowledging the difficulties inherent in generalizing about values in such heterogeneous societies as Tanzania and the United States, some contrasting of value patterns certainly is possible. In fact, the dual processes of making generalizations and comparing are imperative if we are to enhance our understanding of other cultures as well as our own. Whether we live in Massachusetts or California, Oregon or Florida, in a small town or a large metropolis, some common American values stop abruptly at the Rio Grande and somewhat less dramatically at the Canadian border. Over the last several centuries, the United States has woven together threads of culture from all over the world into a quite distinct and recognizable cultural tapestry. Owing to certain common experiences in their enculturation, most Americans share a body of attitudes, values, beliefs, and behavior patterns. As Edward and Mildred Hall have suggested, "You can pick out Americans any place in the world, often very quickly, because of their behavior. Among their most observable traits are openness, friendliness, informality, optimism, creativity, loudness, and vitality" (1990, 140).

In this chapter we look at a number of value contrasts found throughout the world. The approach taken in discussing these fundamental value differences is modeled after the *value orientations* suggested by Florence Kluckhohn and her associates at Harvard in the 1950s (Kluckhohn and Strodtbeck 1961). This approach assumed that certain universal problems and conditions face people in all societies and there are only a limited number of solutions to these problems. Although all potential solutions to these universal problems are present in every society, one solution tends to be preferred by most members of a particular culture. As social scientists, Kluckhohn and her colleagues believe that these different value orientations could be operationalized and presented in a questionnaire format. Once sufficient numbers of questionnaires were administered in a particular culture, dominant value orientations could be identified. Kluckhohn and Strodtbeck (1961, 11) put forth five universal problems (posed as questions) for which all cultures must find solutions:

1. *Human nature orientation*: What is the character of innate human nature? Potential options include innately good, innately bad, or a combination of the two.
2. *Man–nature orientation:* What is the relation of man to nature (and supernature)? Potential options include mastery over nature, subjugation to nature, or harmony with nature.
3. *Time orientation:* What is the temporal focus of human life? Is time directed to the past, present, or future?
4. *Activity orientation:* What is the modality of human activity? Do people value an individual's accomplishments or his/her innate personal traits?
5. *Relational orientation:* What is the modality of man's relationship to other men? Is individualism more highly valued than commitments and obligations to the wider group such as family, neighborhood, or society?

Since Kluckhohn's work on values in the 1950s and 1960s, a number of other scholars have built upon this value-orientated model. In their classic textbook, which essentially launched the eclectic field of intercultural communication, John Condon and Fathi Yousef (1975) added an additional twenty dimensions to Kluckhohn's original five, by looking at such variables as gender (equality vs. male dominance), authority (democracy vs. authoritarianism), social mobility (high vs. low mobility), and formality (low vs. high levels of informality). Dutch social scientist Geert Hofstede (1980) derived four major dimensions of cultural values from his large-scale study of a multinational corporation that employed people from all over the world. Using large amounts of questionnaire data from fifty different cultures, Hofstede was able to relatively rank (1) individualism-collectivism, (2) uncertainty avoidance, (3) power distance, and (4) masculinity-femininity. Terence Brake, Danielle Walker, and Thomas Walker (1995) developed a ten-item value model for understanding international business situations, which included competitiveness versus cooperation, public space versus private space, high versus low context in communication styles, and deductive versus inductive thinking patterns. In 1996 Meena Wilson and Maxine Dalton at the Center for Creative Leadership developed their own set of value orientations, which they called a Learning Framework. While adding little new to the discussion, Wilson and Dalton (1996, 36–37) provide an excellent summary of the various value orientations used by some of the theorists since the groundbreaking work of Kluckhohn and Strodtbeck in 1961.

In this chapter we present a conceptual framework of value differences found in various parts of the world. This framework is designed to help you better understand the value preferences of people from different cultural groups. It will enable you to see how your cultural values compare with other cultural values on a number of important dimensions. It will also give you a set of "hooks" on which you can hang (and better understand) the various cultural traits that you may encounter in the future. This framework assumes that cross-cultural awareness can take place only when you view other cultural values in relation to your own. Since cultural values lie behind breakdowns in cross-cultural communication, such a framework will help you diagnose and hopefully avoid potential miscommunications.

THE INDIVIDUAL–COLLECTIVE DIMENSION

All cultures must ask and answer the following question: To what extent should people pursue their own individual activities and agendas rather than contributing to the success and well-being of the larger group, such as family, neighborhood, clan, team, or compa-

Individualism is so highly developed in North America that most people prefer to drive their own cars rather than rely on public transportation.

ny? Some cultures—such as the United States, Canada, Great Britain, and the Netherlands—place a high value on individualism. These cultures emphasize the worth and dignity of the individual over the group, independence rather than interdependence, and relatively few social obligations. Other cultures—such as Guatemala, Japan, and Taiwan—tend to emphasize the larger group. These cultures encourage people to put the interest of the group above their own, maintain strong ties and obligations to group members, and value long-term social relationships above short-term accomplishments. The individual–collective dimension can be summarized as follows:

Individual-Oriented Societies	Collective-Oriented Societies
Individuals are major units of social perception	Groups are major units of social perception
Explain others' behavior by personal traits	Explain others' behavior by group norms
Success attributed to own ability	Success attributed to help of group
Self defined as individual entity	Self defined in terms of group
Know more about self than others	Know more about others than self
Achievement for one's own sake	Achievement for benefit of group
Personal goals over group goals	In-group goal over personal goals
Values self-assuredness	Values modesty
Values autonomy and independence	Values interdependence
Fears dependence on others	Fears ostracism
Casual connections to many groups	Strong connections to a few groups
Few obligations to others	Many obligations to others
Confrontation is acceptable	Harmony is expected
Task completion is important	Relations are important

How This Value Plays Out in the Two Types of Society

Individual-Oriented Societies

- The ideal of the individual is deeply rooted in the social, political, and economic institutions of such societies as the United States and England. The individual is the source of moral power, totally competent to assess the effects of his or her own actions, and is expected to be responsible for those actions. Since society is seen as an instrument for satisfying the needs of the individual, a political philosophy advocating freedom from coercion by church, state, or traditional authority has developed.
- Family ties tend to be *relatively* unimportant. That is not to say that in the United States the family is unimportant in any absolute sense, for the family remains the primary group to which most Americans have their strongest loyalties. Nevertheless, when compared with other cultures, Americans divide their time and emotional energy between family and a wider variety of social groupings, including church, school, labor union, workplace, and a host of voluntary organizations. Moreover, the constant preoccupation with self has resulted in the truncation of extended family ties, reducing the notion of family to its smallest possible unit—the nuclear family.
- The physical layout of the typical American house, designed to maximize individual space, clearly reflects the emphasis placed on individualism and personal privacy. There are doors on bathrooms and bedrooms, parents are expected to acknowledge the private space and possessions of their children's rooms, and children are usually restricted in their use of space that is considered the domain of the parents.

- The concept of individualism is instilled from an early age in the United States by constant encouragement of children to become self-sufficient. Children are taught to make their own decisions, clarify their own values, form their own opinions, and solve their own problems. Children are encouraged to search out answers for themselves, rather than relying on the teacher or adult. We often tell children, "Go look it up for yourself," a statement that most often reflects our desire to instill the personal qualities of individualism and self-reliance.
- The aim of education is not to serve God or country but to enable the individual to maximize his or her human potential—or in the words of the U.S. Army recruiting campaign, "Be all that you can be!"
- Most U.S. bookstores today have entire sections devoted to literature popularly known as "self-help" books, designed to help the *individual* improve and get ahead. This self-help genre, dating back to Benjamin Franklin's *Poor Richard's Almanac* of 1759, includes books with such cryptic titles as *How to Take Charge of Your Life, Looking Out for Number One,* or simply and directly, *How to Be Rich.* The basic theme of individuality is unmistakable: personal success depends on activating the forces that lie within the individual.
- In the United States, the Bill of Rights protects people against infringement of their individual rights by the state, thus allowing them to express their ideas freely, practice whatever religion they choose, assemble freely, and generally control their own lives to as great a degree as possible.
- The emphasis on individualism in the United States can be seen in the large number of words (approximately 150) found in an American English dictionary that are compounded with the word *self.*
- That such cultures as the United States emphasize individuality can be seen in the American love affair with the automobile. Most Americans express their individuality by becoming fully mobile, capable of traveling in any direction and at any time, rather than being dependent on the schedules and routes of public transportation facilities.

Collective-Oriented Societies

- People tend to identify or define themselves primarily as members of a group rather than as individuals. When asked "Who are you?" most Americans would give their name, profession, and where they live, probably in that order. When asked the same question in Swaziland or Kenya, for example, a person is likely to give his name, his father's name, and his extended family (which may number in the hundreds of people).
- Property, such as land or livestock, is controlled by the larger group rather than being individually owned. Whereas Americans *own* property (to the extent that they have total control over it), people in collectivist societies have only limited rights and obligations to property that is ultimately controlled by the larger group.
- Basic life choices, such as who you will marry or what profession you will follow, are not made exclusively, or even primarily, by the individual. For example, marriages in some parts of the world are arranged by parents and other influential members of the two family groups involved.
- Collectivist societies have a strong sense of responsibility to the group (e.g., country, family, company). In Japan, for example, if an individual does not give his or her best effort, it is seen as letting down the entire group. In other words, both success and failure are "team affairs" in Japan.
- There is considerably less privacy. Children, even in those homes with ample room, frequently share the same sleeping areas with their parents and siblings until well into adoles-

cence. Clearly, they do not adhere to the American value that considers children "disadvantaged" if they must share a room with a sibling.

Implications for Business

Suggestions for Dealing with Collectivist Societies

1. In highly individualistic societies such as U.S. society, it makes sense to hold out incentives to individuals as a way of motivating them. But in collectivist societies, such as Japan, one's primary responsibility is to one's work group, not one's own professional advancement. Thus, to single out an individual member of a Japanese work team for praise is likely to embarrass the individual and demoralize the others on the team.
2. Be aware of the need to build long-term relationships. If building long-term relationships is the only way to do business with people in collectivist societies, then Americans will need to spend time and energy nurturing these relationships.
3. Americans need to develop patience because building the necessary relationships with people takes time and effort. Be patient.
4. Be careful about using the pronoun *I*. Often Americans use the pronoun *I* much more frequently than they use the word *we*. People from collectivist societies sometimes get the impression that Americans are "loose cannons" (John Wayne types, shooting from the hip) and are speaking for themselves rather than the organizations they represent.
5. Expect that rules, policies, and procedures are to be applied in a particularistic way rather than universally.
6. Do not discount family, tribal, or national loyalties, for they may be much stronger than your own.
7. Use third parties to make contacts and introductions.

While on a short-term assignment to Venezuela, Harry Dalton, an upper-level manager for a U.S.-based multinational corporation, was extremely impressed with the performance of one of the local managers. In fact, Harry was so impressed that he offered him a job in the home office in Chicago, which involved a promotion, a handsome increase in salary, and a generous moving allowance. But, much to Harry's surprise, the Venezuelan thanked him but turned down the job offer. Harry began to think that he had seriously misjudged this man's intelligence.

What Harry did not realize, however, was that the Venezuelan manager was making a perfectly intelligent career decision. Coming from a collectivist society, Venezuelans tend to first consider the needs of their family or company before considering their own self-interest. Being offered a promotion and higher salary would not be the most compelling reason for taking a new position. Rather, the Venezuelan manager will think primarily about the interests of extended family members, many of whom probably would not want him to move. Then the employee will consider the interests of the local company, which probably needs him to continue working in Caracas. People are not always motivated by individual benefits when deciding to take a new job.

In the United States, the value of informality extends even to our heads of state.

8. Take extra precautions to safeguard intellectual properties (which are not taken as seriously as in more individualistic societies).
9. Communicate respect for the wider good (for example, environment, whole society) rather than simply the good of the organization. Collectivist societies tend to be more publicly conscious.
10. Emphasize your own sense of loyalty and that of your company because loyalty and the meeting of obligations are important in collectivist societies.

THE EQUALITY–HIERARCHY DIMENSION

This value dimension raises the following question: How should people with different levels of power, prestige, and status interact with one another: equally or unequally? Those cultures that emphasize the equality polarity—such as Canada, Sweden, Australia, and the United States—tend to minimize power and status differences. Power tends to be more diffused, people in higher positions can be questioned, and subordinates want their superiors to consult with them and be accessible. This egalitarian orientation leads to relative informal relations between people of high and low status, a general disregard of protocol, and a high level of delegation of authority. At the other end of the continuum—represented by such countries as Malaysia, Panama, and the Philippines—people expect that status and power hierarchies will be maintained. In fact, hierarchical inequalities are seen as essential for the society's well-being because it satisfies a need for structure, order, and security. People at the higher levels of the hierarchy are treated with great deference by those lower down the ladder. People in authority should not step out of their privileged roles, bosses should not be questioned, and there is little or no delegation of authority. This dimension can be represented in the following way:

Egalitarian Societies

Low-status differences
Power diffused to many people
Delegation of authority
Informal social relations
Minimum deference for superiors
Superior can be questioned
Little respect for old age
Mechanisms to redress grievances

Hierarchical Societies

High-status differences
Power concentrated with few people
Little delegation of authority
Formal social relations
Maximum deference for superiors
Superior cannot be questioned
Great respect for old age
No mechanisms to redress grievances

Alfons Trompenaars and Charles Hampden-Turner (1993) represent this dimension diagramatically by using a series of triangles illustrating varying degrees of social distance. Hierarchical societies are represented by tall triangles (with a small base and relatively long sides) in which the distance between those at the top and those at the bottom is considerable:

More egalitarian societies, on the other hand, are represented by very flat triangles in which there is relatively little social distance between the various levels of the society.

How This Value Plays Out in the Two Types of Society

Egalitarian Societies

- The playing down of status differences, an important theme running through American culture, has its roots in our nation's early history. By moving onto the American frontier, the early settlers gave up much of the formality found in Europe. The hard work required for survival on the frontier was hardly conducive to the preservation of pomp and circumstance.
- Early Americans developed much less formal customs of dress, speaking, etiquette, and interpersonal relationships than found among their European ancestors. To a large extent, this informality and reticence to "stand on ceremony" persists to the present time.
- Americans assume that informality is a prerequisite for sincerity. They become uncomfortable when faced with the type of ceremony, tradition, and formalized social rules found more widely throughout Europe. Moreover, they are likely to feel uneasy when others treat them with too much deference.
- Americans generally take considerable delight when those in particularly high or powerful positions behave just like the everyday person on the street. For example, we are quite reassured when we saw Ronald Reagan chopping wood in his Levi's or Bill Clinton jogging through the streets of Washington in his running shorts.
- Authority figures—such as priests, professors, and supervisors—are often called by their first names rather than their official title and last name.
- In many egalitarian societies, informality (for example, de-emphasizing status differences) is reflected in the structure of everyday language. The distinction between the formal and informal *you*, found in such languages as German and French, requires speakers to make linguistic choices that reflect the social status of the people being addressed. In contrast, the English language makes no such distinctions.
- Authority figures, such as supervisors or college professors, are allowed to admit that they don't have all the answers. They will not lose respect because they admit fallibility.

Hierarchical Societies

- Upper-status people are expected to maintain their high-status and prestige at all costs. Don't expect to see Queen Elizabeth of England wearing Levi's in public or the Emperor of Japan running through Tokyo in his jogging outfit.
- Languages are structured in such a way as to ensure that one's relative status is reflected in the very construction of a sentence.
- High-status people are expected to be addressed by their formal title followed by the last name ("Hello, Dr. Evans") rather than the first name ("Yo, Stan").
- Children defer to their parents, younger defers to older, women defer to men, employees defer to employers, students defer to teachers, sellers defer to buyers, and everyone defers to the head of state.
- Professors (or highly respected authorities) would give a false answer rather than admit they don't know.
- Social rank in hierarchical countries, such as contemporary Japan, is displayed in a number of subtle ways, including the relative depth of the bow, clothing, and seating positions at meetings. In a Japanese office, the type of chair a person sits in reveals his or her status. The chair that carries the highest social status is the one with armrests. Most of the rank-and-file workers sit in chairs without armrests.

- Social order for the Japanese depends on everyone knowing their relative ranking in the society and avoiding any behavior that would threaten that order. The reason that business cards (*meishi*) are so important in contemporary Japan is that they enable individuals who do not know each another to learn the other's relative status so that they will know how to interact.

Implications for Business

Suggestions for Dealing with Hierarchical Societies

1. In egalitarian societies such as the United States, it is expected that high-status people will play down their superior rank. In hierarchical societies, people need to know from the outset what your status is so that they will know how to interact with you in an appropriate fashion. Thus, communicate your status, authority, credentials, expertise, and the like, but without arrogance or boasting.
2. Don't impose equality on your hosts, for it is not expected that all people will be treated democratically. In those societies, the boss is the boss and should be treated as such.
3. The decision-making process takes longer in egalitarian societies where all levels are asked for input. In hierarchical societies, decisions are made more rapidly because some measure of consensus is not expected from all levels.
4. To what extent should you honor, recognize, or respect hierarchies? It is not particularly wise or productive for a manager from an egalitarian society to play down the organizational hierarchies in other countries.
5. To what extent should the boss's decisions be questioned? In hierarchical societies, a boss does not appreciate having his or her decisions or judgments called into question. You exercise your democratic inclinations at your own peril.
6. Pay attention to different levels of social status when dealing with people. Don't expect that lower-status people in your organization can negotiate or conduct business with those of higher status.
7. Don't assume that all people have equal access to information.
8. Use high-status individuals as your agents, contacts, and intermediaries.
9. Expect that there will be a greater level of tension in everyday interactions between high- and low-status people (or between young and old or between men and women).
10. Realize that subordinates expect to be closely supervised.
11. Expect that subordinates will more frequently smile and repress negative emotions.

THE TOUGH–TENDER DIMENSION

The tough–tender dimension helps people define success. Do people in a particular society define success in terms of high-status, material accumulations, and well-rewarded jobs? Or do they define success in terms of less tangible rewards, such as quality time with friends and family, good working relationships, or opportunities for spiritual or personal growth? This value dimension pertains to the extent to which a culture prefers achievement, assertiveness, power, competition, and material posessions versus nurturing, social relationships, and cooperation. Tough societies tend to define gender roles more rigidly than do tender societies. To illustrate, tough societies are more likely to re-

In such 'tender' societies as Sweden, it is not unusual to find 'house husbands'.

strict various occupations to a single gender—for example, male truck drivers and female homemakers; in tender societies, it would not be unusual to find female truck drivers and male homemakers. Tough societies place a high value on doing, achieving external, measurable goals; and accomplishing one's objectives. Tender societies emphasize affiliations, character, personal qualities, nurturing, the quality of life, and the maintenance of social relationships. At the workplace, people in tough societies are primarily interested in task accomplishments, whereas people from tender societies are more concerned with issues of job satisfaction, such as relationships with superiors and peers, the work environment, and how interesting and challenging the job may be. The tough–tender dimension can be represented as follows:

Tough Societies

High occupational segregation by gender
Gender inequality
Careers for males are mandatory
Few women in powerful jobs
Accomplishments highly valued
High level of job-related stress
Highly competitive
Task oriented
Values the art of combat
Bigger is better
Separates family and work life
Live to work

Tender Societies

Little occupational segregation by gender
Relative gender equality
Careers for males are optional
More women in powerful jobs
Nurturing highly valued
Low level of job-related stress
Highly cooperative
Relationship oriented
Values the art of compromise
Smaller is beautiful
Concern for family issues in workplace
Work to live

Elements of the tough–tender dimension have been discussed by a wide range of scholars who have chosen a number of different terms:

1. Kluckhohn and Strodtbeck (1961) distinguish between *doing* (emphasis on accomplishing tasks) and *being* (emphasis on social relationships), a distinction also made by Condon and Yousef (1975) and later by Brake and colleagues (1995).
2. Hofstede (1980) uses the terms *masculine* and *feminine* to refer to this value dimension. Even though Hofstede's research in this area has been considerable, we choose to avoid his terminology, in large part because it overstates the importance of gender. In fact, the use of these gender terms implies, either correctly or incorrectly, that women in whatever culture lean toward one polarity and men toward another. Although gender roles do come into play here, it is misleading to suggest by the use of these terms that gender is the only, or even the major, aspect of this dimension.
3. Another important element of the tough–tender dimension involves varying levels of competition, recognized by Condon and Yousef (1975), Brake and colleagues (1995), and particularly the early studies of anthropologist Margaret Mead (1961) on cooperation and competition among different cultures of the world.
4. The tough–tender dichotomy also incorporates elements of the ascribed versus achieved distinction discussed in the work of Talcott Parsons and Edward Shils (1951), David McClelland (1961), and Trompenaars and Hampden-Turner (1993).

Those societies associated with toughness—such as Austria, Italy, Japan, and Mexico—believe in achievement and ambition, judging people on the basis of their performances, and the right to display the material possessions one is able to acquire. Moreover, people in tough cultures believe in ostentatious manliness and the capacity to be both assertive and decisive. The more tender societies, such as most Scandinavian countries and the Netherlands, are less interested in shows of manliness and are more concerned with making life choices that will improve the quality of life, such as service to others and working with the less fortunate. Countries that scored high on Hofstede's masculinity scale have fewer women in the workforce, have only recently granted women the right to vote, and tend to be more tolerant of wife rape (Seager and Olson 1986).

How This Value Plays Out in the Two Types of Societies

Tough Society

- There is a great deal of gender-role segregation, for women do certain jobs and men do others.
- Fewer women will be in high government positions. To illustrate, in Morocco less than 1 percent of national legislators are women as compared with 43 percent in Sweden.
- Adult women in certain African and Middle Eastern countries cannot receive a driver's license, bank account, passport, or contraceptive without the explicit permission of either their fathers or their husbands.
- People (particularly men) tend to be defined in terms of what they do for a living; that is, one's occupation defines the individual. Consequently, when people retire, they have great problems of adjustment because "who they are" has been taken from them.
- Competition is considered a good thing, even though sometimes the competition can be so fierce that it becomes aggressive and unethical.

- People take relatively few vacations or allow themselves much leisure time with friends and family. When vacations are taken, the phone and laptop are often taken along.
- Teachers reward and praise their best students because academic achievement is highly valued. Male students in particular are highly competitive, assertive, and task oriented.
- The priorities of family and work life are kept as separate as possible. Corporations generally disregard the well-being of employees' families in their strategic planning. For example, employees are transferred without consideration of the disruptive effects on children's education or the workers' obligations to aging parents.
- People (particularly men) display high levels of stress and frequent incidence of high blood pressure and heart disease. Ross Buck (1984) found that men may be generally less healthy physically because they cannot express their emotions as openly as women. This internalizing of emotions, both negative and positive ones, leads to higher blood pressure and higher levels of stress.
- People place a high value on growth for its own sake. Increases in market share take precedence over quality of life, social programs, or environmental protection.
- A strong emphasis is placed on achievement, with the greatest respect given to those who are the high achievers.

Tender Societies

- Employers will likely provide parental-leave programs for both mothers and fathers.
- Survey data have shown that people prefer shorter working hours to higher salaries (Hofstede 1998, 14).
- Men and women are more likely to study the same subjects in college than are men and women in tough societies (Hofstede 1998, 15).
- Students are not praised for their accomplishments because cooperation with others is considered the most important goal. Male students strive to be accommodating and work to develop a sense of community and solidarity with their classmates. Friendships, obligations, and loyalty are all more highly valued than academic brilliance or accomplishments. Courses are selected because of their inherent interest rather than because they might lead to a better job.
- Survey data show a preference for smaller companies over increasingly larger companies (Hofstede 1998, 14).
- People in general and managers in particular acknowledge personal success and accomplishments much less frequently than in tougher societies. It is generally thought that noteworthy achievements in an organization are seldom due to the efforts of a single person. People tend to play down their own strengths and assets while praising those of others.
- Family issues are taken into consideration as part of the corporate decision-making process. Thus, the sanctity of family vacations is preserved at all costs, maternity and paternity leaves are generous, and persons who work abroad are selected, at least in part, with an eye toward family responsibilities. In short, as Wilson and Dalton put it, "The role of the employee as a family member is more clearly recognized and respected" (1996, 11).
- Tender societies spend much more money per capita on foreign aid than do tough societies (Hofstede, 1998, 15).
- Governments lean more toward a welfare state (helping the needy). Progressive income taxes are used to support a wide range of social entitlement programs.
- Dominant religions stress complementarity of the sexes, not male dominance.

Implications for Business

Suggestions for Dealing with Tender Societies

1. Be sensitive to gender issues and the expectation of greater gender equality.
2. Don't assume that all people are motivated predominantly by material gain. When managing employees, understand that issues revolving around general working conditions, hours, and vacation time may be more important than issues of salary.
3. Be prepared for people and the government to be more interested in helping the "underdog" rather than helping the wealthy and powerful.
4. The "hard sell" is likely to meet with less success than the "soft sell."
5. Try to suppress your winner-take-all competitiveness. Don't be offended if people don't want to spend an evening with you playing Monopoly.
6. Be aware that your marketing or management decisions may have a negative impact on the physical environment. Then do everything possible to prevent those negative effects from occurring.
7. When negotiating with people, looking for a win–win situation is always best.
8. Don't be fooled into thinking that men who are nurturing and supportive are necessarily weak.
9. When conducting business of any type, be willing to spend time, demonstrate empathy, and build relationships.
10. Don't be shocked to find women in important positions within the company or within government.

THE UNCERTAINTY-AVOIDANCE DIMENSION

The cross-cultural value dimension of uncertainty avoidance is one of the four original dimensions measured by Hofstede in 1980. Like most of the other dimensions mentioned so far, Hofstede's uncertainty-avoidance measure has been discussed widely in the literature, albeit from different perspectives and by using different sets of terms. Although Hofstede's uncertainty-avoidance dimension is not addressed in the work of Kluckhohn and Strodtbeck (1961), Condon and Yousef (1975, 99–102) discuss significant components of the dimension under the heading of "mutability"; Brake and colleagues (1995, 68–69) use the "order versus flexibility" dichotomy as part of their model; and Wilson and Dalton (1996, 15–17) use the terms *dynamic* and *stable* to make a similar distinction in cultural differences. For purposes of our discussion here, we use Hofstede's terminology of uncertainty avoidance.

According to Hofstede, uncertainty avoidance refers to the lack of tolerance for ambiguity and the need for formal rules and high-level organizational structure. The unpredictability of the future, and the resultant anxiety that this produces, is part of the human experience. Nevertheless, cultures differ in the degree to which they can tolerate ambiguity, cope with uncertainties, and adapt to the future. Hofstede's uncertainty-avoidance measure indicates the extent to which a culture conditions its members to feel either comfortable or uncomfortable in unstructured, ambiguous, and unpredictable situations. Those societies with high uncertainty avoidance—such as Greece, Portugal, and Japan—try to minimize these unstructured situations as much as possible by (1) maintaining strict laws and regulations, (2) providing safety and security measures, (3) adhering to absolute truths, and (4) rejecting unorthodox ideas. At the other end of the continuum—for example, Singapore, Denmark, Hong Kong, and the United States—people from cultures with low uncertainty avoidance tend to be more tolerant of unorthodox opinions, are comfortable with fewer rules and simpler organizational structures, and are more relativistic in their beliefs, philosophies, and religions.

The critical components of the uncertainty-avoidance dimension can be depicted in the following way:

Low–Uncertainty Avoidance Societies	High–Uncertainty Avoidance Societies
Willingness to live day-by-day	Greater anxiety about the future
Less emotional resistance to change	More emotional resistance to change
More risk taking	Less risk taking
Willingness to change employer	Tendency to stay with same employer
Hope for success	Fear of failure
Little loyalty to employer	Considerable loyalty to employer
Sometimes rules can be broken	Rules should not be broken
Conflict is natural and to be expected	Conflict is undesirable
Initiative of subordinates encouraged	Initiative of subordinates discouraged
Differences are tolerated	Differences are considered dangerous
Low stress	High stress
Little emotional expression	Emotional expression is acceptable
Superordinates may say "I don't know"	Superordinates have all the answers
Less formal organizational structures	Formal organizational structures

There is considerable variability across cultures in terms of the extent to which people feel that behavior should follow formal rules. In those societies with high uncertainty avoidance, behavior is rigidly prescribed, either with written laws or unwritten social codes. Even if individuals within such a society occasionally break the rules, they generally believe that it is a good thing that the rules exist. In short, people feel anxious in the absence of formal regulations. At the other polarity, societies with low uncertainty avoidance also have rules and regulations, but they are considered more of a convenience than an absolute moral imperative. People in such societies can live comfortably without strict conformity to social rules and in fact often appreciate their freedom to "do their own thing." In terms of engaging in negotiations, people from societies with high uncertainty avoidance are not very good negotiators because the outcome of negotiations is never predictable. People from societies with low uncertainty avoidance are much more comfortable in negotiating situations in which the outcome is not a foregone conclusion.

A major contribution of Hofstede's work is that it has stimulated an entire body of research from subsequent scholars. One such area has been the examination of the relationship between uncertainty avoidance and innovation. For example, Scott Shane (1995), working with a sample of over 4,400 individuals from sixty-eight countries, found that four different types of innovation-championing roles are significantly more preferred by people from uncertainty-accepting societies than by people from uncertainty-avoiding societies. More specifically, Shane found that the greater the uncertainty acceptance, the more likely people were to prefer the championing role of (1) defending innovators against the inherently conservative organizational hierarchy, (2) persuading others to support innovation, (3) providing innovators with opportunities to violate organizational rules, and (4) providing innovators with the freedom needed to be creative. In an earlier study, Shane (1993) found that uncertainty-accepting societies are more innovative than uncertainty-avoiding societies. These two studies provide empirical evidence to suggest that such cultural values as uncertainty avoidance should be considered in the strategic decision of where innovation efforts (such as research-and-development facilities) are physically located.

Another study that was spawned by Hofstede's conceptualization of uncertainty avoidance, conducted by Lynn Offermann and Peta Hellmann (1997), examined the correlation between uncertainty and leadership. This research drew on a sample of 425 mid-level managers (holding passports from thirty-nine countries) from a single multinational organization. They found that uncertainty avoidance varied positively with the level of control that leaders had over their subordinates and negatively with the approachability of the leader and his or her willingness to delegate authority. In other words, the higher the level of uncertainty avoidance, the greater control leaders had over their subordinates, the less approachable they were, and the less likely they were to delegate power. In the same study, Offermann and Hellmann found a significant correlation between leadership and another one of Hofstede's dimensions, *power distance*, which is equivalent to "the Equality–Hierarchy Dimension." They found that the higher the power distance index, the less likely the leader would be to either delegate authority or encourage team building.

How This Value Plays Out in the Two Types of Societies

Low–Uncertainty Avoidance Societies

- Employees are willing to have their pension funds invested in the stock market rather than a low interest–bearing money-market account.
- Employees are more willing to experiment with new techniques and procedures.
- Employees are not as threatened by workers from other countries as are those from high–uncertainty avoidance societies.
- Employees are better able to function in meetings with a loose agenda.
- Employees have relatively little loyalty to employers because they do not depend on the company for security.
- Employees have a preference for a broad set of guidelines rather than a formal set of rules and regulations.
- Bosses, professors, and other authority figures are not reluctant to say "I don't know the answer to that question." (But, they will take the initiative to find out the answer.)
- Employees are more likely to function effectively in work teams.
- Leaders are more likely to be innovative, creative, and approachable.

High–Uncertainty Avoidance Societies

- Employees would prefer to keep their pension funds in a safe low interest–bearing account (or under the mattress).
- Employees are not likely to want to try anything new because its results are highly unpredictable.
- Employees are likely to resist the hiring of immigrants or others seen to be "outsiders."
- People feel much more secure with a highly structured set of policies, rules, and regulations. Moreover, they have little tolerance for bending the rules under any circumstances.
- Employees have a generally high level of loyalty to their employers and expect the same in return. For this reason, relatively little job turnover will occur.
- Fewer members of the workforce are willing to travel abroad for overseas assignments.
- Employees prefer a manager who they perceive to be competent and whose authority cannot be questioned.
- Employees are considerably less comfortable working in problem-solving teams.
- Leaders are not likely to be innovative or approachable.

Implications for Business

Suggestions for Dealing with High–Uncertainty Avoidance Societies

1. When working with people, try to minimize their anxieties about the future. In other words, build into your proposals and decisions as much predictability about the future as possible.
2. Anticipate and reward your employees for their loyalty to the organization.
3. Make modest proposals for change, not radical ones.
4. Be careful not to appoint managers who are too close to the age of most employees.
5. To help overcome the inherent fear of failure, provide structured work experiences for your employees that are likely to produce successful outcomes.
6. Make certain that organizational guidelines (rules/regulations) are in place, explicitly stated, and followed.
7. Avoid being too unorthodox in your opinions and recommendations.
8. Expect people to be highly rigid during negotiations. Whatever proposal you put on the negotiating table should contain built-in protections that will make the future somewhat more predictable.
9. Don't have unrealistic expectations about your employees' personal initiative, creativity, or ability/willingness to work in teams.
10. Be aware of the fact that most employees are not likely to appreciate a manager who delegates authority.

THE TIME DIMENSION

A major component of any constellation of values is how a particular culture deals with time. We consider this time dimension from three specific perspectives:

1. The importance of a precise reckoning of time
2. The degree to which a culture uses sequential or synchronized time
3. Whether a culture is past, present, or future-oriented

Precise versus Loose Reckoning of Time

For those cultures that reckon time precisely, such as Switzerland and the United States, time is seen as a tangible commodity that must be used efficiently. To ensure this, people are expected to make schedules, establish timetables, and meet deadlines. Much like money, time can be saved, spent, or wasted. In the United States, where punctuality is highly valued, the relationship between time and money is summed up in the expression "Time is money." At the opposite end of the spectrum, in such places as the Middle East and South America, people take a looser, more relaxed approach to time. Schedules and deadlines are seen more as expressions of intent rather than obligations. Rather than reacting to the arbitrary positions of the hands on a clock, people are more likely to respond to social relationships that are occurring in the present. People from cultures with relaxed notions of time see those who deal with time very precisely as being rude because they are willing to cut off social relationships for the sake of keeping their next appointment. The time dimension can be represented in the following way:

Precise-Reckoning-of-Time Societies	**Loose-Reckoning-of-Time Societies**
Punctuality	Little punctuality
Rigid schedules	Loose schedules
Time is scarce/limited	Time is plentiful
"Time is money"	Social relationships

Even though people from most cultures understand the meaning of clock time (hours, minutes, and seconds), each culture has its own vocabulary of time and its own pace of life. In one rather ingenious cross-cultural study of social time, Robert Levine and E. Wolfe (1985) compare the temporal pace in six cultures—England, Indonesia, Italy, Japan, Taiwan, and the United States. This study utilized some creative unobtrusive measures for quantifying how seriously time is taken in these cultures. These included (1) the accuracy of bank clocks, (2) the average length of time it took pedestrians on a clear day to walk 100 feet on a city street during business hours, and (3) the average length of time it took to buy a single stamp from a postal clerk. The findings suggested considerable differences across these six cultures on these three time indicators. A quick pace of life and concern for speed and accuracy were most noticeable in Japan, followed closely by the United States, whereas Indonesia scored consistently at the other extreme.

Sequential versus Synchronized Time

In some respects, time speaks more plainly than words, for time conveys powerful messages about how people relate to the world and to each other. In addition to some societies having either a precise or loose reckoning of time, they also must

With increased business relations between the United States and Mexico, many U.S. businesspeople are becoming keenly aware of the differences in how these two cultures deal with time. According to Jay and Maggie Jessup,

> The mañana syndrome is basic to Mexican business. The word "mañana" is translated literally as "tomorrow." But figuratively, the word has a different meaning. The naive U.S. businessperson uses mañana derogatorily, suggesting that Mexicans procrastinate. But what at first seems to be procrastination is merely the different way Mexican businesspeople prioritize their lives and activities. The Mexican businessperson's system of priorities is family and social obligations first and business later. . . . It is absolutely wrong for the visiting United States businessperson to try to overcome . . . [the Mexican] concept of mañana. . . . In a country where business is done only with "friends," the (2–4 hour) ritual business lunch is an opportunity for the Mexicans to take your measure, judging you by your cool and by your attention to family and social concerns. Thus, this indeed is a business lunch. Your response to the mañana attitude tells the Mexicans about you as a person and enables them to decide whether you will be an asset to their business or an unnecessary annoyance. (1993, 34–35)

choose whether to do things sequentially (one thing at a time) or synchronically (a number of things at the same time). This dichotomy between sequentially and synchronically oriented societies uses terms suggested by Trompenaars and Hampden-Turner (1998, 126–28). However, others have used different terminology to refer to the same phenomenon. For example, Brake and colleagues (1995, 50–51) use the terms *single focus* and *multifocus*, whereas years earlier Edward Hall (1976, 14–18) spoke of *monochronic time* (M-time) and *polychronic time* (P-time). The person from a sequential, or M-time, culture conceives of time as a straight, dotted line with regular spacing. Tasks are routinely accomplished one at a time, meetings have highly structured agendas, and schedules are rigidly followed. Since everything has its own time and place for the sequential thinker, any changes in the normal sequence are likely to be anxiety producing. In such sequentially oriented societies as England, the United States, and the Netherlands, one should never jump ahead of others waiting in line. According to Trompenaars and Hampden-Turner, "In the Netherlands you could be the Queen, but if you are in a butcher's shop with number 46 and you step up for service when number 12 is called, you are still in deep trouble . . . (after all) order is order" (1998, 126).

Those people in sequentially oriented societies would argue that proceeding in a straight line is reasonable because it is orderly, efficient, and involves a minimum of effort. However, this type of straight-line thinking may not always be the best way of doing something, for it is blind to certain efficiencies of shared activities and interconnections. Sometimes juggling a number of different tasks at the same time may in fact be the most time efficient. Continuing with the butcher shop analogy, Trompenaars and Hampden-Turner cite the example of the shop in Italy (a more synchronically oriented society) where the butcher unwraps and slices an order of salami for one customer, and then yells out, "Anyone want salami before I rewrap it?" Even though each customer is not served in order, the whole process is more efficient because it involves far less unwrapping and rewrapping of the various types of meat.

Thus, the person from a synchronically oriented society conducts a number of activities in parallel, without being thrown off his or her rhythm. By way of contrast, those people that are sequentially oriented envision a crucial path from which they do not want to deviate. Both approaches to time are usually so well ingrained in people that a person of one style will have difficulty when interacting with a person accustomed to the opposite style. To illustrate, a New Yorker is likely to think a salesclerk in Buenos Aires is extraordinarily rude when she is writing up his sales order while talking on the phone, drinking a diet cola, and flirting with another customer. Someone from a synchronically oriented society, however, will think that his American colleague (who is talking on the phone) is rude because the American does not greet him when entering his office, for it is considered a serious slight not to be greeted even while still talking on the phone.

Most North Americans tend to take time very seriously.

The differences between those who are sequentially oriented (M-time) and synchronically oriented (P-time) can be summarized as follows:

Sequentially Oriented Societies	Synchronically Oriented Societies
One task at a time	Multiple tasks at a time
Concentration on task	Easily distracted
Schedules taken very seriously	Schedules not taken seriously
Many short-term relationships	Long-term social relationships
Time is a threat	Time is a friend

Past, Present, and Future Orientations

A third aspect of the time dimension concerns the extent to which people focus on the past, the present, or the future. To be certain, all three alternatives must be recognized, but as Kluckhohn and Strodtbeck (1961, 14) argue, one time orientation is likely to predominate. Past-oriented societies regard previous experience and events as the most important and in fact use the past as a guide to the present. Traditional wisdom that has been passed down from previous generations is given a primary emphasis. Since the elders are the link with the past, they are afforded the highest level of deference in the present. Events in such societies are seen as circular or recurring; consequently, the tried-and-true solutions to problems are the ones most likely applied to present-day problems. In such cultures, the leaders are expected to carry the vision of the past into the present and future.

Present-oriented societies tend to emphasize spontaneity, immediacy, and experiencing each moment to its fullest. According to this perspective, people do not do things because it reflects a glorious past or because it will bring about some gain in the future. Rather, people do things because of the inherent pleasure they will derive in the here and now. This perspective on time can be summed up in the adage "Take care of today, and tomorrow will take care of itself." Since people with a present orientation typically believe that their lives are controlled by external forces (such as fate or luck), they have developed a number of ways of appreciating the simple pleasures of daily activities. Business organizations in such present-oriented societies formulate short-term plans, allocate resources based on present demands, and train their personnel to meet current goals.

People from future-oriented societies believe that it is far more important to trade off short-term gains in the present for more long-term benefits in the future. One does not engage in activities today for the sole reason of benefiting from the immediate rewards, but rather from the potentially greater benefits that will be realized in the future. In other words, people are willing to invest now and defer gratification until the future. For example, rather than buying a Yugo automobile today, you should leave the money in a high-interest mutual fund so that you will be able to buy a BMW next year. In the event of premature death, future-oriented parents are willing to pay life insurance premiums today so that their dependent children are protected from financial catastrophe. People from future-oriented societies—such as the United States, Canada, and a number of European countries—believe that they have a good deal of control over their lives and can to some degree influence the course of future events. Business organizations in future-oriented societies plan work and resources to meet long-term goals that will be directed to future needs.

Although the United States is a future-oriented society, the American view of the future—which, it is believed, can be controlled from the present—is relatively short term. American businesspeople tend to emphasize gains in the immediate future, not the distant future. Other societies have much deeper conceptions of the future. For example, in Japan it is not at all unusual for a couple to take out a 100-year mortgage on a house. Moreover, Japanese companies are likely to include projections for the next two centuries in their business plan, not just for the next decade as is typical in Europe and the United States. The notion of a future-oriented society can only become meaningful when we realize that some societies have a very truncated view of the future. According to John Mbiti, many traditional African societies have essentially a two-dimensional notion of time, "with a short past, a present, and virtually no future" (1969, 17). Since African time is composed of a series of events that are experienced, the future must be of little meaning because future events have not yet occurred. Mbiti supports his argument with linguistic data from the Gikuyu and Kikamba languages of Kenya. Both languages contain three future tenses covering a period not exceeding two years from the present. If future events do not fall within this shallow range, virtually no linguistic mechanisms can conceive or express them. Given these linguistic structures, it is safe to assume that speakers of these East African languages have little or no interest in those things that might occur in the distant future.

How This Value Plays Out in Different Types of Societies

Precise/M-Time Societies

- People pay close attention to their watches and tend to divide time in very precise units.
- People tend to eat meals because "it's time to eat."
- Business deadlines are taken very seriously.
- People move rapidly.
- Meetings start pretty much on time, usually no later than five minutes after the designated time.
- People do one thing at a time, rather than a number of things at the same time.
- People tend to emphasize getting contracts signed and then moving on to some new endeavor.

Loose/P-Time Societies

- Few people pay close attention to the clock.
- People eat because of the "need to share food," rather than because of the position of the hands on the clock.
- Business deadlines are hoped for, but people will not get overly upset if something prevents the deadline from being met.

- People move at a more leisurely pace.
- Meetings start after an appropriate amount of time is devoted to socializing.
- People do many things at the same time.
- A greater emphasis is placed on building social relationships, rather than on completing the task on time.

Past-Oriented Societies

- People have a great concern for history and origins of their families, businesses, and social institutions.
- Employees are motivated by examples from the "golden past."
- Predecessors and older people are looked to as role models. Even though they may not have had the most recent formal education, their wisdom and experience are highly valued.
- Business hosts will want to share their cultural history with you (via museums, monuments).

Present-Oriented Societies

- People live in the here and now and look for immediate gratification.
- Everything is evaluated in terms of its immediate impact.
- People are not particularly effective at deferring gratification or planning for the future.

Future-Oriented Societies

- People tend to be enthusiastic planners.
- There is a considerable willingness to defer present gratification for even more gratification later on.
- People are generally optimistic about progress in the future.
- People place a high value on being youthful, because the young have more of a future than the more senior members of the society.

Implications for Business

Suggestions for Dealing with Loose/P-Time Societies

1. Suppress the urge to get things done quickly (because "Faster is better" and "Time is money"). Be willing to spend time building long-lasting relationships.
2. Don't show impatience. You may be viewed as untrustworthy and as someone who wants to cheat your business partners.
3. Become more flexible in your scheduling and broaden your concept of what is an acceptable range of tardiness.
4. Be aware that high-status people can keep lower-status people waiting, but the opposite is not true.
5. Don't be put off when business associates do more than one thing at a time. Be prepared to be in several different conversations at the same time.
6. Understand and respect local traditions and long-term commitments.
7. Use role models and situations from the past as ways of motivating your employees.
8. Sell the reputation of your company and its success over time.

CONCLUSION

In this chapter, we have set forth a framework to help you better understand different value systems found in the world's many cultures. The conceptual framework (derived from the work of many scholars over the last thirty years) is composed of five major dimensions, which raise important questions that need to be answered when encountering a new and different culture. These questions include the following:

1. Do people identify themselves primarily as individuals or as members of a larger collective?
2. Do people with different levels of power and prestige treat one another equally or unequally?
3. To what extent do different cultures emphasize combat (tough) or compromise (tender)?
4. How do cultures differ in terms of taking risks, tolerating ambiguity, and needing relatively little organizational structure?
5. How precisely do people from different cultures deal with time?

These five value dimensions should serve as a starting point for better understanding the dynamics of interacting cross-culturally. We must keep in mind that these dichotomies are not a precise description of reality. There are no cultures that embody absolutely all the traits associated with any of these basic polarities. Instead, we should view this framework as a set of continua on which different cultures fall relative to one another. Viewed as such, the framework will help us better understand that reality. In other words, it should help us get a better feel for someone else's values *relative to our own*. To illustrate, before a lawyer from Boston can conclude that a rural Colombian is too lazy to be on time, he must first come to grips with the importance that his own culture puts on schedules, deadlines, and punctuality. In short, before we can begin to understand other cultures, we must first understand how our own culture influences our cognitive and behavioral assumption. This framework of values should enable us to get a better handle on both sets of values, theirs as well as our own.

If these dichotomies are taken too seriously, they can be just another form of uncritical stereotyping. But, as Nancy Adler (1997, 75–76) suggests, they can be "helpful stereotypes," provided we recognize their limitations. We must see them as being more useful for comparing *between* cultures than in understanding the wide differences that exist *within* a single culture. They must be seen as describing cultural norms, not the exact behavior of all people within a cultural group. They should be subject to revision, and they should constitute the best "first guess" about a culture before having all the facts.

Finally, we must remember that the way we view ourselves and our own values is often quite different from the way others view us. Americans might take pride in describing themselves as individualistic, autonomous, and self-reliant, but people from other cultures might view us as egocentric or self-absorbed. We may see ourselves as informal, friendly, and casual, but others might see us as undisciplined and insensitive to legitimate status differences. Also, our desire to "tell it like it is" (direct communication) can be interpreted as rude or excessively blunt. In other words, it is only natural for all people, including ourselves, to consider their own values as natural and good, while those values that are different or opposite from their own are strange and less good. The value differences discussed in this chapter, however, are neither good nor bad. Rather, they should be viewed as a way of better understanding the values of others, as well as our own. The good news is that no one expects you to adopt the values of other cultures. In fact, no one is even asking you to like them. But, it is imperative to *understand* the value differences found throughout the world so that you will be in the best position to make the most informed international business decisions.

CROSS-CULTURAL SCENARIOS

Read the following cross-cultural scenarios. In each mini-case study, a basic cultural conflict occurs between the actors involved. Try to identify the source of the conflict and suggest how it could have been avoided or minimized. Then see how well your analyses compare to the explanations in Appendix A.

5-1 Tom Forrest, an up-and-coming executive for a U.S. electronics company, was sent to Japan to work out the details of a joint venture with a Japanese electronics firm. During the first several weeks, Tom felt that the negotiations were proceeding better than he had expected. He found that he had very cordial working relationships with the team of Japanese executives, and they had in fact agreed on the major policies and strategies governing the new joint venture. During the third week of negotiations, Tom was present at a meeting held to review their progress. The meeting was chaired by the president of the Japanese firm, Mr. Hayakawa, a man in his mid-forties, who had recently taken over the presidency from his eighty-two-year-old grandfather. The new president, who had been involved in most of the negotiations during the preceding weeks, seemed to Tom to be one of the strongest advocates of the plan that had been developed to date. Also attending the meeting was Hayakawa's grandfather, the recently retired president. After the plans had been discussed in some detail, the octogenarian past president proceeded to give a long soliloquy about how some of the features of this plan violated the traditional practices on which the company had been founded. Much to Tom's amazement, Hayakawa did nothing to explain or defend the policies and strategies that they had taken weeks to develop. Feeling extremely frustrated, Tom then gave a fairly strongly argued defense of the plan. To Tom's further amazement, no one else in the meeting spoke up in defense of the plan. The tension in the air was quite heavy, and the meeting adjourned shortly thereafter. Within days the Japanese firm completely terminated the negotiations on the joint venture.

How could you help Tom better understand this bewildering situation?

5-2 Jeff Walters, owner and manager of a highly successful bookstore in Philadelphia during the 1960s and 1970s, had gone on a three-week safari to East Africa. He and his wife had been so struck by the beauty of the area that they had decided soon after returning to the United States to sell the bookstore and start a book distribution company based in Nairobi that would supply books from all over the world to eastern and southern African countries. Although the new business was only four years old, Jeff's enthusiasm for combining his love of books with his newfound love of East Africa was largely responsible for the great success of the new enterprise. In only four years, Jeff, as president of the company, had put together a professional and administrative staff of eighteen local Kenyans.

Jeff found that he was behind schedule in preparing a lengthy proposal for a possible government contract due in the USAID office in Nairobi the next day. The deadline was so critical that he had to work very closely with some of his staff to make sure that it was met. In the final hours, Jeff found himself helping the secretaries make copies, collate, and assemble the multiple copies of the proposal. But minutes after pitching in to help, he noticed that his staff became very noncommunicative, and he seemed to be getting a lot of cold stares. Jeff couldn't understand why his attempts to be helpful were so unappreciated.

How could you help Jeff better understand this cross-cultural problem?

5-3   For the past three years, Ned Ferguson has served quite successfully as the manager of a U.S.-owned manufacturing company in Taiwan. Shortly after Ned's arrival in Taipei, he instituted a number of changes in the plant operation that increased both production and worker satisfaction. However, within the last several months, a series of what seemed to Ned to be unrelated incidents had occurred. First, there had been a fire in the warehouse, which fortunately was contained before too much damage had been done. On the following day, the wife and two children of the local plant supervisor were killed in a spectacular automobile accident. Finally, within the past several weeks, there had been a rash of minor accidents on the assembly line, quite uncharacteristic given the plant's excellent past safety record. Ned heard that rumors were running rampant about the plant being cursed by evil spirits, and absenteeism had increased dramatically. To try to deal with these problems, Ned called together his chief supervisors. His American staff recommended that some experts from the insurance company come in to review the safety procedures, which, they argued, would show the workers that the company was taking their safety needs seriously. But the Taiwanese supervisors considered this step to be inadequate and instead suggested that a local religious priest be brought in, during company time, to pray for the workers and ward off any evil forces. Ned and his U.S. staff thought that such an action would do nothing but give official company support to superstition. The meeting ended without any substantial agreement between U.S. and Taiwanese supervisors.

How would you explain this basic cultural conflict?

5-4   Within the past decade, Ray Cisneros had worked hard to become the top salesperson for the entire West Coast district of his company, which manufactures and distributes vinyl floor coverings. When his company received an invitation to make a marketing presentation to a large distribution firm in Buenos Aires, Ray's Hispanic background, fluency in Spanish, and excellent salesmanship all made him the logical choice for the assignment. Ray had set up an appointment to make his presentation on the same day that he arrived from Los Angeles. But upon arrival, the marketing representative of the host firm, who met him at the airport, told him that the meeting had been arranged for two days later so that Ray could rest after the long trip and have a chance to see some of the local sights and enjoy their hospitality. Ray tried to assure his host that he felt fine and was prepared to make the presentation that day. Ray could see no good reason not to get on with the business at hand. Eventually, the marketing representative (somewhat reluctantly) intervened on Ray's behalf, and the meeting was reset for later that afternoon. But once the meeting began, Ray noticed that the Argentinean executives never really got beyond the exchange of pleasantries. Finally, the vice president in charge suggested that they meet again the next afternoon. Ray was feeling increasingly frustrated with the excruciatingly slow pace of the negotiations.

How could you help Ray gain some clarity on this cross-cultural situation?

5-5   Stefan Phillips, a manager for a large U.S. airline, was transferred to Dhahran, Saudi Arabia, to set up a new office. Although Stefan had had several other extended overseas assignments in Paris and Brussels, he was not well prepared for working in the Arab world. At the end of his first week, Stefan came home in a state of near total frustration. As he sat at the dinner table that night, he told his wife how exasperating it had been to work with the local employees, who, he claimed, seemed to take no responsibility for anything. Whenever something went wrong they would simply say *"Inshallah"* ("If God wills it"). Coming from a culture that sees no problem as insolvable, Stefan could not understand how the local employees could be so passive about job-related problems. "If I hear one more *inshallah*," he told his wife, "I'll go crazy."

What might you tell Stefan to help him better understand the cultural realities of Saudi Arabia?

CHAPTER 6

Negotiating across Cultures

In a very general sense, the process of negotiating is absolutely fundamental to human communication and interaction. If we stop to consider it, we are negotiating all the time. We negotiate with our spouses, children, co-workers, friends, bosses, landlords, customers, bankers, neighbors, and clients. Because negotiating is such an integral part of our everyday lives, it becomes largely an unconscious process, for we do not spend a lot of time thinking about how we do it. As with so many other aspects of our behavior, the way we negotiate is colored by our cultural assumptions. Whether we are effective negotiators or not, our culturally conditioned negotiating styles are largely operating at an unconscious level.

When negotiating within our own culture, it is possible to operate effectively at the intuitive or unconscious level. However, when we leave our familiar cultural context and enter into international negotiations, the scene changes dramatically. There are no longer shared values, interests, goals, ethical principles, or cultural assumptions between the negotiating parties. As we demonstrated in previous chapters, different cultures have different values, attitudes, morals, behaviors, and linguistic styles, all of which can greatly affect the process and outcome of our negotiations. To illustrate, researchers Jeanne Brett and Tetsushi Okumura (1998) studied the effects of culture on the process of negotiating between Japan and the United States. They found that the basic value differences of individualism versus collectivism (see Chapter 5) is reflected in differential levels of self-interest in the negotiation process. The more individualistic Americans (who come from a culture where the definition of self is less dependent on group membership) are more likely to emphasize their own personal self-interests when negotiating. The Japanese, by way of contrast, are more likely to suppress their personal self-interest in favor of the interests of the group and the need to honor their social obligations. Moreover, the direct versus indirect way of communicating (see Chapter 3) that distinguishes Japanese and Americans can affect the process of negotiations. In general, the Japanese tend to communicate much more indirectly than Americans; that is, they leave much information unstated about their needs, positions, and priorities. Americans, on the other hand, state their positions very explicitly and expect those on the other side of the table to do like-wise. This results in the Japanese negotiators understanding the priorities of the Americans, while the opposite is not true. Americans conclude (erroneously) that the Japanese are sneaky and covert, while the Japanese conclude (equally erroneously) that their American counterparts are not very intelligent because they cannot understand the subtle and indirect messages that the Japanese are sending.

Thus, as is obvious, we cannot negotiate across cultural lines without being conscious of how the basic features of different cultures can influence the negotiation process. In this chapter, our aim is to analyze the cross-cultural negotiation process, for by heightening our awareness of some of the potential pitfalls, we may become more effective international negotiators.

THE NATURE OF CROSS-CULTURAL NEGOTIATION

Because the act of negotiating is so central to our lives, we frequently fail to define it. Those who write about the process of negotiation, on the other hand, do define it—sometimes in excruciating detail—but fail to agree on a common definition. But, as Robert Moran and William Stripp (1991, 71–72) remind us, the common theme running through all definitions is that two or more parties, who have both common and conflicting interests, interact with one another for the purpose of reaching a mutually beneficial agreement.

Effective negotiation does not involve bludgeoning the other side into submission. Rather, it involves the more subtle art of *persuasion*, whereby all parties feel as though they have benefited. There is no simple formula for success; each situation must be assessed within its own unique set of circumstances. The successful negotiator must choose the appropriate strategy, project the correct personal and organizational images, do the right type of homework, ask the most relevant questions, and offer and request the appropriate types of concession at the right time. Negotiating within one's own culture is sufficiently difficult, but the pitfalls increase geometrically when one enters the international/intercultural arena.

Being a skilled negotiator in any context entails being an intelligent, well-prepared, creative, flexible, and patient problem solver. International negotiators, however, face an additional set of problems/obstacles not ordinarily encountered by domestic negotiators. As we have tried to establish from the outset of this book, one very important obstacle to international negotiations is culture. Because culture involves everything that a people have, think, and do, it *will* influence or color the negotiation process. The very fact that usually one party in a negotiation will travel to the country of the other party establishes a foreign negotiating setting for at least one party, and this "strangeness" can be a formidable barrier to communication, understanding, and agreement.

There are other barriers as well. For example, international negotiation entails working within the confines of two different and sometimes conflicting legal structures.

Unless the negotiating parties can both understand and cope with the differing legal requirements, a joint international contract may be governed by two or more legal systems. Another barrier may be the extent to which government bureaucracies in other countries exert their influence on the negotiation process, a problem not always understood by Westerners whose governments are relatively unobtrusive in business negotiations.

Finally, an additional obstacle that goes beyond cultural differences is the sometimes volatile, or at least unpredictable, geopolitical realities of the two countries of the negotiating parties. Sudden changes in governments, the enactment of new legislation, or even natural disasters can disrupt international business negotiations either temporarily or permanently. For example, the disintegration of the Soviet Union, Iraq's invasion of Kuwait, or an earthquake in Mexico could all have far-reaching implications for Western businesspeople who were in the process of negotiating business deals in those parts of the world.

While we recognize the importance to international negotiations of these noncultural obstacles (different legal structures, interference by government bureaucracies, and geopolitical instability), our discussion of international business negotiation will focus on the cultural dimension.

It should be apparent by now that success in negotiating international business contracts requires a deep understanding of the culture of those on the other side of the table. The reason for this cultural awareness, however, is not for the purpose of bringing the other side to its knees—to make them do what we want them to do. Nor is it to accommodate them by giving up some of our own strongly adhered-to principles. Rather, an appreciation of the important cultural elements of the other side is essential if one is to get on with the business at hand so that all parties concerned can feel as though they are better off after the negotiations than before. Moreover, it is equally the responsibility of both sides in the negotiating process to understand the cultural realities of their negotiation partners. Intercultural communication, in other words, is a two-way street, with both sides sharing the burden and responsibility of cultural awareness.

WHERE TO NEGOTIATE

Earlier we defined *negotiation* as a process between people who share some common interests, people who stand to benefit from bringing the process to a successful conclusion. Both sides have a stake in the outcome, so it stands to reason that the place of negotiations could be on the home turf of either party or in a neutral environment. The selection of a site for the negotiations is of critical importance because there are a number of advantages of negotiating in your own backyard. In the world of international diplomatic negotiations, the question of where a summit meeting will occur is taken very seriously because it is assumed that the location will very likely affect the nature and the outcome of the negotiations. The business negotiator who travels abroad is confronted with an appreciable number of problems and challenges not faced by those who negotiate at home. Let's consider some of the difficulties encountered when negotiating abroad.

First, and perhaps most important, the negotiator abroad must adjust to an unfamiliar environment during the days, weeks, or even months of the negotiations. This involves getting used to differences in language, foods, pace of life, and other aspects of culture. The negotiator who is well prepared will make a relatively smooth and quick adjustment, yet not without moments of discomfort, awkwardness, and general psychological disorientation. Time and effort must be spent learning about the new environment, such as how to make a telephone call, where to find a fax machine, or simply how to locate the rest room. For those who are less well prepared, the adjustment process may be so difficult that there is little energy left for the important work of negotiating.

Second, the business negotiator cannot avoid the deleterious effects of jet lag. Even for those international travelers who heed all conventional wisdom concerning minimizing jet lag (avoid alcohol and eat certain foods), an intercontinental flight will nevertheless take its toll on one's physical condition. Thus, the traveling negotiator is likely not to be as rested or alert as his or her counterpart who doesn't have to cope with jet lag.

Third, the negotiator has little or no control over the setting in which the discussions take place. The size of the conference room, the seating arrangements, and the scheduling of times for both negotiating and socializing are decisions made by the host negotiating team. The side that controls these various details of the process can use them to their own advantage.

Fourth, the negotiator working in a foreign country is further hampered by being physically separated from his or her business organization and its various support personnel. Frequently, before negotiators can agree to certain conditions of a contract, they must obtain additional information from the manufacturing, shipping, or financial department of their home office. Those negotiating at home have a marked advantage over the traveling negotiator because it is always easier to get a question answered by a colleague down the hall than by relying on transcontinental telephones or fax messages.

Finally, negotiators working on foreign soil are under pressure to conclude the negotiations as soon as possible, a type of pressure not experienced by those negotiating at home. The longer negotiations drag on, the longer the negotiator will be away from the other operations of the office that need attention, the longer his or her family and social life will be disrupted, and the more it will cost the firm in terms of travel-related expenses. Given these very real pressures, negotiators working abroad are more likely to make certain concessions than they might if they were negotiating at home.

It would appear that negotiating abroad has a number of distinct disadvantages as compared with negotiating at home, including the hassle of an unfamiliar cultural setting, uncertain lines of communication with the home office, lack of control over the negotiating setting, and considerable expenditure of both time and travel funds. There is little doubt that, given the choice, most Western businesspeople would opt to conduct their negotiations at home. Yet, more often than not, Westerners are attempting to sell their products and ideas abroad. And if the potential international customers are to learn about the products or services, it is essential that Westerners go to them. Moreover, in many parts of the world, particularly in developing areas, potential customers from both the private and public sectors have very limited resources for traveling. Thus, in many cases, if Westerners desire to remain competitive in the international marketplace, they will have no other choice than to do their negotiating on foreign soil.

EFFECTIVE STRATEGIES FOR INTERNATIONAL NEGOTIATORS

In keeping with the conceptual nature of this book, this chapter does not attempt to list all the do's and don't's of negotiating in all the cultures of the world. Such an approach—given the vast number of features found in each culture—would be well beyond the scope of this book and certainly beyond any single individual's capacity to comprehend. Whereas some works have taken a country-by-country approach to international negotiating (Kennedy 1985; Moran and Stripp 1991), here we focus on certain general principles of cross-cultural negotiating that can be applied to most, if not all, international situations. This chapter does not provide a cookbook-style guide for avoiding negotiating faux pas in all the major cultures of the world, but it will draw upon some of the most positive experiences of successful intercultural negotiators.

Concentrate on Long-Term Relationships, Not Short-Term Contracts

If there is one central theme running through the literature on international business negotiations, it is that the single most important consideration is building relationships over the long run rather than focusing on a single contract. At times, U.S. businesspeople have been criticized for their short-term view of doing business. Some feel that they should not waste time; they should get in there and get the contract signed and get on to other business. If the other side fails to meet their contractual obligations, the lawyers can sue. Frequently, this approach carries with it the implicit analogy of a sports contest. Negotiating across cultures is like a football game, the purpose of which is to outmaneuver, outmanipulate, outsmart, and generally overpower the other side, which is seen as the opponent—and the wider the margin of victory, the better. But conventional wisdom, coupled with the experience of successful negotiators, strongly suggests that international business negotiating is not about winning big, humiliating the opposition, making a killing, and gaining all the advantages. Rather, successful international business negotiating is conducted in a cooperative climate in which the needs of both sides are met and in which both sides can emerge as winners.

To be certain, considerable variation exists throughout the world in terms of why people enter into business negotiation in the first place. In some societies, such as our own, businesspeople may enter into negotiations for the sake of obtaining the signed contract; other societies, however, view the negotiations as primarily aimed at creating a long-standing relationship and only secondarily for the purpose of signing a short-term contract. As Jeswald Salacuse (1991, 60) reminds us, for many Americans a signed contract represents *closing* a deal; to the Japanese, signing a contract is seen as *opening* a relationship. With those cultures that tend to emphasize the relationship over the contract, no contract will likely be signed unless a relationship of trust and mutual respect has been established. And even though relationship building may not conform to the typical American's time frame, the inescapable truth is that, because relationships are so important in the international arena, negotiations are unlikely to succeed without them.

Building relationships requires that negotiators take the time to get to know one another. Frequently, this involves activities—eating, drinking, visiting national monuments, playing golf—that strike the typical American as being outside the realm of business and consequently a waste of time. This type of ritual socializing, however, is vital because it represents an honest effort to understand, as fully as possible, the needs, goals, values, interests, and opinions of the negotiators on the other side. The two sides need not have similar needs, goals, and values in order to have a good relationship, for it is possible to disagree in a number of areas and still have a good working relationship. However, both parties need to be willing to identify their shared interests while working at reconciling their conflicting interests in a spirit of cooperation and mutual respect. This twofold task, which is never easy to accomplish, has the very best chance of succeeding if a relationship built on trust and mutual respect has been established between the negotiating parties.

Focus on the Interests behind the Positions

After the parties in a negotiation have developed a relationship, the discussion of positions can begin. This stage of negotiating involves both sides setting forth what they want to achieve from the negotiations. From a seller's perspective, it may involve selling a certain number of sewing machines at x dollars per unit. From the perspective of the purchaser, it may involve receiving a certain number of sewing machines within a month's time at x minus $30 per unit. Once the positions have been clearly stated, the effective international negotiator will then look behind those positions for the underly-

When building long-lasting relationships with international business associates, it helps to get to know them as people.

ing needs of the other party. The stated position is usually one way of satisfying needs, but often the position of one side is in direct opposition to the position of the other side. If the negotiators focus just on the positions, they will not likely resolve or reconcile their differences. However, by looking beyond the position to the basic needs that gave rise to those positions in the first place, creative solutions can likely be found that will satisfy both parties.

The need to distinguish between a *position* and the *needs underlying the position* has been effectively illustrated by Dean Allen Foster (1992, 286–87). The representative of a U.S. telecommunications firm had been negotiating with the communications representative from the Chinese government. After months of relationship building and discussing terms, the finalization of the agreement appeared to be in sight. At the eleventh hour, however, the Chinese representative raised an additional condition that took the American by surprise. The Chinese representative argued that since they were about to embark on a long-term business relationship between friends, the U.S. firm should give its Chinese friends a special reduced price that it would not give to other customers. The problem with this request was that the U.S. firm had a strict policy of uniform pricing for all countries with which it did business.

If we look at this situation solely in terms of the positions of the two parties, it would appear to be an impasse. For anything to be resolved, one party would have to get what it wanted, while the other would have to abandon its position. But, by understanding the basic needs behind the positions, both sides have more room to maneuver so that a win–win situation can result. Let's consider the needs behind the positions. The Chinese position was based on two essential needs: to get a lower price, thus saving money, and to receive a special favor as a sign of the American's friendship and commitment to the relationship. The position of the U.S. firm was based on its need to adhere to the principle of uniform pricing. By looking at the situation from the perspective of underlying needs rather than positions, it now became possible to suggest some alternative solutions. The U.S. negotiator offered another proposal: to sell the Chinese some new

---

During negotiations on a joint venture with a Japanese company, Tom Clancy, representing a company from Seattle, was listening intently to a presentation made by one of the Japanese negotiators. Although Tom was very interested in what was being said, he was becoming increasingly annoyed with his Japanese counterpart, who kept pausing to ask Tom if he understood. Tom began to think that his Japanese colleague thought he was either inattentive or stupid.

This cross-cultural misunderstanding occurred because the role of the listener in Japan is quite different than in the United States. It is customary in Japan for listeners to use certain replies (known as *aizuchi*) such as *hai* (yes) to indicate that one is listening and understanding what is being said. Americans do this as well by saying yes or grunting "umhum," but the Japanese use these to a much greater extent. Since Tom was not giving off any *aizuchi*, his Japanese counterpart kept seeking reassurance that his message was being understood.

additional equipment at a very favorable price in exchange for sticking with the original pricing agreement. Such an arrangement met all the needs of both parties. The Chinese were saving money on the new equipment, *and* they were receiving a special favor of friendship from the U.S. firm. At the same time, the U.S. company did not have to violate its own policy of uniform pricing. In this example, a win–win solution was possible because the negotiators concentrated on the needs behind the positions rather than on the positions themselves. Once the negotiators were willing to look beyond a prepackaged, nonnegotiable, unilateral position for having their own needs met, they could explore new and creative ways of satisfying each other's needs.

Avoid Overreliance on Cultural Generalizations

The central theme of this book has been that success in any aspect of international business is directly related to one's knowledge of the cultural environment in which one is operating. Simply put, the more knowledge a person has of the culture of his or her international business partners, the less likely he or she will be to misinterpret what is being said or done, and the more likely one's business objectives will be met. Communication patterns—both linguistic and nonverbal—need to be mastered as well as the myriad of other culture-specific details that can get in the way of effective intercultural business communication. But just as it would be imprudent to place too little emphasis on cultural information, being overdependent on such knowledge is equally inadvisable.

As was pointed out in Chapter 2, cultural "facts" are generalizations based on a sample of human behavior and as such can only point out *tendencies* at the negotiating table. Not all Middle Easterners engage in verbal overkill, and not all Japanese are reluctant to give a direct answer. If we tend to interpret cultural generalizations too rigidly, we run the risk of turning the generalizations into cultural stereotypes. We may chuckle when we hear heaven defined as the place where the police are British, the cooks are French, the mechanics are German, the lovers are Italian, and it's all organized by the Swiss; conversely, hell is defined as the place where the cooks are British, the mechanics are French, the lovers are Swiss, the police are German, and it's all organized by Italians. Such cultural stereotypes can be offensive to those being lumped together uncritically, but they can be particularly harmful in the process of international business negotiations because they can be wrong. Sometimes negotiators on the other side of the table do not act the way the generalization would predict.

To be certain, people's negotiating behavior is influenced by their culture, but there may be some other factors at work as well. How a person behaves also may be conditioned by such variables as education, biology, or experience. To illustrate, a Mexican business negotiator who has an M.B.A. from the Wharton School may not object to discussing business at lunch, as most other Mexicans might. We should not automatically assume that all Mexicans will act in a stereotypical way. Owing to this particular Mexican's education and experience, he has learned how to behave within the U.S. frame of reference. It is therefore important that we move beyond cultural stereotyping and get to know the negotiators on the other side not only as members of a particular cultural group but also as individuals with their own unique set of personality traits and experiences.

Be Sensitive to Timing

Timing may not be everything, but in international negotiations it certainly can make a difference between success and failure. As pointed out in Chapter 5, different cultures have different rhythms and different concepts of time. In cultures like our own, with tight schedules and a precise reckoning of time, it is anticipated that business will be conducted without wasting time. But in many parts of the world, it is not realistic to expect to arrive one day and consummate a deal the next before jetting off to another client in another country. The more likely scenario involves spending what may seem like inordinately long periods on insignificant details, frustrating delays, and unanticipated postponements. Bringing the U.S. notion of time into an international negotiation will invariably result in either frustration or the eventual alienation of those with whom one is negotiating.

As a general rule, international negotiations, for a number of reasons, take longer than domestic negotiations. We should keep in mind that McDonald's engaged in negotiations for nearly a decade before it began selling hamburgers in Moscow. In another situation, a high-level salesperson for a U.S. modular office furniture company spent months negotiating a deal in Saudi Arabia. He made frequent courtesy calls, engaged in long discussions on a large number of topics other than office furniture, and drank enough coffee to float a small ship. But the months of patience paid off. His personal commission (not his company's profit) was in excess of $2 million! The lesson here is clear. An international negotiator must first understand the local rhythm of time, and if it is slower than at home, exercise the good sense to be patient.

Another important dimension of time that must be understood is that some times of the year are better than others for negotiating internationally. All cultures have certain times of the year when people are preoccupied with social or religious concerns or when everything having to do with business simply shuts down. Before negotiating abroad, become familiar with the national calendar. To illustrate, do not plan any global deal making with the Taiwanese on October 10, their national day of independence; or with the Japanese during "Golden Week," when most people take a vacation; or anywhere in the Islamic world during Ramadan, when Muslin businessmen are more concerned with fasting than with negotiating. Any attempt to conduct negotiations on these holidays, traditional vacation times, or times of religious observance will generally meet with as much success as a non-American might have trying to conduct business negotiations in the United States during the week between Christmas and New Year's day.

Still another consideration of time has to do with the different time zones between one's home office and the country in which the negotiations are taking place. Owing to these different time zones, an American negotiating in Manila cannot fax the home office in New York and expect an answer within minutes, as might be expected if the negotiations were taking place in Boston. If at 4:00 P.M. (Manila time) a question is raised in the negotiations that requires clearance or clarification from the home office, an answer will not likely be received until the next day because in New York it is 3:00 A.M. Thus, attempting to operate between two distant time zones can be frustrating for most Americans because it tends to slow the pace of the negotiations.

Remain Flexible

Whenever entering an international negotiating situation, the Western negotiator, despite the best preparation, will always have an imperfect command of how things work. In such an environment, some of the best laid plans frequently go unexecuted: Schedules change unexpectedly; government bureaucrats become more recalcitrant than predicted; people don't follow through with what they promise. When things don't go as expected, it is important to be able to readjust quickly and efficiently. To be flexible does not mean to be weak; rather, it means being capable of responding to changing situations. Flexibility means avoiding the all too common malady known as "hardening of the categories."

The need for remaining open and flexible has been well illustrated by Dean Allen Foster (1992, 254–55), who tells of a U.S. businessman trying to sell data-processing equipment to a high-level government official in India. After preparing himself thoroughly, the American was escorted into the official's office for their initial meeting. Much to the American's surprise, seated on a nearby sofa was another gentleman who was never introduced. For the entire meeting, the host-government official acted as if the third man were not there. The American became increasingly uncomfortable with the presence of this mystery man who was sitting in on the negotiations, particularly as they discussed specific details. After a while, the American began having paranoid delusions. Who was this man listening in on these private discussions? He even imagined that the man might be one of his competitors. The American negotiator became so uncomfortable with this situation that he lost his capacity to concentrate on the negotiations and eventually lost the potential contract. Here was a perfect example of a negotiator who was unsuccessful because he could not adjust to an unfamiliar situation. In India, as in some other parts of the world, it is not unusual for third parties to be present at negotiations. They may be friends, relatives, or advisors of the host negotiator, invited to listen in to provide advice—and perhaps a different perspective. Unaware of this customary practice in India, this U.S. negotiator began to imagine the worst until it had irreparably destroyed his capacity to focus on the negotiations at hand.

We can see how flexibility is important in order to most effectively adapt to unfamiliar cultural situations that are bound to emerge when negotiating internationally. Remaining flexible has another advantage as well. Flexibility creates an environment in which creative solutions to negotiating problems can emerge. We have said earlier that negotiations should be a win–win situation, whereby both sides can communicate their basic needs and interests, rather than just their positions, and then proceed to brainstorm on how best to meet the needs of both sides. A win–win type of negotiation is most likely to occur when both sides remain flexible and open to exploring nontraditional solutions.

Prepare Carefully

It is difficult to imagine any undertaking—be it in business, government, education, or athletics—where advanced preparation would not be an asset. Nowhere is this more true than in the arena of international negotiating where the variables are so complex. There is a straightforward and direct relationship between the amount of preparation and the chances for success when engaging in global deal making. Those who take the rather cavalier attitude of "Let's go over and see what the Japanese have to say" are bound to be disappointed. What is needed is a substantial amount of advanced preparation, starting, of course, with as full an understanding as possible of the local cultural realities. In addition, the would-be negotiator needs to seek answers to important questions concerning his or her own objectives, the bottom-line position, the types of information needed as the negotiations progress, an agenda, and the accessibility of support services, to mention a few. These and many other questions need to be answered *before* getting on the plane. Failure to prepare adequately will have at least two negative consequences. First, it will communicate to the other side that you don't consider the negotiations sufficiently important to have done your homework. Second, ill-prepared negotiators frequently are forced into making certain concessions that they may later regret.

We often hear the old adage "Knowledge is power." Although most Americans would agree, we are a society that tends to downplay, at least in principle, status distinctions based on power. Our democratic philosophy, coupled with our insistence on universal education, encourages people from all parts of society to get as much education (and information) as possible. Even the recent computer revolution in the United States now puts vast quantities of information into virtually anyone's hands. Consequently, Americans usually do not equate high status or power with the possession of information. In some other cultures, however, there is a very close association

A good deal of the preparation for International negotiations can now be done over the Internet.

Sometimes cross-cultural negotiations can be affected by differences in communication style. To illustrate, a wide range of stylistic differences is found throughout the world in terms of emotional self-disclosure. In certain Asian societies, proper communication is dispassionate and unemotional. But in many parts of South America, people speak more excitedly, with frequent tone changes, and often overlapping one another's speech. Americans typically have difficulty with both of these extremes in communication style. We frequently see Asians as being "inscrutable," an interpretation based on our inability to "read" them emotionally. We often see South Americans as overemotional, irrational, and, in some cases, rude because they are always interrupting. But if we understand these stylistic differences before the negotiations begin, we can give these behaviors a more positive spin. Asians are being emotionally reserved, not to be sneaky but out of respect for both you and the seriousness of the negotiations. The emotional style of South Americans reveals their commitment to the negotiation process with their hearts as well as their minds.

between knowledge and power. Unless Americans negotiating in such cultures have as much information as possible, they are likely to be seen as weak and, by implication, ineffectual negotiators.

A basic part of preparing for negotiations is self-knowledge. How well do you understand yourself, the assumptions of your own culture, and your own goals and objectives for this particular negotiation? If you are part of a negotiating team, a number of questions must be answered: Who are the team members? How have they been selected? Is there general consensus on what the team hopes to accomplish? Is there a proper balance between functional skills, cross-cultural experience, and negotiating expertise? Has a rational division of labor been agreed upon in terms of such tasks as note taking, serving as a spokesperson, or making local arrangements? Has there been sufficient time for team building, including discussions of strategies and counterstrategies?

A particularly important area of preparation has to do with getting to know the negotiators on the other side of the table. At the outset, it must be determined if the organization is the appropriate one to be negotiating with in the first place. Once that has been decided, it is important to know whether their negotiators have the authority and responsibility to make decisions. Having this information *before* the negotiations begin can eliminate the possibility of long delays stemming from the last-minute disclosure that the negotiators on the other side really cannot make final contractual decisions. But once involved in the negotiating process, it is important, as a general rule, to get to know the other team's negotiators as people rather than simply as members of a particular culture.

Learn to Listen, Not Just Speak

The style of oral discourse in the United States is essentially a very assertive one. Imbued with a high sense of competition, most Americans want to make certain that their views and positions are presented as clearly and as powerfully as possible. As a consequence, they tend to concentrate far more on sending messages than on receiving them. Many Westerners treat a discussion as a debate, the objective of which is to win by convincing the other party of the superiority of their position. Operating under such an assumption, many Americans are concentrating more on their own response than what the other party is actually saying. They seem to have a stronger desire to be heard than to hear. Although public speaking courses are quite common in our high schools and colleges, courses on how to listen are virtually nonexistent. Because effective listening is a vital component of the negotiating process, Westerners in general, and Americans in particular, are at a marked disadvantage when they appear at the negotiating table.

If, as we have tried to suggest throughout this chapter, the best negotiator is the well-informed negotiator, then active listening is absolutely essential for understanding the other side's positions and interests. The understanding that comes from your active listening can have a positive persuasive effect on your negotiating partners in at least two important ways. First, the knowledge gleaned through listening can convince your negotiating partners that you are knowledgeable and thus worthy of entering into a long-term relationship. Second, the very fact that you made the effort to really hear what they were saying will, in almost every case, enhance the rapport and trust between the two parties.

Developing good listening skills may be easier said than done. Nevertheless, some general guidelines, if followed, can help us receive oral messages more effectively:

1. Be aware of the phenomenon that psychologists call *cognitive dissonance*, the tendency to discount, or simply not hear, any message that is inconsistent with what we already believe or want to believe. In other words, if the message does not conform to our preconceived way of thinking, we subconsciously tend to dismiss its importance. It is important to actively hear *all* messages—those that you agree with and those that you don't. You don't have to agree with everything being said, but it is important to hear the message so that you will then be in a position to seek creative ways of resolving whatever differences may exist.
2. Listen to the whole message before offering a response. Focus on understanding rather than interrupting the message so that you can give a rebuttal/response. Because no one likes to be cut off before he or she is finished speaking, it is vital for the effective negotiator to practice allowing other people to finish their ideas and sentences.
3. Concentrate on the message rather than the style of the presentation. It is easy to get distracted from what is being said by focusing instead on how it is presented. No matter how inarticulate, disorganized, or inept the speaker might be, try to look beyond those stylistic features and concentrate on the content of the message.
4. Learn to ask open-ended questions, which are designed to allow the speaker to elaborate on a particular point.
5. Be conscious of staying in the present. All people bring into a negotiation session a wide variety of "baggage from the past." It is tempting to start thinking about yesterday's racquetball game with a friend, this morning's intense conversation with your boss, or the argument you had with your spouse at breakfast, but to do so will distract you from actively hearing what is being said.
6. Consider the possibility of having a friend or close associate serve as an official listener whose job it is to listen to the other side with another set of ears. Such a person can provide a valuable new perspective on what is being said and can also serve as a check on your own perceptions.

7. In almost all situations, taking notes will help you become a more effective listener. Provided you don't attempt to record every word, selective note taking can help highlight what is being said. Not only will note taking help document the messages, but when the speaker notices that you are taking notes, he or she will in all likelihood make a special effort to be clear and accurate.

THE USE OF INTERPRETERS

Throughout this book, we have stressed the importance of knowing as much as possible about the language and culture of the people with whom one is doing business. Speaking the language of your business partners gives you an enormous advantage, in that it enhances rapport and allows you to understand more fully the thought patterns of your business partners. However, when deciding on which language to use in the negotiation, do not be guided by the principle that a little knowledge is better than none at all. In other words, unless you are extremely well versed in a foreign language, do not try to negotiate in that language directly but rather rely on the services of a competent interpreter. Even if you have a relatively good command of the language, working through an interpreter may be helpful because it allows you more time to formulate your response. On the other hand, use of an interpreter has certain disadvantages, such as increasing the number of people involved, increasing the costs of the negotiations, and serving as a barrier to the two sides really getting to know one another.

When considering the use of a linguistic intermediary in cross-cultural negotiations, it is important to make the distinction between a translator and an interpreter. Although both roles are aimed at turning the words of one language into the words of another language, the *translator* usually works with documents, whereas the *interpreter* works with the spoken word in a face-to-face situation. Translators have the luxury of using dictionaries and generally are not under any great time constraints. Interpreters, on the other hand, must listen to what is being said and then instantaneously translate those words into the other language. Interpreting is a demanding job, for it requires constant translating, evaluating, and weighing the meaning of specific words within the specific social context. A good interpreter not only will need to be aware of the usual meaning of the words in the two languages but also must consider the intent of the words and the meanings of the nonverbal gestures. Because of these special demands, language interpretation is more exhausting—and consequently less accurate—than language translation.

When selecting an interpreter, it is important for that person both to be intimately knowledgeable of the two languages and have a technical expertise in the area being negotiated. For example, although a U.S. university professor of Spanish literature may have an excellent command of the language, he or she may not be particularly effective at translating scientific terms or highly technical data on weaving equipment. It is this type of shortcoming that could lead an interpreter to translate the term *hydraulic ram* into the term *wet sheep*.

Because the use of an interpreter involves placing an additional person between the two primary negotiators, one should take a number of precautions to ensure that the interpreter clarifies communication rather than obscures it. First, the negotiator and the interpreter should allow sufficient time, before the negotiations begin, to get to know one another. This involves reviewing your own notes, slides, and technical terms that may cause misunderstandings. Only when the interpreter understands your goals and expectations can he or she represent your interests to the other side and be on the lookout for the type of information that you need. Second, help the interpreter by speaking slowly and in discrete sentences. By pausing momentarily between sentences, you are actually providing a little more time for the interpreter to do his or her job. Third, because interpreting is an exhausting job that requires intense concentration, interpreters should be given breaks periodically to recharge their intellectual batteries. Fourth, plan your words carefully so as to avoid ambiguities, slang, or other forms that do not translate well. Finally, it is imperative that interpreters be treated with respect and acknowledged as the highly qualified professionals that they are. The purposeful development of cordial relations with your interpreter can only help facilitate the process of communication at the negotiating table.

THE GLOBAL NEGOTIATOR

We have examined, in a very general way, some of the problems and challenges of negotiating abroad. This chapter is not intended to be a cookbook for the would-be international negotiator. Rather, it is offered as a set of general guidelines for those who find themselves negotiating across cultures. Bear in mind that no two negotiating situations are exactly alike, but most of the strategies suggested here are applicable to whatever type of cross-cultural negotiating session one can imagine. We have suggested that international negotiators should (1) concentrate on building long-term relationships rather than short-term contracts, (2) focus on the interests that lay behind the positions, (3) avoid overdependence on cultural generalizations, (4) develop a sensitivity to timing, (5) remain flexible, (6) prepare carefully ahead of time, (7) learn to listen effectively, and (8) know when to use interpreters.

A major theme running through the contemporary literature is that, because negotiating across cultures involves mutual interdependence between the parties, it must be conducted in an atmosphere of mutual trust and cooperation. Quite apart from your position on the issues that are being negotiated, maintaining a high degree of personal respect for those on the other side of the table is important. Even though the negotiators on the other side of the table likely view the world very differently than you do, always approach them with respect and with a willingness to learn. Do not try to reform the other culture at the negotiating table in hopes that they will eventually be more like yourself, for the simple reason that it will *not* work. On the other hand, do not go overboard in the other direction by "going native." Most people tend to be suspicious of anyone imitating their gestures or behaviors. The soundest advice is to learn to understand and respect cultural differences while retaining one's own. This spirit of mutual respect and cooperation has been cogently expressed by Salacuse:

At times the two sides at the negotiating table are like two persons in a canoe who must combine their skills and strength if they are to make headway against powerful currents, through dangerous rapids, around hidden rocks, and over rough portages. Alone they can make no progress and will probably lose control. Unless they cooperate, they risk wrecking or overturning the canoe on the obstacles in the river. Similarly, unless global deal makers find ways of working together, their negotiations will founder on the many barriers encountered in putting together an international business transaction. (1991, 164)

CROSS-CULTURAL SCENERIOS

Read the following cross-cultural scenarios. In each mini-case study, a basic cultural conflict occurs between the actors involved. Try to identify the source of the conflict and suggest how it could have been avoided or minimized. Then see how well your analyses compare to the explanations in Appendix A.

6-1   Fred Gardener, a thirty-one-year-old sales manager for a small boat-building firm in Connecticut, decided to stop off in Lisbon to call on several potential clients after a skiing trip to Switzerland. Having set up three appointments in two days, he arrived for the first two scheduled meetings at the appointed times but was kept waiting for over a half-hour in each instance. Based on these two experiences, Fred assumed that the Portuguese, like other "Latin" types, must be *manana* oriented and not particularly concerned with the precise reckoning of time. With this in mind, he was not particularly concerned about being on time for his third appointment. Instead, he extended his visit to the local museum and arrived at his third appointment more than forty minutes late. However, Fred sensed that the Portuguese businesspeople were quite displeased with his tardiness.

How would you explain this reaction?

6-2   Margaret Errington, a corporate attorney for a San Francisco department store chain, was responsible for negotiating leases for their outlets abroad. Because she had been particularly successful in similar negotiations in Europe, she was looking forward to securing attractive leasing agreements from a shopping mall developer in Osaka, Japan. She was especially optimistic because of her successful telephone communications with her counterparts in Japan. But when she arrived with her two assistants, John Gresham and Mel Watt, she was told by her Japanese hosts how surprised they were that she should come to negotiate in person. Margaret was usually not included in the after-hours socializing, and frequently the Japanese negotiators would direct their questions to John or Mel rather than to Margaret.

Can you explain why Margaret was treated as she was?

6-3   Harold Josephson, an electronics engineer for an American satellite manufacturer, had spent weeks negotiating with a Japanese parts distributor in Yokohama. The Japanese executive, Mr. Kushiro, was tough in the negotiations, so progress had been slow. Eventually, Harold felt they had found common ground and an equitable deal could be worked out to the advantage of both companies. On the final day of negotiations, Harold was pleased to announce to Kushiro that their thinking was parallel and he was ready to draw up the contract. Kushiro pleasantly thanked Harold for his time and left the meeting without further discussion.

What happened?

6-4   Roger Brown, marketing vice president for a Seattle-based lumber company, was making a sales presentation to a plywood wholesaler in Tokyo. Roger had just proposed what he considered to be a fair price for a large shipment of first-quality plywood. Much to his amazement, the three Japanese executives did not respond immediately but rather sat across the table with their hands folded and their eyes cast downward, saying nothing. Fifteen seconds passed, then thirty, and still no response. Finally, Roger became so exasperated that he said with a good deal of irritation in his voice, "Would you like for me to repeat the offer?" From that point onward, the talks were stalled, and Roger never did successfully negotiate a contract for plywood.

What advice would you give Roger for future negotiations?

6-5   Frank McDougal had been chosen to set up a branch office of his engineering consulting firm in Seoul, Korea. Although the six engineering consultants who would eventually be transferred to Seoul were Americans, Frank was interested in hiring local support staff. He was particularly interested in hiring a local person with excellent accounting skills to handle the company's books. He was confident that he would be able to find the right person for the job because his company was prepared to offer an excellent salary and benefits package. After receiving what he considered to be several excellent leads from a friend at the Rotary Club, he was surprised to be turned down by all four prospective candidates. They were very appreciative of being considered for the position, but all preferred to stay with their current employer. Frank just couldn't understand why all four of these Koreans chose to pass up an increase in salary and fringe benefits.

How would you explain this situation to Frank?

CHAPTER 7

Coping with Culture Shock

Preparing for a two-year overseas assignment in Lagos, Nigeria, a U.S. businessperson during the 1970s submitted to no fewer than twenty-seven shots as a protective measure against everything from yellow fever to hepatitis. Although he managed to avoid any dreaded tropical disease during his assignment, he contracted one malady for which there was no known vaccination. The disease was culture shock, that psychological stress resulting from trying to adjust to major differences in lifestyles, living conditions, and business practices in another cultural setting.

THE NATURE OF CULTURE SHOCK

Culture shock, a term first popularized by anthropologist Kalvero Oberg, refers to the psychological disorientation experienced by people who suddenly find themselves living and working in radically different cultural environments. Oberg describes culture shock as the anxiety that results when all familiar cultural props have been knocked out from under a person who is entering a new culture:

> Culture shock is precipitated by the anxiety that results from losing all our familiar signs and symbols of social intercourse. These signs or cues include the thousand and one ways in which we orient ourselves to the situations of daily life: when to shake hands and what to say when we meet people, when and how to give tips, how to give orders to servants, how to make purchases, when to accept and when to refuse invitations, when to take statements seriously and when not. Now these cues which may be words, gestures, facial expressions, customs, or norms are acquired by all of us in the course of growing up and are as much a part of our culture as the language we speak or the beliefs we accept. All of us depend for our peace of mind and our efficiency on hundreds of these cues, most of which we do not carry on the level of conscious awareness. (1960, 177)

Culture shock ranges from mild irritation to a deep-seated psychological panic or crisis. Culture shock occurs when U.S businesspeople abroad, all of a sudden, try to play a game in which they have little or no understanding of the basic rules. They must struggle to uncover what is meaningful in this new cultural environment, while acknowledging that many of their own familiar cultural cues may be irrelevant. They are forced to try out new and unfamiliar modes of behavior, all the while never really knowing when they might be unwittingly committing a gross social indiscretion. Culture shock usually carries with it feelings of helplessness and irritability, while producing fears of being cheated, injured, contaminated, or discounted. Even though everyone, to some extent, suffers the anxiety of culture shock when first having to struggle in an unfamiliar cultural setting, the very success or failure of an overseas living assignment depends largely on how well one can make the psychological adjustment and get beyond the frequently debilitating effects.

Both social scientists and laypeople use the term *culture shock* to define in very broad terms the unpleasant consequences of experiencing a foreign culture. Since the 1960s a number of writers in the field have attempted to elaborate on Oberg's (1960) original formulation by using such terms as *role shock* (Byrnes 1966), *culture fatigue* (Guthrie 1975), and *pervasive ambiguity* (Ball-Rokeach 1973). Yet despite these variations on Oberg's original theme, there is general agreement that culture shock involves the following dimensions:

- A sense of confusion over expected role behavior
- A sense of surprise, even disgust, after realizing some of the features of the new culture
- A sense of loss of the old familiar surroundings (friends, possessions, and so on) and cultural patterns
- A sense of being rejected (or at least not accepted) by members of the new culture
- A sense of loss of self-esteem because the inability to function in the new culture results in an imperfect meeting of professional objectives
- A feeling of impotence at having little or no control over the environment
- A strong sense of doubt when old values (which had always been held as absolute) are brought into question

Despite the use of the word *shock*, which implies a sudden jolt, culture shock does not occur quickly, nor is it the result of a single event. Rather, it results from a series of cumulative experiences. When first arriving in a new culture, usually flying into a major city, the cultural contrasts do not seem too obvious. There are usually traffic lights, taxis, tall buildings with elevators, banks, and modern hotels with English-speaking desk clerks. But before long, the very real cultural differences become painfully apparent. People push in front of you in line rather than lining up in an orderly fashion; when people say yes, they don't always mean yes; you try to be thoughtful by asking about the health of your business partner's wife, and he acts insulted; you cannot buy things that you are accustomed to having every day at home; people promise to have something done by tomorrow, but it doesn't get done; you try to be friendly, but people don't respond. As those first days and weeks pass, the differences become more apparent, and the anxiety and sense of frustration build slowly. Eventually, the cultural differences become the focus of attention. The foreign ways of thinking and acting are no longer quaint and fascinating alternative ways of living but rather are pathological, clearly inferior to your own. When this occurs, culture shock has set in.

Robert Kohls (1984, 65) provides a fairly comprehensive list of the major symptoms that have been observed in relatively severe cases of culture shock:

- Homesickness
- Boredom
- Withdrawal (for example, spending excessive amounts of time reading; seeing only other Americans; avoiding contact with host nationals)
- Need for excessive amounts of sleep
- Compulsive eating
- Compulsive drinking
- Irritability
- Exaggerated cleanliness
- Marital stress
- Family tension and conflict
- Chauvinistic excesses
- Stereotyping of host nationals
- Hostility toward host nationals
- Loss of ability to work effectively
- Unexplainable fits of weeping
- Physical ailments (psychosomatic illnesses)

Since culture shock is characterized by a large and diverse set of symptoms, the malady is frequently difficult to predict and control. It is important to point out, however, that not everyone will experience all the symptoms, but almost all people will experience some. Moreover, some symptoms, or combination of symptoms, will vary in severity from one case to another. Yet whenever any of the symptoms manifest themselves while one is living and working abroad, one can be sure that culture shock has set in.

Individual international businesspeople vary greatly in the extent to which they suffer from culture shock. A few people are so ill suited to working in culturally different environments that they repatriate shortly after arriving in the host country. Others manage to get by with a minimum of psychological discomfort. But for most Westerners, operating abroad involves a fairly severe bout with culture shock. According to Oberg (1960), culture shock usually occurs in the following four stages:

1. *The honeymoon stage:* Most people begin their foreign assignment with a positive attitude, so this initial stage is usually characterized by euphoria. At this point, all that is new is exotic and exciting. Attitudes about the host country, and one's capacity to operate in it successfully, are unrealistically positive. During this initial stage, which may last from several days to several weeks, the recent arrival is probably staying temporarily at a Western-style hotel or staff guesthouse where food, conditions of cleanliness, and language are not appreciably different from those at home. The sojourner's time is devoted to getting established—finding a house, a maid, and perhaps schools for the children. It is possible that the family's standard of living in this foreign land will be more opulent than they were accustomed to while living in the United States. By and large, it is the similarities between this new country and the United States that

stand out—which leads one to the erroneous conclusion that people are really all alike under the skin.

2. *Irritation and hostility*: But as with marriages, honeymoons do not last forever. Within several weeks or perhaps months, problems arise at work, at home, and at the marketplace. Things taken for granted at home simply don't occur. A number of small problems become insurmountable obstacles. Now, all of a sudden, it is the cultural differences, not the similarities, that loom so large. For the first time it becomes clear that, unlike a two-week vacation, one will be in this situation for the next twelve to eighteen months. The second stage of culture shock has set in; this second stage represents the crisis stage of a disease. Small problems are blown out of proportion. It is during this stage that one or more of the symptoms mentioned are manifested to some degree. A commonly used mode for dealing with this crisis stage is to band together with other expatriates to disparage the local people: "How can they be so lazy?" "So dirty?" "So stupid?" "So slow?" Now is when ethnic jokes proliferate. The speed with which one passes through this crisis stage of culture shock will vary directly with the ultimate success of the international assignment. Unfortunately, some never get past stage 2, and they become premature return statistics or somehow manage to stick it out but at a high cost to themselves, their families, and their companies.

3. *Gradual adjustment*: Stage 3 marks the passing of the crisis and a gradual recovery. This stage may begin so gradually that the "patient" is unaware that it is even happening. An understanding slowly emerges of how to operate within the new culture. Some cultural cues now begin to make sense; patterns of behavior begin to emerge, which enable a certain level of predictability; some of the language is becoming comprehensible; and some of the problems of everyday living—which seemed so overwhelming in stage 2—are beginning to be resolved. In short, the culture seems more natural and more manageable. A capacity to laugh at one's situation is a sure sign that adjustment—and ultimate recovery—is well under way.

4. *Biculturalism*: The fourth and final stage, representing full or near full recovery, involves the ability to function effectively in two different cultures. The local customs that were so unsettling months earlier are now both understood and appreciated. Without having to "go native," the international businessperson now accepts many of the new cultural ways for what they are. This is not to imply that all strains in intercultural relationships have disappeared, but the high-level anxiety caused by living and working in a different cultural environment are gone. Moreover, in a number of situations, those making a full recovery from culture shock find that there are many local customs to which they have become accustomed and which will be missed upon returning home. Again, many people never reach stage 4. It is possible to "get by" with a modicum of success by never going beyond stage 3. But for those who do become bicultural, the international assignment can be a truly positive, growth-producing experience.

The description of culture shock presented here so far paints a rather bleak picture of the helpless victim suffering from the debilitating psychological effects of a serious illness. Although not glossing over the very real deleterious consequences of culture shock, we can view it more positively as a potentially profound experience leading to cultural learning, self-awareness, and personal growth. For example, Peter Adler (1975) contends that the conflicts, problems, and frustrations associated with culture shock can result in "transitional experiences" for the international businessperson, which "can be the source of higher levels of personality development." Cultural learning is most likely to occur under situations of high anxiety, such as is com-

Adjustment to different cultures involves a willingness to get out and explore the cultural landscape.

mon in moderate to severe cases of culture shock. At lower levels of anxiety, the motivation to learn about the host culture is absent. But when anxiety, frustration, and pain are high, the motivation will be powerful to acquire new knowledge and skills, which can be used to reduce the anxiety. Moreover, culture shock encourages the sufferers to confront their own cultural heritage and to develop a new awareness of the degree to which they are products of it. Although we are indebted to Adler for reminding us of the more positive consequences of culture shock, the suggestion that it can be growth producing does have its limitations. As Richard Brislin has suggested, if the anxiety of culture shock is too high, "people may be so upset that they are unable to focus on new learning possibilities" (1981, 158).

As has been too often the case, many Western businesspeople fail to meet their overseas objectives because they are ill prepared to cope with culture shock. Yet even for those who are successful at managing culture shock during their foreign assignment (that is, by reaching stage 3 or 4), the phenomenon has an additional surprise in store—reverse culture shock, or what has come to be known as *reentry shock*. Most Westerners are not prepared for the enormous letdown they feel when returning home after an overseas assignment. In some cases, reentry shock—the disorientation faced when trying to reorient oneself to life and work in the United States—can be more anxiety producing than the original culture shock.

Although most international businesspeople will anticipate a certain number of problems and discomfort when entering a new cultural environment, they are frequently unprepared for the myriad of problems they will face when returning home. First, many U.S. businesspeople, after returning from a long assignment abroad, soon realize that one problem is finding a new niche in the corporate structure at home. Those who originally decided to send them abroad may no longer be on the scene; consequently, the corporation's plan for how it would use them now may no longer exist.

Second, while trying to overcome the original dose of culture shock, many U.S. businesspeople tend to embellish (in some cases, grossly exaggerate) their fond memories of life in the United States. They remember that things are better made, cheaper, and cleaner and people are more efficient, polite, and competent. But upon reentry to the United States, many of these myths are shattered. One of the by-products of a successful adjustment to the host culture is that our old notions of our culture will never again be the same. After one lives for a while in Switzerland or Germany, the United States no longer seems to be the epitome of cleanliness; when compared with the Japanese, the typical American seems loud and boisterous; after a stint in a developing nation, people in the United States seem rushed and impersonal. Somehow home isn't what one had remembered.

Third, one's standard of living may actually decrease when returning to the United States. Such luxuries as servants, large company houses, chauffeurs, live-in baby-sitters, and other perks used to entice people into an international assignment are likely to disappear. One is now faced with cutting one's own lawn and spending several hours a day on a commuter train.

Fourth, in those cases in which the U.S. businessperson has made a successful adaptation to a third-world cultural environment, there can be additional problems of adjustment. The returnee has seen, on a daily basis, the economic standards of people living in the host country. Per capita income may be no more than several hundred dollars a year; infant mortality may be fifteen times as high as it is in the United States; disease and lack of medical facilities keep the average life expectancy to less than forty years of age; government attention to human rights might be nonexistent; and the prospects of changing these conditions in any meaningful way are highly unlikely. And then, upon return, they encounter friends, colleagues, neighbors, and relatives complaining bitterly that they are unable to find at the grocery store the correct color of toilet tissue for the downstairs bathroom. Such complaints stir up (1) considerable anger at how unaware and unappreciative most Americans are of their own material well-being and (2) guilt for having mouthed many of these same inane complaints at an earlier time.

Fifth, and perhaps the most unsettling aspect of reentry shock, there is an almost total dearth of psychological support for the returnee. When encountering the initial stage 2 culture shock during the foreign assignment, there were (it is hoped) some preparation, an understanding (however inadequately developed) that there would be rough times, and other expatriates (who were experiencing many of the same frustrations) who could provide reassurance and support. But when returning home, U.S. businesspeople and their families feel alone and unable to express their feelings with someone who has not been through the same type of experience. Friends and relatives whom they have not seen for months or even years will say, "Oh, I can't wait to hear about your stint in Singapore." But after listening half-heartedly for about five minutes, they will change the subject to a new TV show they have just seen. In short, returnees have a great need to share their overseas experiences (some of which may have been life altering) with others, but frequently no one seems to be interested. Since they have had the unusual experience of living and working abroad, many of their friends and acquaintances, whose lives may have gone on uninterrupted or changed in other ways, have no way of relating to these experiences. The result is a feeling of alienation from the returnees' own culture because they feel that they are not being understood.

MINIMIZING CULTURE SHOCK

Just about everyone living and working abroad for extended periods of time can expect to experience culture shock to some degree. Tourists and occasional (short-term) business travelers are by and large shielded from some of the more debilitating effects of culture shock because their experiences are limited to hotels and restaurants geared to Americans. Yet those who must live and work in a foreign culture for a year or two are faced with new ways of behaving, thinking, and communicating. Even U.S. businesspeople who have lived and worked in a number of different countries claim that they have experienced culture shock in each country. For some, each subsequent assignment becomes a little easier, but for many, culture shock must be confronted for each new situation. Although there is no "quick fix" for culture shock, you can take a number of purposeful steps to minimize its negative impact.

One very effective way of totally avoiding culture shock is to choose (or have your employer choose) to stay at home rather than enter the international business arena. Some people simply do not have the desire, inclination, or temperament for international business. There may be others who are suited for some foreign cultures but not others. The old Greek adage "Know thyself" could not be more appropriate than in the process of self-selection for an international assignment. Before deciding to live abroad, it is imperative to have a realistic grasp of your motives and feelings. If people decide to move into the international arena solely on the basis of the lure of more money or possible promotion, they will probably do themselves (and their organizations) a favor by staying home. The international businessperson who is most likely to do well abroad is the person who (1) has a realistic understanding of the problems and promises of international business, (2) possesses a number of important cross-cultural coping skills, and (3) sees the world marketplace as providing vast opportunities for professional and personal growth. Those who cannot meet these criteria may be so ill suited to working in an international business setting that they would be virtually unable to overcome the more deleterious effects of culture shock.

For those who do select the international business arena, the best single piece of advice for minimizing culture shock is to be prepared. The more thorough the preparation for an overseas assignment, the fewer surprises there will be, and, consequently, the smaller will be the accumulated negative effect. A major factor in adjusting to a foreign cultural environment is the degree of familiarity with the host culture, or as William Gudykunst and Y. Y. Kim (1984, 217) suggest, knowledge about the host culture adds to the individual's capacity to adjust. It is important to recognize that culture shock will never be totally avoided, but it can be minimized through careful preparation. To prepare for an international business encounter, refer to the major substantive chapters of this book (Chapters 2 through 6), which really suggest a fourfold approach.

First, as suggested in Chapter 2, a general understanding of the concept of culture can provide a fuller appreciation of other cultures, regardless of where one might be conducting business. For example, that cultures are learned (as opposed to being acquired genetically) should remind the international businessperson that although culturally different people have learned different things, they are no less capable of learning efficiently. The concept of an integrated culture—where many or most of the parts of the culture are interconnected—should serve to convince us that all cultures, no matter how incomprehensible they may appear at first, do in fact have a consistently logical structure and should not be given such disparaging epithets as "primitive," "savage," "crazy," "stupid," and so on. And we should realize that our culture is so thoroughly internalized that it can have very real effects on our physiological functioning. These and other general concepts—which hold equally true for Indonesians, the French, Bolivians, or Japanese—can be helpful in gaining a greater understanding of the foreign cultural environment.

A second way of preparing for culture shock (see Chapters 3 and 4) is to become familiar with local patterns of communication, both verbal and nonverbal. Since any type of business depends on communication to such a significant degree, learning to communicate in a foreign business context is absolutely essential. It enhances rapport with native colleagues who have bothered to learn English; it enables the international businessperson to understand the full context of the negotiations and transactions; it frequently gives access to otherwise exclusive realms of local business; and it opens a window onto the rest of the culture. But proficiency in communications can also play a major role in adjusting to culture shock. Since living in a foreign culture involves doing hundreds of things a day—from taking taxis, to making appointments, to having a watch repaired—knowing how to communicate efficiently can both minimize the frustrations, misunderstandings, and aggravations that always face the linguistic outsider and provide a sense of safety, mastery, and self-assurance. In addition to the mastery of the local language, a vital part of communicating in an international business situation involves being able to send and receive nonverbal messages accurately. As mentioned in Chapter 4, any communication event is incomplete without a consideration of the additional layers of meaning conveyed by nonverbal behavior.

The third segment of the fourfold approach, as spelled out in Chapter 5, involves a healthy dose of cultural self-awareness. Before it is possible to understand the internal structure and logic of another culture, it is essential to first understand our own culture and how it influences who we are and what we do. We are as much products of our culture as the Japanese, French, and Cubans are products of theirs. All people face a number of universal societal problems, from how to make decisions to how to help young people make the transition to responsible adulthood, from how to gain a livelihood to how to explain the unexplainable. How any particular culture solves these problems varies widely. Middle-class Americans have worked out one set of cultural patterns, whereas the Indonesians may have developed a radically different solution. In most cases, one solution is probably not more inherently rational than another. They simply represent different answers to similar societal problems. Only after we understand why we do the things we do can we appreciate the internal logic of why other, culturally different people do what they do.

Finally, before entering the international business scene, it is important to become familiar with as much specific cultural information as possible about the country or countries with which one is conducting business (see Appendix B). There is no shortcut to the acquisition of culture-specific data. It will take time, effort, and no small amount of creativity, but the effort will be worth it. It is important not to be limiting when learning about a new culture. The number of sources of culture-specific information are nearly endless. There are, for example, many scholarly sources (books, journal articles, and so on) from such disciplines as anthropology, religious studies, intercultural communication, cross-cultural psychology, and comparative sociology. Besides the scholarly literature (which is not always easily accessible or comprehensible), there are many other sources of excellent information, including commercially published sources for the business traveler, State Department publications, newspapers, and information published and distributed by the various foreign embassies. In addition to publications, people are also valid sources of information. In short, it is advisable to draw on as wide a range of culture-specific sources as possible. The more cultural information at hand, the fewer surprises there are likely to be; consequently, serious culture shock can more likely be avoided.

This fourfold approach to understanding the cultural environment constitutes the cornerstone of the cognitive approach. By conscientiously pursuing these four content areas—general cultural concepts, local communication patterns, cultural self-awareness, and culture-specific information—the international businessperson will have touched on the major areas of cultural knowledge, thereby avoiding total alienation and some of the more debilitating consequences of culture shock. But one's preparation for coping with and eventually adjusting to radically different cultural environments involves more than the mere acquisition of information. Also required are developing certain skills, acquiring new attitudes, and modifying old ways of doing things. What follows are some additional suggestions for enhancing the international business experience by reducing clashes with the local culture.

1. *Understand that learning about the host culture is a process that continues throughout your stay in the host culture, and beyond.* Far more learning will occur after your arrival in the country than prior to leaving home. Make certain that you use a wide variety of information sources to learn about the host culture. Include local people, newspapers, tourist information, libraries, and your own observations. Find a friend or colleague (either a local

resident or an experienced expatriate) to serve as a guide and mentor in helping you learn as quickly as possible.

2. *As soon after arrival as possible, become familiar with your immediate physical surroundings.* Armed with a good map of the vicinity, leave your hotel and walk in a number of different directions, exploring the city or town on foot. Identify local buildings, what they are used for, where they are in relation to one another, the pattern, if any, of how streets are configured, and where people seem to congregate. A familiarity with the "lay of the land," while very tangible and concrete, will provide an excellent base for learning about other aspects of the culture.

3. *Within the first several days of arrival, work on familiarizing yourself with some of the basic, everyday survival skills that your hosts take for granted.* These include such capacities as using the local currency, using the public transportation system, buying stamps, using the telephone system, and ordering from a menu. By mastering these seemingly simple tasks, you will minimize frustrations and embarrassment quickly, as well as gain the self-confidence to master some of the more subtle aspects of the host culture.

4. *As difficult as it may be, try to understand your hosts in terms of their culture rather than your own.* When you encounter a behavior or an attitude that appears strange or even of-

One way of minimizing the negative effects of culture shock is to take care of yourself physically.

fensive, try to make sense of it in terms of their cultural assumptions rather than your own. This is not to suggest that you should adopt their attitudes or behaviors, or even like them, but you will better understand them when viewed from within their proper cultural context.

5. *Particularly in the beginning, learn to live with the ambiguity of not having all the answers.* Trying to operate in a new culture is, by definition, a highly ambiguous situation. The person who insists on having immediate and clear-cut answers for everything is likely to be frustrated. Just like the person who is expected to play a game without knowing all the rules, it is important for the cultural neophyte to know that there will be many unanswered questions. By being patient and learning to live with ambiguity, the new arrival is both preserving his or her mental health and "buying time" to learn more answers, reduce the ambiguity, and thus eventually adjust to the new culture.

6. *As a way of enhancing your relationships with your hosts, make a conscious effort to be empathetic; that is, put yourself in the other person's shoes.* It is only natural for people to be attracted to those individuals who can see things from their point of view. Empathy can be practiced by becoming an active listener. First try to understand—then try to be understood.

7. *Understand that flexibility and resourcefulness are key elements to adapting to a new culture.* When living and working in a different culture, the best-laid plans often are not realized. When plans do not work out as expected (as they have a tendency to do more than at home), you need to make and execute new plans quickly and efficiently without becoming overstressed. Resourceful people are familiar with what is available in the host culture, are comfortable calling on others for help, and know how to take advantage of available opportunities.

8. *Learn to postpone making a judgment or decision until you have all the required information.* Effective administrators in the United States are defined by their ability to decide quickly and effectively and to bring successful closure to problem-solving tasks. When operating in another culture, however, the capacity of "wrapping things up" or "getting the show on the road" can be a liability rather than an asset. Since people have an imperfect grasp of the rules, norms, and procedures in the host culture, they need to postpone decisions and conclusions until all facts are at hand.

9. *At least at the beginning of your stay, don't evaluate yourself according to your usual standards of accomplishment.* Any recent arrival to a new culture is bound to be less efficient, productive, or socially competent. The learning curve takes time, so don't be unrealistically hard on yourself.

10. *Don't lose your sense of humor.* People in any situation, either at home or abroad, tend to get themselves in trouble if they take themselves too seriously. When struggling to learn a new culture, everyone makes mistakes that may be discouraging, embarrassing, or downright laughable. In most situations, your hosts will be disarmingly forgiving of your social faux pas. The ability to laugh at your own mistakes (or at least not lose sight of the humorous side) may be the ultimate defense against despair.

11. *Avoid U.S. ghettos abroad.* Perhaps the best way to ensure an unsuccessful international experience is to limit your social life to an isolated and insulated U.S. enclave where you can get a hamburger and ice in your soft drink but little else. Ghettos are formed when some U.S. travelers attempt to re-create their former lifestyle, while complaining about the lack of amenities, pace of life, and inconveniences of the host culture. Ghetto dwellers might as well have stayed home, for they are not learning much about the host culture. By remaining isolated in an American ghetto, expatriates send the local population the message that they feel superior. At the same time, they reinforce their own negative stereotypes.

12. *Be adventurous.* All too often, Americans abroad view their overseas assignments as a hardship post that must be endured and will eventually pass, particularly if they become im-

mersed in the job. But living and working abroad should be much more than an experience to be endured. Instead, it can and should be a positively life-altering experience. As long as there is a willingness to experiment and learn about new things, an overseas experience can provide an exciting new world. There are places to explore, people to meet, customs to learn, food to eat, music and art to experience. All of these are available if the traveler is willing to experiment and take risks.

13. *Learn how best to manage stress.* Culture shock results from the anxiety brought about by (a) the loss of familiar cultural cues and (b) trying to operate in an unfamiliar cultural setting. How one responds to such anxiety varies considerably, as do the techniques for coping with stress. Some manage stress through regular physical exercise, such as jogging, playing tennis, or taking an aerobics class. Others use such techniques as biofeedback, yoga, or meditation. Still others rely on more spiritual techniques for reducing stress, such as prayer and worship. Whatever technique you choose, it is important to have an effective mechanism for reducing stress, which will in turn enhance the adjustment process.

14. *Take appropriate health precautions.* There is nothing that can ruin an international assignment quicker than serious illness or death. While we cannot eliminate the possibility of illnesses, a number of preventive measures will reduce their occurrence. For example, prior to leaving home, be certain that all required and recommended immunizations are current. If traveling to a malaria-infested area, be certain to take the required malarial suppressant(s) prior to, during, and after your stay abroad. While away from home, follow the same good health habits recommended generally—eat well-balanced meals, allow yourself sufficient rest, exercise regularly, and avoid excesses of alcohol, tobacco, and drugs. Moreover, obtain accurate information about which local foods can be eaten safely and which should be avoided.

15. *Let go of home (for now).* Before leaving home, it is important to properly say goodbye to friends, relatives, and your familiar way of life that you are temporarily leaving behind. Saying goodbye provides the traveler with a symbolic way of moving from home, a necessary step before you can step into a new culture. This is not to say that you need to cut yourself off from home. In fact, it is advisable to work out ways ahead of time to maintain contact with people at home through letters, telephone calls, or e-mail. Also, before leaving, travelers need to understand that they (and those remaining at home) will have changed in significant ways upon return to the United States.

16. *Keep in mind that when studying other cultures there are no absolutes.* In a sense, every culture is unique, as is every situation and person within a culture. Moreover, each sojourner brings her or his own unique perceptions based on past experiences. In other words, there is no way of predicting with absolute certainty how people will behave in any given situation. The generalizations that we read in books written by social scientists should not be viewed as ironclad rules but rather as general statements that are valid for most people, most of the time. The advice we get in training sessions and in our reading should not be viewed as a step-by-step set of prescriptions to be used like a cookbook.

17. *Keep the faith.* After preparing yourself for an international assignment as thoroughly as possible, you need to have confidence in yourself as well as in your hosts. All new arrivals are bound to experience frustrations and make mistakes. Yet, eventually your goodwill and basic humanity will come across to the local people—provided, of course, you make an honest effort to participate in the local culture. At the same time, having faith in the inherent goodwill of the local population is important. By and large, people the world over are tolerant of our indiscretions when they result from an honest attempt to learn about the local culture. If you genuinely communicate that you are the student (interested in learning about their culture) and they are the teachers, very few people in the world would refuse to share their expertise. They are the experts, while the visiting Americans are the uneducated, at least in terms of local cultural knowledge. If the sojourner is able to acknowledge openly

his or her own subordinate position when dealing with local people, many doors of learning and friendship will be open.

To be certain, no bottled remedies for culture shock are to be found at the pharmacy. But, by simply knowing that culture shock exists, that it happens to everyone to some extent, and that it is not permanent is likely to reduce the severity of the symptoms and speed the recovery. Don't think you are pathological or inadequate if you experience some culture shock. The anxiety resulting from trying to operate in a different environment is normal. Give yourself permission to feel frustration, homesickness, or irritability. Eventually, you will work through these symptoms and emerge with a much richer appreciation of the host culture. But it is also important to remain realistic. There will be some people, for whatever reason, who will not become close friends. There may be others who, for purely personal reasons, you will not like and vice versa. And there are some things that may never be understood. But once you understand that these problems, while real and frustrating, are perfectly normal reactions for any sojourner, then you can begin to search for solutions.

CROSS-CULTURAL SCENARIOS

Read the following cross-cultural scenarios. In each mini-case study, a basic cultural conflict occurs between the actors involved. Try to identify the source of the conflict and suggest how it could have been avoided or minimized. Then see how well your analyses compare to the explanations in Appendix A.

7-1 Tom Putnam, the president of a Boston publishing company, had been working for several months with a French architectural firm that was designing the company's new printing facility in Fontainbleau, France. However, Tom was becoming increasingly frustrated with the many delays caused by the French architects. When the preliminary plans for the building—which the architects had promised by a certain date—had not arrived, Tom called them to inquire when he would be receiving the plans. The architects, somewhat indignant that he had called, felt that Tom doubted their integrity to deliver the plans. Tom was equally annoyed because they had missed the deadline, and what was worse, they didn't seem to be the least bit apologetic about it. By the end of the phone call, Tom was convinced that his company's relationship with the French architectural firm had suffered a major setback.

How might you explain the conflict in this case?

7-2 Howard Duvall, an up-and-coming accountant with a New York-based firm, was on contract in Mombasa, Kenya, for three months, setting up an accounting system for a local corporation. Since he had never been out of the United States before, he was interested in learning as much as possible about the people and their culture. He was fascinated by the contrasts he saw between the traditional and the modern, relations between Africans and Europeans, and the influence of the Arabic language and the Muslim religion. Every spare moment, he had the company's driver take him to see the interesting sights both in town and in the rural villages. To document the sights for friends back home, he brought his 35-mm camera wherever he went. Although Howard was able to get a number of good pictures of game animals and buildings, he became increasingly frustrated because people turned their backs on him when he tried to take their pictures. Several people actually became quite angry.

What advice could you give Howard?

7-3   Jim Ellis, vice president of a North Carolina knitwear manufacturer, was sent by his company to observe firsthand how operations were proceeding in their Korean plant and to help institute some new managerial procedures. Before any changes could be made, however, Jim wanted to learn as much as possible about the problems that existed at the plant. During his first week he was met with bows, polite smiles, and the continual denial of any significant problems. But Jim was enough of a realist to know that he had never heard of any manufacturing operation that didn't have some problems. So after some creative research, he uncovered a number of problems that the local manager and staff were not acknowledging. None of the problems were particularly unusual or difficult to solve, but Jim was frustrated that no one would admit that any problems existed. "If you don't acknowledge the problems," he complained to one of the managers, "how do you expect to be able to solve them?" And then to further exasperate him, just today when a problem was finally brought to his attention, it was not mentioned until the end of the workday when there was no time left to solve it.

How could you help Jim better understand the dynamics of this situation?

7-4   Bill Higgins had served as the manager of a large U.S. timber company located in a rather remote rain forest in a South American country. Since it began its logging operations in the 1950s, a major problem facing the company has been the recruitment of labor. The only nearby source of labor is the sparsely populated local Indian groups in the area. Bill's company has been in direct competition for laborers with a German company operating in the same region. In an attempt to attract the required number of laborers, Bill's company has invested heavily in new housing and offered considerably higher wages than the German company, as well as a guaranteed forty-hour work week. Yet the majority of the available workers continued to work for the German company, despite its substandard housing and a minimum hourly wage. Bill finally brought in several U.S. anthropologists who had worked among the local Indians. The answer to Bill's labor recruitment problem was quite simple, but it required looking at the values of the Indian labor force rather than simply building facilities that would appeal to the typical U.S. laborer.

What did the anthropologists tell Bill?

7-5   Directly after completing a master's degree in international business, Dick Sutton decided to accept a job with a firm in Tokyo. He had studied Japanese for a year and was most interested in immersing himself in Japanese culture. Within the first month of his arrival, he was invited to an office party. As was the custom, most of the employees were expected to entertain the group with a song, poem, or joke. Knowing the keen interest the Japanese have in baseball, Dick recited the poem "Casey at the Bat," which seemed to be well received. Dick was having a good time at the party and was secretly congratulating himself on his decision to come to Japan. In fact, he couldn't help thinking how informal and playful all his colleagues were, including the upper-level executives, a far cry from all the descriptions he had read of the Japanese as austere and humorless businesspeople. Later in the evening, Dick found himself talking with two of his immediate superiors. Wanting to draw on the informality and good humor of the moment, Dick casually brought up some plans he had for a new marketing strategy, only to be met with near total indifference. For the remainder of the evening, Dick felt as though he was not being included in the party.

What advice could you give Dick?

CHAPTER

8

Developing Global Managers

Within the past decade, there has been a rapidly growing literature on global leadership, international management, expatriate excellence, global assignments, and the globalization of the human resources function. Yet, despite this literature, little consensus occurs among the practitioners "in the trenches," concerning what is meant by the overused term *global*. Senior executives at major U.S. corporations are struggling to define what "going global" means for their specific operations. According to preliminary findings of Meena Wilson and Maxine Dalton of the Center for Creative Leadership, "Other than a handful of organizations, the truly global company is hardly to be found; other than a handful of CEOs and maybe several hundred senior executives, the truly global manager is more projected image than real human being" (1996, 1).

Most chief executive officers (CEOs) consider foreign markets to be a key factor in their company's future success (Gates 1994, 6). Moreover, an increasing number of these same CEOs believe that developing global managers must be an integral part of their long-term strategic planning. This involves taking very purposeful steps to develop future executives with appropriate global perspectives and the experience to implement competitive strategies. Developing global leaders for the twenty-first century involves having a long-term strategy—a well-integrated system for dealing with selection, training, overseas support, appropriate appraisal, suitable compensation packages, and a deliberate process of repatriation.

The gap, however, between what "is" and what "ought to be" remains wide indeed. Strong evidence suggests that over the past several decades there has been a reduction in the use of American expatriates abroad (Kobrin 1992, 264). Instead, U.S. multinationals are finding competent host-country nationals to manage their overseas operations. By contrast, Asian multinational corporations use their own expatriates more extensively than do their U.S. counterparts. To illustrate, according to a recent Price Waterhouse Coopers report (Figg 2000, 13), 70 percent of the U.S./European companies surveyed outsource all or part of their international management function. The report also found that an increasingly number of managers are circumventing long-term overseas assignments by relying on more frequent business trips and such technology as e-mail and teleconferencing.

To be certain, there are a number of good reasons for reducing the use of U.S. expatriates. For example, it tends be more cost effective to use host-country nationals as compared to transferring American employees and their families; the use of local people is well received by host-country governments; an increasing number of local people are well qualified to manage large operations, particularly since they are well versed in the local language and culture. Yet some have suggested a somewhat less flattering interpretation for the reduction of U.S. expatriates over the years. For example, Stephen Kobrin (1992) argues that, despite some compelling reasons for using host-country nationals, U.S. firms have cut back too drastically on using expatriates because they have had problems with their overseas assignments. Failure rates among expatriates from the United States are considerably higher than for Europeans and Japanese expatriates. To illustrate, Rosalie Tung (1988, 16) reports that 76 percent of the U.S. companies in her sample (as compared with 3 percent of Western European and 14 percent of Japanese companies) revealed expatriate failure rates of over 10 percent.

There are at least two major disadvantages to cutting back too precipitously on the use of one's own managers abroad. First, by relying too heavily on host-country nationals, the parent company may become isolated from its overseas subsidiaries. If the reduction of expatriates proceeds far enough, the result could be a multinational corporation that is little more than a loose federation of semiautonomous units located throughout the world.

A second and equally important disadvantage of reducing the number of expatriates too severely is that parent-company nationals have little opportunity to develop valuable managerial skills that can best be gained through international experiences. Moreover, it tends to reinforce provincialism and discourages the development of a cadre of global managers—those who have the agility to operate in a rapidly changing marketplace and those with experience at working with different legal systems, political structures, languages, tax systems, customs, and ethical systems.

The majority of expatriates sent abroad by U.S.-based firms are essentially tactical assignments to meet a specific and immediate need. It is, in other words, a quick fix to get a specific job accomplished with little or no attention to such strategic issues as providing valuable experience for future leaders, coordinating relationships between the home office and subsidiaries abroad, and increasing the flow of international information. Moreover, the entire expatriate process itself has not in the past been handled in a systematic fashion. To illustrate: Most expatriates received little or no cross-cultural training prior to assuming their overseas assignments, and much of what training was received was generally superficial and of limited duration; the majority of expatriates, and the overwhelming majority of their families, received no repatriation preparation to help them adjust to living and working back in the United States; many returning expatriates have no specific job to which to return, and for many who do, they frequently involve less authority, status, and compensation than the overseas jobs; relatively few returning expatriates have a chance to utilize their newly acquired international/cross-cultural skills;

and a surprisingly large number of returning expatriates become so disenchanted with their reception home that they wind up taking jobs elsewhere.

What seems painfully clear is that many U.S. companies fail to manage expatriate assignments in a systematic or comprehensive way. Most companies do not pay sufficient attention to all the different phases of the expatriation process, such as selection, training, in-country support, and repatriation. Frequently, assignments are seen as necessary evils that must be made in order to put out temporary "brush fires." Given such an ad hoc approach, international assignments are not viewed by and large as valuable from a strategic, long-term organizational perspective. Consequently, for too many U.S. companies, global assignments are not seen as very effective mechanisms for developing global leaders over the long run.

This is not to suggest, however, that there are no U.S. companies that deal with expatriate assignments systematically. There is a small yet growing number of firms that are approaching the topic in an integrated, comprehensive fashion. It is these exemplary firms that serve as a standard for best practices. Organizations that are dealing with overseas transfers in the most efficacious way start from a strong and unequivocal global focus that is built into the very fiber of the corporate culture. Employees with international experience are seen as valuable assets. Employees willing to accept international assignments are encouraged, supported, and rewarded appropriately. Top management, in other words, sends a clear message that international/cross-cultural experience is valued and has a positive impact on one's career trajectory. Moreover, these exemplary firms understand that international assignments provide a fertile training ground for developing the type of leader needed for managing global companies in the twenty-first century.

To make the most of global assignments, companies must follow the lead of the handful of companies that are doing it the right way. They must take a more holistic (long-term) approach to management development by paying close attention to all the various phases of making international (global) transfers, including selection, cross-cultural preparation, repatriation, and the utilization of the skills and competencies gained while abroad to the benefit of both the individual and the organization. In the remainder of this chapter, we explore each of these aspects of expatriate assignments.

SELECTION

Although all companies that send employees abroad go through some sort of selection procedure, some are more effective than others. All too often, personnel are chosen for expatriate assignments too hastily, according to an insufficient set of criteria, and with little attention to long-term strategic considerations. A number of studies have identified those selection criteria that predict both cultural adjustment and job effectiveness (see, for example, Teagarden and Gordon 1995; Black, Gregersen, and Mendenhall 1992; Mendenhall, Dunbar, and Oddou 1987). These range from technical job skills to spousal adaptability to a wide range of personal and interpersonal skills. Despite the fact that all these studies suggest strongly that a wide range of criteria need to be applied to the selection process, most U.S. multinational firms continue to make their selections on the basis of technical competence primarily, if not exclusively; that is, an engineer expected to be an expatriate in Indonesia will be selected largely on skills and past performance as an engineer at home. A study of fifty major U.S. global firms showed that, in nine of every ten cases, expatriates were selected primarily on the basis of their demonstrated technical expertise for a specific job (Solomon 1994, 51–54). The assumption is that if one can perform effectively in the United States, he or she can do so equally well abroad.

Although technical expertise certainly is an important selection criterion, it should not be the only one. The professional literature is clear that expatriates fail not because of technical incompetence but because they (or their accompanying family members) have not adjusted to the foreign culture. In other words, their professional effectiveness is diminished by the fact that they are suffering from culture shock or are otherwise unable to get along with their local business associates. Thus, technical competency is a necessary but not sufficient selection criterion. Expatriate selection must be made on a number of criteria that go beyond technical competency and serve as effective predictors of cultural adjustment and consequently expatriate success. These selection criteria can be grouped into four major categories: communication skills, personality traits, motivation, and family circumstances.

Communication Skills

Since communication is so vitally important for conducting business at home, it should come as no surprise that it is equally important for successful business abroad. The single best way to become an effective communicator as an expatriate is to learn the local language. This seems like a sophomorically naive statement, but it remains a fact that most U.S. expatriates never develop their second-language proficiency. Although it is unrealistic to expect expatriate candidates to be proficient in the local language prior to being selected, one important selection criterion should be their willingness to take language training before leaving home and during their overseas assignments. Besides knowing how to speak another language, expatriate candidates should demonstrate a willingness to use it. For a variety of reasons, some people lack the motivation, confidence, or willingness to throw themselves into conversational situations. Even though they may have some technical competence in the language, they prefer to communicate through interpreters or intermediaries and rarely seek out opportunities to communicate directly with their foreign business associates. Thus, communication skills must be assessed in terms of language competency, motivation to learn another language, and willingness to use it in professional and personal situations.

Personality Traits

Research in the area of intercultural communications has identified a number of personality characteristics associated with successful overseas experiences. Some of these traits—in no particular order of significance—include tolerating ambiguity; bouncing back from disappointment; being nonjudgmental, intellectually flexible, nonethnocentric, perceptually aware, and culturally empathetic; and willing to experience new things. Unfortunately, many human resources personnel responsible for expatriate placements shy away from such selection criteria because they are not sure how to measure such personality traits. In recent years, however, a number of effective standardized inventories have been designed to provide information on an individual's potential for cross-cultural effectiveness. To illustrate, the Cross Cultural Adaptability Inventory (CCAI), originally developed by Colleen Kelley and Judith Meyers (1995) in 1987, examines four basic dimensions that contribute to intercultural effectiveness: emotional resilience, flexibility/openness, perceptual acuity, and personal autonomy. The CCAI is not intended to predict with absolute certainty the success or failure in overseas assignments. Instead, after exploring their strengths and weaknesses along these four dimensions, potential expatriates (and their employers) can assess their readiness for an overseas assignment. Since the inventory can identify those skills needing further development, it is useful for making choices about expatriate training.

Motivation

Yet another critical variable for expatriate success is the level of motivation to take the assignment in the first place. Some employees view overseas transfers as necessary evils that must be endured. These "hardship posts" are seen as potentially dangerous to one's career path and, at the very least, entail a disruption of normal life for themselves and their families. Others, by way of contrast, see expatriate assignments as opportunities for professional advancement, learning, and personal growth. They have a general interest in working and living abroad, a specific interest in the host culture, and generally believe that overseas assignments are career enhancing rather than career threatening. Evidence suggests that those with greater motivation for and more positive attitudes about overseas assignments are more successful than those without them (Feldman 1991). It is important to point out, however, that one's motivation for an expatriate assignment can be greatly influenced by the message that the potential expatriate receives from his or her organization; that is, a candidate's lack of motivation could be the result of a very realistic assessment of the value that the firm places on the assignment. Nevertheless, the motivational state of the expatriate candidate is an important dimension, which should not be overlooked, of the selection process.

Family Circumstances

A growing number of studies over the past decade have emphasized the importance of the accompanying spouse for expatriate success. In many respects, the unemployed spouse faces a greater number of challenges of adjusting to the new culture than does the expatriate employee. While the employee has the security and familiarity of the organizational structure, the accompanying spouse is faced with dealing with the butcher, getting the TV repaired, and enrolling the children in school—all without any institutional support. In addition, whereas the expatriate employee may see the international transfer as a positive career move, the accompanying spouse may see the move as little

Organizations need to make certain that all members of the family make a smooth adjustment to the new international assignment.

more than the disruption of his or her own career. In addition to spouses, the special circumstances that can influence the cross-cultural adjustment of teenage children must also be considered. It is not hard to imagine how an unhappy or maladapted spouse or child can negatively affect the morale and performance of the expatriate employee. One study has in fact cited poor spousal adjustment as the most common explanation of ex-

---

Being an effective global manager in the twenty-first century requires more than technical competence alone. It also requires a full understanding of the international business environment, the use of culturally diverse teams, and a heavy dose of cultural and linguistic sensitivity. Professor Jose De La Torre of UCLA's Graduate School of Management offers a worst-case and a best-case scenario:

> In 1969, Coca-Cola proudly assigned one of its toughest and most successful U.S. managers to France to deal with its newly acquired distribution system. He spoke no French, had never visited France and took pride in the fact that he would "Americanize" the French market. Eighteen months later, he was reassigned home. It was not that his ideas were wrong or badly implemented, but that his lack of cultural awareness got in the way of his effectiveness.
>
> Contrast that story with Squibb's decision to hire the head of the Chinese language department at Cornell University to head its new subsidiary in Shanghai. Although ignorant of the technical aspects of the business, he was supported by an excellent U.S. staff, and his language and cultural skills allowed him to surround himself with the best local managers, whether they spoke English or not. (1994)

patriate failure (Tung 1981). The implication of such studies is that, in addition to the expatriate employee, spouses and children should be assessed as well on those criteria found to be critical for overseas success.

Based on a thorough review of the literature, a number of general recommendations emerge as "best practices" for selecting employees for overseas assignments. First, use as wide a variety of criteria as possible, including technical competence, as well as some of the "softer" predictors of success, such as communication skills, personality traits, motivation, and family situation. Once technical competence has been determined, these other dimensions are the best predictors of success in overseas assignments, particularly for those employees who will be expected to interact frequently with host nationals. Second, companies should avoid a "quick and dirty" selection process in an attempt to cut corners and save money. Given the considerable costs of making an international posting, companies need to protect their long-term investment by maximizing their chances for selecting successful expatriates. Third, realizing that all candidates will not score high on all selection criteria, firms should be prepared to enhance those weaker areas in either the predeparture preparation phase or during the in-country posting phase. Finally, intensive interview data from candidates and their families are significantly more valid than data collected from supervisors' evaluations (Teagarden and Gordon 1995, 29).

CROSS-CULTURAL TRAINING

Once the expatriate has been selected, the next step is to equip that individual with as much preparation as possible so as to maximize his or her chances for successfully meeting professional objectives. To be certain, a vital part of that preparation involves information about the nature of the job description, how it fits into the overall organizational structure, and the relationship between this particular job and the wider objectives of the company. But since business is always conducted within a cultural context, and since the expatriate will be expected to operate within a different cultural context, an essential part of the preparation must involve an understanding of the new cultural realities.

For decades, cross-cultural training (CCT) has been advocated as essential for adjusting to new cultural environments, irrespective of whether we are diplomats, missionaries, Peace Corps volunteers, health professionals, or businesspeople. By facilitating adjustments to the host culture, CCT increases job performance, reduces the number of incorrect attributions of behavior, increases an understanding of one's own culture, reduces stereotypic thinking, helps in intercultural team building, decreases the social ambiguity that can lead to culture shock, develops cross-cultural competencies, and generally leads to more fully accomplishing one's professional objectives. Despite what appears to be a compelling case in favor of CCT, the majority of firms still do not provide it for those about to assume an international assignment. It has been estimated that only about one-third of U.S. expatriates receive predeparture CCT, as compared with approximately 69 percent for European firms and 57 percent for Japanese firms (Brewster 1995, 57). Of those firms that do offer predeparture CCT, much of it is short term and not particularly rigorous.

Although many U.S.-based corporations have doubted the value of cross-cultural preparation, expatriates themselves tend to be considerably more positive, and the scientific literature tends to support these expatriates in their more positive assessment. Examining a number of studies on the effectiveness of CCT, Stewart Black and Mark Mendenhall (1990, 117–19) found the following results:

- Nine of ten studies showed a positive relationship between CCT and self-confidence (in terms of one's ability to function abroad).
- Nineteen of nineteen studies showed that CCT positively affected relational skills in a cross-cultural context.
- Sixteen of sixteen studies concluded that CCT helps in developing more accurate cross-cultural perceptions.
- Nine out of nine studies found a positive relationship between CCT and adjustment to new cultures.
- Eleven of fifteen studies found a positive correlation between CCT and job performance.

When attempting to answer the question, "What is the syllabus for cross-cultural training?" we should not expect a simple or singular answer. No generic or packaged program would be appropriate for all situations. Rather, each company must carefully design its own CCT programs to meet its specific needs and the particular needs of its trainees. To determine the content, length, intensity, and rigor of a particular CCT program, certain critical issues need to be considered, including previous international experience, previous host-country experience, nature of the job, language capability, and the extent of the cultural differences.

Whatever form CCT might take, preparing people to function effectively in a different cultural environment requires a multifaceted approach. Taking our lead from the relatively wide CCT literature and following the basic structure of Chapters 2 through 5, pedagogically sound programs should include the following major components, to one degree or another:

1. *Culture-general component*: A general understanding of the concept of culture provides a fuller appreciation of other cultures, regardless of where one might be conducting business. To illustrate, the notion that cultures are learned (as compared with being genetically transmitted) should remind the trainee that, although culturally different people have learned different things, they are no less capable of learning efficiently. The concept that all cultures are integrated—where many or most of the parts are interconnected—should serve to convince the trainee that all cultures, no matter how incomprehensible they might appear at first, do in fact have a consistently logical structure and should not be given such disparaging epithets as "primitive," "savage," "crazy," or "stupid." Moreover, we should realize that our culture is so thoroughly internalized that it can have very real effects on our psychological functioning. These and other general concepts—which hold true for Koreans, Germans, Bolivians, and Iowan farmers—can be helpful in gaining a greater understanding of a foreign cultural environment.

2. *Mastering patterns of communication*: Another component of understanding another culture is familiarization with its patterns of communication, both verbal and nonverbal. Effective communication between people from the same cultural and linguistic group is often difficult enough. But when one tries to communicate with people who speak little or no English—and have different ideas, attitudes, assumptions, perceptions, and ways of doing things—the opportunities for miscommunicating increase enormously. Becoming fluent in another language would be the ideal way to get inside of another culture, but few corporations are willing to take the time and expense of total immersion language training. In the absence of a language-proficiency program, however, there is much that one can learn about a language that will provide insights into the culture. For example, how does a language influence people's perception? How does language affect culture and vice versa? Is one learning about a high-context or a low-context culture? How direct or indirect is the language? What can you learn about the social hierarchy in another culture by studying its language? Moreover, a significant part of learning about communication patterns involves the study of nonverbal communication, including such modes as facial expressions, eye contact, hand gestures, touching, posture, and proxemics.

3. *Cultural self-awareness*: To maximize our chances for success in the international business arena, it is imperative that we examine cultural values—theirs as well as ours. It is necessary to recognize the cultural influences on our own thinking and how they conform to or contrast with those of culturally different peoples. For example, before we can conclude that a vegetable vendor in Nairobi, Kenya, is offensively smelly, we must first realize how much emphasis U.S. culture places on eliminating odors of all kinds; before we think that a Mexican is too lazy to ever be on time, we must first understand the incredible importance we place on the precise reckoning of time. In other words, a heightened awareness of their own culture will enable trainees to better diagnose problems of intercultural communication.

4. *Culture-specific component*: Before entering an international business environment, it is important to become familiar with as much culture-specific information as possible. There is a wide range of published sources on different cultures of the world; these include scholarly sources (books, journal articles) from such disciplines as cultural anthropology, comparative sociology, and cross-cultural psychology and other sources such as State Department publications, commercially published sources for business travelers, newspapers, and information put out by foreign embassies. It is advisable to draw on as many solid sources of data as possible because the better we can equip a soon-to-be sojourner with culture-specific facts, the fewer surprises there will be and the quicker he or she will adjust to the new environment.

5. *Developing cross-cultural skills*: The preceding four components of a CCT program are all cognitive in nature. Yet adjusting to a new cultural environment involves more than the acquisition of information. Also required is the development of certain skills, acquiring new attitudes, and modifying old ways of doing things. In other words, a number of competencies are associated with effectiveness in cross-cultural business settings. These include developing the capacity to tolerate ambiguity, display empathy, show resourcefulness, be nonjudgmental, maintain a sense of humor, be patient but persistent, improve one's perceptual acuity, and become more emotionally resilient. Also, in terms of useful skills, trainees should learn how to collect useful cultural data while they are living and working within the host culture.

In addition to having a number of content components, CCT can be conducted using different methodological approaches. These approaches differ in terms of levels of active participation (that is, experiential learning), which in turn affects the level of train-

Sometimes insensitivity to the local political situation can be costly. According to Neal Goodman (1994, 43), a Western electronics firm had 40,000 twenty-five-page full-color brochures produced for a trade show in the Peoples' Republic of China (PRC). As part of the very attractive brochure, the company had included a list of its international manufacturing facilities, including one in the Republic of China, located on the Island of Taiwan. The government of the PRC, however, does not officially recognize the existence of the Republic of China but considers it a renegade province of its own government. Had the brochure listed the company's manufacturing site as being located in Taiwan, not the Republic of China, there would have been no potential source of embarrassment for the PRC. Shortly before the opening of the trade show, the inappropriate listing was noticed by an alert executive. To avoid embarrassing the host government (the PRC), the company discarded the brochures that had cost more than $500,000 to produce.

ing rigor. As one moves from less to more experiential methods, the training becomes more rigorous and consequently more effective. At the least rigorous end of the continuum is the approach that emphasizes the simple imparting of factual information, using such passive techniques as assigned readings, lectures, and videos. At a more intermediate level would be the analysis of minicase studies or scenarios (attribution training), which involves trying to determine why people in other cultures think and act the way they do. This approach is predicated on the fact that cross-cultural misunderstandings frequently occur because of the natural tendency to explain (attribute meaning) the behavior of others based on our own values and cultural assumptions. At the highest level of interactivity are such experiential training strategies as role playing, simulations, field

Pre-departure cross-cultural training is just the beginning of the learning proceess for the future expatriate.

trips, and interactive multimedia CD-ROMS, which actively involve the individual trainees to as great an extent as possible.

Even though CCT needs to be custom designed to meet the unique needs of individuals and organizations, some general principles are basic to most good expatriate orientation programs:

1. Learning to relate effectively to people from different cultural backgrounds requires specific knowledge about both the cognitive (thinking) and affective (feeling) domains. Thus, training programs should deal with facts and concepts on the one hand and feelings and perceptions on the other.
2. Since people learn most effectively when they are actively involved in their own learning, training programs should be designed for active participation on the part of the trainees.
3. It is important for trainees to see how their learning relates to their jobs. Therefore, training programs should be practical by emphasizing the relevance of learning to specific work situations.
4. Since cultural awareness training is a lifelong process, trainees should be given (a) packages of the latest and most relevant cultural information to take with them after the training session and (b) data-gathering skills that can be used in any cross-cultural situation in the future.
5. CCT can never expose trainees to every detail of every culture of the world. Therefore, training sessions should offer a balance between specific cultural information and more general theories, concepts, and methods that can be applied to a variety of cross-cultural settings.
6. Since learning about other cultures must be preceded by an understanding of one's own culture, one important component of any training program is cultural self-awareness.
7. CCT involves changes in behavior and attitudes that can occur only when people feel comfortable taking risks. Thus, training sessions need to be conducted in a positive and supportive environment, allowing trainees to take risks and experiment with new behaviors.
8. When employees are given overseas assignments, often the unemployed spouse experiences the greatest problems of cultural adjustment. Thus, unemployed spouses and children need to be included in the predeparture training.
9. Although predeparture training is an important part of a successful overseas assignment, the most effective learning takes place after several weeks of being in the overseas assignment. At no other time are sojourners more receptive or better motivated to learn because they must deal with real cross-cultural encounters rather than the more theoretical or simulated situations presented in the predeparture phase of the training. Thus, it is imperative that in-country CCT be provided.
10. In general, orientation and support activities are most effective when they are provided by sojourners' co-workers as well as by outside specialists. Thus, to reduce feelings of social isolation so common in overseas assignments, experienced colleagues in both the home and host offices should be involved in orientation and support activities.
11. The learning activities of any cross-cultural orientation program need to be compatible with the learning styles of the trainees. Learning activities that conflict with the trainees' educational styles are likely to be ineffective in imparting the skills and knowledge needed for a successful overseas working and living assignment.

REPATRIATION

While many expatriates anticipate dealing with a host of adjustment problems when entering a new culture, few are prepared for the adjustments they face when coming home. Most returning expatriates—particularly those who have successfully acclimated to their overseas assignments—expect to be given a ticker-tape parade upon returning home. They have, in many cases, made enormous sacrifices by uprooting themselves and their families, managed to adjust to many new situations, and generally succeeded in meeting their personal and professional objectives. They view themselves, quite correctly, as having accomplished some major achievements. Yet if they expect to be seen as "conquering heros" by their employers, colleagues, friends, and loved ones, they are in for a rude awakening.

Returning home is oftentimes as challenging as the original adjustments of the foreign assignment. Ideally, preparation for repatriation should be taken as seriously as predeparture preparation. Coming home should be treated as yet another foreign assignment. Since successful expatriates have experienced some life-altering changes while abroad, they are different people than they were when they left home. Moreover, home is not the same. During one's time away, many changes have occurred at the home office, in the neighborhood, at the children's school, in the economy, and even in the physical surroundings. Expatriates who left the United States during the first months of the Clinton administration in 1993 would come home to a very different political climate three years later after the Republicans took control of both houses of Congress. Leaving the country at a time of rapid stock market growth and returning during a Dow Jones downturn can be jolting. Even the amount of commercial development (and the resulting traffic congestion) in one's old neighborhood can seem startling upon returning after a four-year assignment abroad. Whereas the expatriate may have been a "big fish in a little pond," he or she may be just the opposite back at the home office. One's status, authority, and even physical amenities may be somewhat diminished after returning home from an overseas assignment. There are bound to be a number of changes at the home office in terms of personnel, strategy, leadership, technology, and even corporate culture. Little wonder that returning expatriates may feel that they are coming back to a foreign environment.

Unfortunately, the track record of U.S. firms in dealing with repatriation leaves a good deal to be desired. General inattention to the reentry process has negative consequences for both the returnee and the organization. Based on research they conducted on a number of U.S. expatriate executives, Stewart Black, H. B. Gregersen, and Mark Mendenhall (1992) provide some insight into the dimension of the problem. For example, they found the following:

1. Sixty-four percent of all repatriating employees and over 90 percent of their spouses received no repatriation preparation.
2. Most were given very little lead time before ending their overseas assignments. Only 4.3 percent were given more than six months notice; most received under three months, which meant very little time to prepare for repatriation.
3. Between 60 percent and 70 percent of repatriates did not have a specific job to return to by the time they returned home.
4. Forty-six percent of returning Americans wound up with jobs with less authority and autonomy than they had in the overseas assignments.
5. Only 11 percent of returnees received a promotion, while 77 percent were demoted to lower-level positions.

6. Only 39 percent of the returnees had an opportunity to use their internationally acquired skills in their next position. (*Message*: Most employers do not recognize or appreciate the skills that are developed overseas or how they can be applied to helping the company in the future.)

7. Twenty percent of all U.S. expatriates left the company within the first year of returning to the states.

If these data are even remotely accurate, the message that U.S.-based multinational corporations send is both clear and unfortunate: Overseas assignments are detrimental to one's long-term career development. Since most expatriates make considerable sacrifices for the company by disrupting their personal and professional lives (and those of their families), they expect to be rewarded upon their return. Not only are most not rewarded, but many are actually penalized! In the end, it is the company that suffers as well. After making an enormous investment in the international transfer, the company sees many of its returning expatriates, feeling unappreciated and undervalued, take their valuable assets somewhere else—perhaps to a competitor! What an inexcusable waste of talent.

What needs to be done to ensure that the returning expatriate (a corporate asset far more valuable upon return than before the international assignment) is integrated smoothly back into the corporate mainstream and retained over the long haul? The answer to this question goes beyond merely looking at the issue of repatriation. Instead, it requires that the company understand and attend to the larger issue of why it is making the international transfer in the first place. What is the strategic purpose of the foreign assignment? What will it accomplish? If it is no more than filling a position, it may well make more sense to hire a host-country national to accomplish a specific task. But, if the company (in addition to filling a job position) wants to achieve greater control over a foreign subsidiary, then it will need to know how the expatriate executive will accomplish that. If the company is interested in executive development, it will need to be very explicit up front about what skills and capacities should be nurtured during the overseas assignment. If the company is hoping to use the overseas transfer as a mechanism for increasing its flow of international information, then it must be purposeful in identifying what information will be transferred and how best to use the expatriate in that capacity to the company's benefit. Unless the company takes this more holistic (that is, strategic) approach to expatriate assignments, it is likely to overlook the value of its human resources and consequently is not likely to take the appropriate steps to repatriate and retain its returning employees.

If an international assignment is handled as an integral part of the overall strategic planning of the organization, then the company will attend to all aspects of the assignment from selection to training, to in-country support, to repatriation, and to reintegration. All too often, expatriates are selected on inappropriate criteria, inadequately prepared, poorly supported during the assignment, and given little preparation for repatriation. When this occurs, the overseas assignees become discouraged and disillusioned, and whatever strategic objectives the company may have had will, in all likelihood, go unmet. Thus, the best insurance against loosing valuable human resources after returning home is for the company to be meticulous about all aspects of the expatriation process. More specifically, the corporation should take a number of purposeful steps to enhance the successful repatriation and ultimate retention of the returning expatriate:

1. A common complaint of many returning expatriates is that they felt disconnected from the parent company, or as some have put it, "Out of sight, out of mind." Some have suggested that companies should assign a "godparent" (an experienced expatriate) to each expatriate for the sake of mentoring, keeping them informed, monitoring their assignments for problems, and generally looking out for the expatriates' interests. Although the idea of a godparent is a good idea, a more effective mechanism might be a repatriation team composed of two or more godparents.

2. Whenever people leave the comfort of their own cultural surroundings, they experience the feeling of being slightly out of control. Not only are many of the familiar props missing, but also it is natural to feel some anxiety because everything seems so new and different. You are expected to play the game without understanding all the rules. There is, in other words, a noticeable lack of information on most subjects. Thus, one way to relieve the anxiety and ensure a more effective adjustment is to provide expatriates (and their families) with as much information as possible at every step of the expatriate process. In addition to providing both predeparture and in-country training, this involves a prereturn trip home, prereturn orientation, and repatriate debriefing upon return. One very cost-effective way of providing information that will help repatriates adjust to coming home involves sending them copies of their hometown newspapers for several months prior to their return.

3. It is particularly important for companies to be sensitive to the needs of high-risk returnees—those returning from unusually long stays abroad or those coming back from very different cultures, such as Nigeria or Egypt. Assuming that the returnees have made successful adjustments while abroad, the problems of repatriation will be appreciably more severe for those coming from radically different cultures or those having been away from home for an extended period of time.

4. One of the best ways of keeping repatriates from leaving the company is to ensure that they in fact have a job to which to return. As was pointed out earlier, approximately two-thirds of all repatriates in the Black and colleagues (1992) study did not have a specific job waiting for them upon return. While some did have jobs, there are tales of those who waited as long as four months to get their own office (Osland 1995, 193–94). Not only is it important for the repatriate to have a specific job upon return, but the job should also utilize the skills and competencies gained while abroad. To do otherwise is certainly not in the best interest of the organization because it will fail to maximize the company's original investment in the transfer. Moreover, it sends a clear message to the repatriate that his or her hard-won competencies are not valued by the organization.

5. The company needs to attend to some of the "nuts and bolts" of coming home, such as finding a place to live or helping the repatriated family with repairing and/or redecorating their home that had been rented during their time abroad. The company needs to make sure that families spend as little time as possible in "transitional housing" before getting permanently resettled.

6. Prior to starting the new home-based assignment, companies should provide several weeks of leave to readjust. All too often, repatriates returning home from overseas, suffering from jet lag and reentry shock, are expected to be at work the day after they arrive back in the States. A certain amount of "decompression time" is necessary for returnees to adjust to the myriad of changes they will face both at the office and in the community. This time should be devoted to taking care of personal matters, engaging in official debriefing/repatriation sessions provided by the company, reflecting and writing about the overseas expe-

rience, and spending time with family members to process and bring closure to what was a meaningful—and, in some cases, life-altering—experience. This "downtime" should also be used for family members to meet with and discuss their experiences with other expatriate families.

7. Finally, it is imperative that returning expatriates be made to feel appreciated for what they have accomplished. Returning expatriates frequently express their disappointment that their organizations do little or nothing to explicitly thank them for the many sacrifices they have made on its behalf. Public forms of appreciation—such as welcome home banquets or write-ups in the company newsletter—not only facilitate the reintegration of the repatriate back into the firm but also make an unequivocal statement to others that the company appreciates and rewards those willing to take overseas assignments.

GLOBAL MANAGERS FOR THE TWENTY-FIRST CENTURY

As we enter the new century, the management literature is becoming increasingly inundated with descriptions of behavioral traits for successful management in the twenty-first century (see, for example, Brake, Walker and Walker 1995; Howard 1992; Weeks 1992; Wills and Barham 1994). Although each commentator puts a slightly different spin on his or her list of characteristics, there remains a basic core of competencies upon which most would agree. These, discussed in some detail below, involve developing a broad perspective; appreciating points of view other than one's own; being able to balance contradictions and operate comfortably in ambiguous situations; working effectively in cross-cultural teams; becoming emotionally resilient, open-minded, autonomous, and perceptually aware; and being willing to make decisions in the absence of all of the facts. These are the traits that leaders will need in a world that is becoming increasingly more global and multicultural. This represents a good inventory of competencies that could be used as selection criteria (or predictors of success) for overseas assignments, and they are the very competencies that are best developed by overseas assignments. As one human resources professional queried, "I know that our company's future leaders need to develop the capacity to tolerate ambiguity, but how do you train for that?" Perhaps the best single strategy for developing that competency (and others mentioned above) is to send them abroad for a several-year assignment.

CCT—which should occur before and during an international assignment—also can contribute to the development of these management/leadership competencies. Predeparture CCT can put trainees through a series of cross-cultural simulations that can serve as the beginning phase of internationalizing the desired skills. Moreover, one of the benefits of CCT is that it makes explicit the competencies and skills that an individual should be working on in the overseas assignment in order to maximize success in that assignment. Sometimes the very awareness that trainees should be working on these carry-over skills will ensure that they will be internalized to a greater degree than if there were no such awareness. It is similar to making it very clear at the beginning of a class that students should be working on certain carry-over skills (such as speaking, writing, making connections, and research competencies) in addition to mastering the mere content of the course. While students would in all likelihood develop some of those skills without

Serving in overseas assignments is the best single way of developing the executive leadership skills needed for the twenty-first century.

such an awareness, their level of skill development will be higher if they are purposeful about their education and personal growth.

What follows is a brief discussion of the major competencies needed for leadership in the twenty-first century and their relationship to both CCT and the expatriate experience. The first four competencies, which establish a *global mind-set*, provide the base of the learning pyramid. The next three competencies provide *personal stability* needed to function effectively in any cross-cultural business environment. The next two competencies provide the *professional confidence* needed for international assignments. These three levels of competencies provide a firm foundation for *successful leadership*, which is the capstone competency needed for effectiveness in the global economy in the twenty-first century.

1. *Broad perspective:* Unlike the more traditional domestic manager, the global manager needs to develop the broadest possible perspective. The emphasis should be on seeing the big picture. This involves a type of systems thinking whereby one can see how the various parts are interconnected to make a systematic whole. A fundamental generalization from the discipline

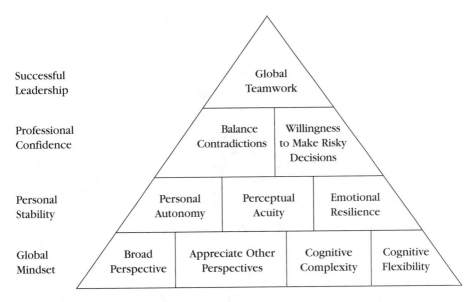

The author is indebted to Dr. R. Boyd Johnson of Indiana Wesleyan University for suggesting this hierarchy of competencies.

of anthropology is the functional interrelatedness of the parts of culture; that is, any culture is composed of a number of parts, many of which are interconnected to form a systemic, well-integrated whole. A major goal of CCT is to make explicit how the parts of a culture are integrated/interrelated. It helps trainees see the part (idea, thing, value, custom, and so on) in its proper cultural context in order to better understand why it exists.

2. *Appreciate other perspectives:* A key aspect of learning for global leaders is being able to make the bridge from their own point of view to many different points of view. Perhaps the best way to truly understand other points of view is to learn other languages, a vital part of CCT. Languages are more than simply communication mechanisms, allowing people to send and receive messages with relative efficiency. Rather, languages establish mental categories that force us to distinguish between what we consider similar from those things we consider different. Since every language is unique, the linguistic categories of one will never be identical to the categories of any other. Consequently, the speakers of any two different languages will not categorize in the same way, nor will they perceive reality in exactly the same way. In other words, they will, because of their language, have different frames of reference or views of the world. Thus, learning a second or third language provides entry into another set of categories, way of thinking, paradigm, or frame of reference.

3. *Cognitive complexity:* Global leaders need what Stefan Wills and Kevin Barham (1994, 50) refer to as "cognitive complexity," composed of the twin abilities to differentiate and integrate. *Differentiation* involves being able to see how a single entity is composed of a number of different parts; *integration* involves the capacity to identify multiple relationships between the different parts. The truly complex thinker—needed for success as a global manager—is the person who can engage in both types of thinking and can move comfortably between the two. CCT and cross-cultural experiences encourage the examination of (a) your

own culture and your host culture, (b) how both compare and contrast with one another, and (c) how both relate to the generalized concept of culture. The cognitively complex global manager feels comfortable moving from the specific parts to the whole and back again. In terms of the organizational structure, the successful international manager has the ability to focus on the unique needs of the local situation while maintaining a good grasp of how it fits into the overall operations of the parent organization.

4. *Cognitive flexibility:* On most lists of competencies for international managers is the need to be curious, nonjudgmental, and open to new ways of thinking and explaining phenomena. This essentially means that the individual is willing to learn and postpone making evaluations until more facts are known. Such a capacity involves the suppression of your ego and the letting go of old paradigms. In a sense, the expatriate experiences a psychic transformation that entails letting go of cultural certainty, learning how other cultures view us, and being willing to see the internal logic of another culture. This type of cultural literacy actually enables us to understand our own culture and those of others, mobilize diverse people, serve diverse clients and customers, and operate across cultures with maximum success. This is really the only way that anyone can learn about a new culture. Only by remaining open and flexible will it be possible to understand why culturally different people act and think the way they do. Being a successful leader abroad involves being sufficiently open and receptive to learning, to be able to adapt to the new environment. It is only when a successful adaptation has been made that you can hope to meet your personal and professional objectives.

5. *Personal autonomy:* Another important competency of the successful global leader is personal autonomy. To be open, flexible, and nonjudgmental does not entail adopting the

Managers for the twenty-first century need to know how to manage cross-cultural teams.

thoughts and behaviors of others as your own; nor do you even need to like them. But while remaining open minded (to learn more about another culture), you must not abandon your own identity in favor of theirs. With high self-esteem and a well-developed self-concept, personally autonomous global leaders are not threatened by culturally different people, nor are they overdependent on cues from the environment for their identity. They have high self-esteem, they value their cultural roots, and they come to the international arena as mature adults. Any good CCT program makes a deliberate effort to make certain that trainees do not fall into the trap of "going native" or resorting to such destructive coping mechanisms as drugs or alcohol.

6. *Perceptual acuity:* Successful leaders need to be perceptually acute in a number of ways. They need to accurately derive meaning from interactions with people from a wide variety of cultures and subcultures. This involves being attentive to both verbal and non-verbal communication by (a) being an active listener, (b) deriving meaning from social context, and (c) being sensitive to the feelings of others and to your effect on others. CCT provides experiential practice at analyzing cross-cultural scenarios in which communication between people from different cultures breaks down. This forces the trainee to focus on alternative explanations rather than relying on explanations that might seem logical or obvious from one's own cultural perspective. You have to consider not only the words exchanged in these scenarios but also the nonverbals, the social context, and the assumptions embedded in the other culture. Such predeparture simulations serve as effective practice for when the international assignee must deal with real-life cross-cultural encounters.

7. *Emotional resilience:* Things rarely go as planned when living and working in a culturally different environment. Frustrations are frequent and stress is high. Although unanticipated problems occur in any leadership situation, they occur with greater regularity when operating in an environment in which the rules are imperfectly understood. Thus, the international assignment becomes a training ground for learning how to deal with unanticipated problems, frustrations, and stress. To succeed in the international assignment, the international manager must learn to bounce back rapidly after disappointment or frustration. This involves maintaining a positive, up-beat attitude in the face of adversity. Thus, practicing effective stress-reducing techniques (which should be part of any good CCT program) is essential for becoming an effective global manager.

8. *Balance contradictions:* A major requirement for being an effective global manager is being able to balance contradictory needs and demands rather than prioritizing or attempting to eliminate them. Contradictions and conflicts should be seen as opportunities, not as unqualified liabilities. Conflicting values, behaviors, and ideas are a fact of life in the world today, and they are not diminishing in number. The world is not becoming culturally homogenized into a monolith. If anything, the cultures of the world are becoming increasingly more diverse and insistent upon maintaining their unique identities. CCT provides insights into the nature of the world's diversity and allows the trainees to see how different cultures work (that is, how each culture is a logical and coherent system). When exposed to logical alternatives to their own way of thinking and behaving—and understanding the nature of those alternative systems—cross-cultural trainees can learn to cope with the contradictions and actually use these differences for the sake of achieving synergy. In other words, grasping multiple perspectives can lead to a wider range of options and approaches to problems and challenges.

9. *Willingness to make risky decisions:* Making decisions, as all leaders must, always involves a certain amount of risk. Being a new global leader entails being an adventurer. It often requires a willingness to act on "gut feelings," and, if unsuccessful, bounce back before anyone notices. Because leaders in cross-cultural situations often need to act with less than a perfect grasp of all the facts, the range of risks is frequently greater than in a more cultur-

ally familiar environment. International assignments—and the CCT that should precede them—provide a laboratory for experimenting with different levels of comfort and discomfort associated with risk. In other words, living and working in another culture familiarizes the individual with the risks inherent in decision making and, perhaps more importantly, provides the opportunity for taking risks, experiencing failure on some occasions, but learning from those failures.

10. *Global teamwork:* Global leaders need to emphasize cultural awareness and cross-cultural teamwork, not just personal awareness and individual mastery. With the ubiquity of foreign subsidiaries, joint ventures, and offshore facilities, global manager/leaders need to be able to value and facilitate multicultural teamwork. Yet, before one can build fully effective multicultural teams within an organization, people must first understand the cultural assumptions and ways of behaving of others in the group. This understanding, if lacking, can best be developed by way of CCT. We should, however, keep in mind that an intimate connection exists between personal awareness and cultural awareness—they are hardly mutually exclusive enterprises. Before you can understand another culture, you must first understand the influence your own culture has on your thinking and behavior. Conversely, the only way to really understand who you are is to first understand your own culture—and you can only do that once you have been exposed to other cultures. So, in a sense, the personal and cross-cultural awareness needed for multicultural team building are mutually reinforcing.

Thus, a number of skills considered to be essential for effective global leaders of the future can be mastered through international (expatriate) experiences. To be certain, the mastery of these skills is not ensured by the expatriate experience itself. As we have seen, those expatriates who become "premature return statistics" have not, in all likelihood, developed those skills. Yet, under the proper circumstances, the expatriate experience is the single best "classroom" for developing these leadership/management skills. This expatriate "testing ground" becomes most effective when the whole process of expatriation is treated in a holistic or systematic fashion; that is, close attention must be given to issues of selection, preparation, in-country support, and repatriation. The assignment must be well planned strategically, to benefit both the individual and the corporation. The leadership skills to be obtained must be made explicit from the very beginning and reinforced throughout the experience.

In many ways, the development of global leaders through expatriate assignments is greatly enhanced when a global perspective has been built into the fabric of the corporate culture. Despite the fact that international operations constitute a significant segment of their operations, many firms still do not truly "think" globally. They are not particularly adept at collecting, disseminating, and utilizing international information; they too infrequently treat international assignments in a strategic fashion; they often fail to reward international/cross-cultural competence; and they frequently overlook opportunities (at all levels of the organization) to expose their personnel to growth-producing international activities.

For U.S. multinational corporations to manage international transfers effectively, they will need to create a corporate culture in which global competencies can thrive. In some cases, this involves assessing or reassessing the long-term goals for training, leadership development, and human resources management. This involves dealing with global issues in a systematic fashion, while encouraging and rewarding international competence at all levels. Creating a global climate within an organization often involves a series of small steps, none of which are particularly expensive, but when taken together can have a positive cumulative effect. For example, companies can (1) reward globally oriented behavior among all employees, such as taking foreign-language classes, serving on local boards of international nonprofit organizations, and attending international/cross-cultural seminars; (2) sponsor "brown bag" lunches (open to all) where employees can present information on recently completed international travel; (3) use in-house non-American employees as part of the cross-cultural predeparture training of American expatriates; (4) create a regional focus in upper-level management by expecting top leaders to become experts in a particular part of the world in which the company has an interest; (5) subscribe to relevant international materials for the company library, including books, newspapers, journals, and CD-ROMs on different parts of the world; (6) establish foreign-language conversation hours at lunch where people can practice their foreign-language skills; (7) liberally publicize the global activities of employees in the company newsletter; (8) when internationals are visiting the company, have them stay with host families chosen from within the home office rather than housing guests in a hotel; (9) bring in speakers from corporate divisions in other countries or from other global organizations; and (10) offer courses for all employees on how to do business in other countries. Although any one of these suggestions by itself might seem fairly insignificant, they all send an unequivocal message to employees: The organization is seriously committed to its global mission over the long haul.

CROSS-CULTURAL SCENARIOS

Read the following cross-cultural scenarios. In each minicase study, a basic cultural conflict occurs between the actors involved. Try to identify the source of the conflict and suggest how it could have been avoided or minimized. Then see how well your analyses compare to the explanations in Appendix A.

8-1   Tom Bennett, a senior accountant with a major New York accounting firm, had just arrived in Bogotá, Colombia, to assume a two-month assignment to set up an accounting procedure for a middle-sized local business. On his way to the office, Tom stopped to cash a check at the main branch of the largest bank in the country where he had just opened an account a week earlier. Tom approached the least crowded teller's window, which had about eight people crowded around it. After about five minutes of jostling, Tom worked his way in front of the teller's window and handed the teller his check. While he was waiting for his money, several other people elbowed their way up to the window and handed the teller their checks, and the teller took them. Tom was getting increasingly annoyed with the rudeness of these people who kept interrupting his banking transaction. While Tom waited for his money, a number of people kept trying to get in front of him, and what made things even more infuriating was that they seemed to be angry at him. And to think that people from the United States are always accused of being impatient! When his money finally arrived, he couldn't wait to get out of that very unfriendly situation. As he walked on to his office, he was already thinking about the letter of complaint he would send to the bank president.

How might you explain Tom's frustraton at the bank?

8-2 Steve Lee, an executive with a Hartford insurance company, was sent to Kuwait immediately after the 1990 Gulf War to investigate damage claims to several hotels his company had insured. Back in the States, Steve had the reputation of being extremely affable and sociable. The day after Steve arrived in Kuwait City, he met with Mr. Said, the manager of one of the insured tourist hotels. His previous telephone conversations with Said were upbeat and had led him to expect that Said was interested in getting the claims settled quickly and efficiently. His initial meeting with Said went extremely well, with both men agreeing on most of the issues discussed. At the end of that first meeting they shook hands, and to emphasize the depth and sincerity of his goodwill, Steve grasped Said's hand with two hands and shook vigorously. For reasons that Steve never understood, the subsequent meetings with Said were never as cordial and friendly as that first meeting.

What explanation might you give to Steve?

8-3 Martha and Ted Harding, owners of the largest travel agency in Salt Lake City, were invited on a "familiarization" tour of Australia by that country's Ministry of Tourism. They were part of a group of eight U.S. travel agents who were being wined and dined and shown all the major tourist attractions by the ministry in hopes that they would recommend Australia as a vacation spot to their clients. Shortly after their arrival, they attended a lavish cocktail party sponsored by the Association of Hotels and Restaurants in Sydney. Everyone seemed to be very cordial and good spirited. Yet Martha noticed that she got some cool glances from some of their Australian hosts when she declined a drink. Moreover, Martha noticed that the party was segregated sexually, the men talking at one end of the room and the women talking among themselves at the other end. Martha was beginning to feel increasingly uncomfortable at the cocktail party.

What could you tell Martha that might have made her feel a bit more at home?

8-4 Andy Ross, an electrical engineer for a Chicago firm on a contract with the Turkish government, had been living with his wife in Istanbul for several months. When Andy had to spend several weeks in Ankara, he thought it was a good opportunity to combine business with pleasure. Since he was entitled to some vacation time, he decided to travel leisurely to Ankara by car with his wife in order to spend some time in rural Turkey and get a better feel for village life. Living in Istanbul had been very enjoyable, for both Andy and his wife had found it to be a sophisticated and interesting European city. But when traveling in the outlying regions, they began to feel uneasy for the first time since coming to Turkey because the local people seemed hostile. On their second day out of Istanbul, they stopped in a small coffeehouse that they had heard was a focal point of social activity in rural Turkey. But shortly after arriving, they sensed that they were not welcome. People stared and stopped talking to one another. They could not understand why people were so hostile, particularly since people seemed so friendly in Istanbul.

What explanation might you offer Andy and his wife?

8-5 John Harmon, a vice president of a U.S.-based courier service, was sent to open an office in Madrid. The company had recently expanded its overnight delivery services to several other countries in Europe (including the Netherlands), and these were doing very well. The company's "bread and butter" service was overnight delivery any- where in Europe, provided that the package was in the pickup box by 5:00 P.M. Even though John and his wife, Linda, were getting along well in Spain, he could not un- derstand why the Spanish people were not responding more favorably to the compa- ny's services.

Why was the overnight delivery system not catching on in Spain?

APPENDIX

Cross-Cultural Scenario Discussions

CHAPTER 2

2-1 In the United States, public humiliation is one of a number of techniques that can be used quite effectively to change people's behavior. In the world of Islam, however, where the preservation of dignity and self-respect is absolutely essential, public reprimand will be totally counterproductive. If Arabs feel that they have suffered a loss of personal dignity because they have been criticized in public, they take it as a dishonor to both themselves and their families. And when Sam insisted on using this "motivational" technique, he was alienating not only the individual to whom the reprimand was directed but also all his fellow workers, who felt hurt on his behalf. When this happens, the person giving the reprimand loses the respect of those witnessing it.

2-2 The employee–employer relationship in Japan is very different than in the United States. When a Japanese firm hires an employee, he or she becomes part of the corporate family. Whereas labor and management in the United States operate largely from an adversarial perspective, the relationship between the Japanese worker and the company is based on loyalty and a long-term commitment to one another. Not only do most employees expect to stay with the firm for the duration of their careers, but also the firm takes an active role in the personal lives of its employees and their families. Housing, recreation, and schooling for the children are just some of the areas arranged by the employers for their workers. Moreover, far less separation of business and personal matters occurs between Japanese employees and their supervisors. Thus, it is little wonder that the Japanese mechanics thought that George was not acting like a responsible supervisor because he was unwilling to become involved in their personal lives.

2-3 In most of Europe when people write the date as 6/5/01, they are placing the day first, month second, and year last. So Stefan's request for information by 6/5 was not for June 5 but for May 6. Therefore, Bernice was not three and one-half weeks early but five days late!

2-4 Although Bob thought he was giving a straightforward answer to a rather mundane question about his father's health, his response, from Saade's perspective, made Bob appear to be a very undesirable business partner. Coming from a society that places a very high value on family relationships, Saade thought it quite inhumane to leave one's aging father at a nursing home in the care of total strangers. If Bob couldn't meet his primary obligations to his own family members, Saade reasoned, how could he be trusted to meet his obligations to his business partners?

2-5 Although this fertilizer company did a good deal of research in developing its product, it was woefully lacking in cultural information that would have enabled the company to market it. First, the company tried to convince the village men to accept an agricultural innovation when in fact it was the women who were the farmers. That they failed to understand this basic ethnographic fact did little for their general credibility. Second, many East Africans have two important beliefs that can help explain their reaction: (a) the theory of *limited good,* which assumes that there is a finite amount of good in the world (such as fertility), and (b) witchcraft, the notion that evil forces embodied in people can harm members of the community. Given these two beliefs, any individual East African farmer would never participate in any scheme that promises to produce considerably more per acre than her neighbor, for to do so would open her up to charges of having bewitched the fertility from the neighbor's soil. In short, to continue to grow the same amount as one had in the past is a far preferable alternative to being killed for witchcraft.

CHAPTER 3

3-1 The key to understanding this apparently innocent exchange, which left LeBec offended and Wayne confused, revolves around the use of personal questions. People in the United States think it perfectly natural to ask a number of personal questions early on in one's initial conversation, this is considered a normal way of finding a common ground on which to build a relationship quickly. Given the highly mobile nature of U.S. society, it is imperative to build relationships quickly because next week our new friends may be transferred across the country. In less mobile societies like France, people move to establish social relationships at a slower pace. The personal life of the French, and that of their families, is considered private. They will be quite reluctant to make any moves toward intimacy until there has been sufficient time to assess the newcomer. Thus, Wayne's questions appeared overly personal to LeBec, whose culture handles such introductory amenities much more slowly.

3-2 Saudis do not budget their time in the same way that Americans do. Time is considered to be a much more flexible commodity. The best piece of advice we might give Bill is to be patient and allow more time when conducting business affairs in Saudi Arabia than would be normal in the United States. Moreover, what Bill considered to be "small talk" is a very important part of the process of doing business in Saudi Arabia. Trust is an important ingredient in business affairs. Before engaging in meaningful business relations, most Saudis need time to get to know those with whom they are about to do business. They feel that there is no better way to do this than to discuss a wide variety of nonbusiness topics while drinking coffee. Finally, Saudis define private and public space somewhat differently than they do in Dallas. Although Saudis are extremely private in their personal lives, they are quite open in those things they consider to be public, and business is thought to fall into the public domain. Thus, even though the Western businessperson may want to discuss confidential business matters, it is not at all uncommon for a "personal" appointment to be conducted with other people in the room.

3-3   Having graduated near the top of his class, Eric had always met with academic success and high-level achievement. Unlike many of the courses that he had taken in the past (for example, mathematics, sciences, and engineering), this language course produced few concrete results in the early stages. Anyone ever taking a foreign language for the first time will feel incompetent and "lost" for the first several months. Eric's dissatisfaction with the language course and the project resulted from his strong need to achieve, which he felt was not being satisfied.

3-4   Even though Fred and his company thought they had been well prepared for the presentation, they made two tactical errors. First, despite Fred's knowledge of the product and his proficiency in German, he had one important factor working against him, namely, his age. By and large, managers in German corporations tend to be older than their U.S. counterparts. A young U.S. executive, however bright and charming, making a presentation before a group of older German executives may not be taken seriously because he is seen as relatively inexperienced. Second, Fred did not win any points by trying to set an informal, relaxed atmosphere by telling a few jokes. Although this may be an acceptable approach for an after-lunch speech at the Rotary Club, it was viewed as quite inappropriate in a German business setting.

3-5   France is one of the few nations in the world where an *attempt* to speak the language is not appreciated. There are many nuances in the French language that are difficult to grasp by anyone not very accomplished in the language. Clearly, Betty's three years of college French, although perhaps adequate to give directions to the cab driver, fell far short of being sufficient for conducting business. As a general rule, if you do not speak French well, it is best to use English (if possible) or work through an interpreter.

CHAPTER 4

4-1   In any society, gifts are given as a way of symbolizing certain thoughts. Yet like other aspects of culture, certain gifts symbolize different thoughts in different cultures. In the United States, chrysanthemums are given for a number of general purposes. But in Italy and in some other European countries, chrysanthemums are used traditionally as funeral flowers. Also, Don's flowers sent another unintended message. Although it is appropriate to take flowers as a gift when invited to someone's home for dinner, to present flowers at other times to the mother of an unmarried woman is seen as an expression of a man's serious intentions toward the daughter.

4-2   Actually, according to Saudi Arabian culture, the landlord was treating Lorna with respect and utmost politeness. Since her husband was absent, it would have been considered an invasion of her privacy to speak to Lorna.

4-3   France, along with other European countries, still suffers the memories of Hitler's reign of terror. Uniformity in logos, slogans, or signs are reminiscent of the German swastika and the humiliation of the period of occupation. The "gifts," coupled with the hostile takeover, started the Fortune 500 corporation off on shaky ground, considering French history.

4-4 In a sincere but misguided attempt to convey to their Japanese counterparts their interest in the project, the Americans made two serious cultural blunders. First, by taking off their jackets and rolling up their sleeves, they were trying to communicate sincerely, in a nonverbal way, that they were interested in working hard to arrive at a satisfactory agreement between the two corporations. The Japanese, however, who tend to be much more formal in dress, interpreted this symbolic gesture as most unbusinesslike and inappropriate, a breach in professional protocol. The second faux pas resulted from Harry's invitation to start their discussions off on a first-name basis. Although by making such a suggestion Harry was genuinely interested in facilitating their work relationship, he failed to realize that Japanese business relationships tend to be based on quite rigid status differences. In the eyes of the Japanese, being on a first-name basis involved an unacceptable level of informality and egalitarianism.

4-5 Here is another example of how certain nonverbal actions—in this case, the pounding of one's fist into one's palm—have a very different meaning in a foreign country than in the United States. In Singapore, as well as in several other Southeast Asian countries, such a gesture is a sexual insult, comparable in the United States to extending the middle finger.

CHAPTER 5

5-1 The demise of these joint-venture negotiations cannot be explained by the fact that contemporary Japanese firms are inextricably wedded to traditional practices. Present-day Japanese firms have shown an enormous willingness to adopt innovative policies and strategies, which has contributed to their rapid rise in the world economy. Yet, equally high on the Japanese list of cultural priorities is the value placed on respect for elders and saving face. Even though Hayakawa may have disagreed with his grandfather's position, it would have been totally inappropriate for him to have disagreed with his grandfather in a *public* meeting. The Japanese way would have involved private discussions between Hayakawa and his grandfather to try gently to convince the former president of the need for these innovative policies. Tom's impassioned attempt to change the old man's mind in the public meeting was seen as a serious breech of etiquette, which caused the old man to lose face.

5-2 In Nairobi, as in many other parts of the world, status and rank are important elements of social and business relationships. In the United States, where people have a tendency to play down status differences, the boss may often roll up his or her sleeves and start working alongside those of lower rank and position. In fact, the boss in the United States is likely to become more popular by engaging in manual labor alongside the workers, for it shows a true spirit of empathy and democracy. In Kenya, however, a boss doing manual labor is seen as a deliberate rejection of self-respect. If those in high positions are not willing to maintain their high status and self-respect, they will unlikely continue to receive the respect of their employees. To the African employees, it would have been far preferable to have missed the deadline than to have their boss lose his self-respect by engaging in manual labor.

5-3 This scenario illustrates the high value Americans place on science, logic, and rational thought. Since there were no logical links between any of these unfortunate happenings at the plant, Ned and his fellow Americans concluded that they were just an unfortunate yet unrelated series of accidents. The local workforce, on the other hand, believed that sinister forces were at work which required the services of a religious special-ist. This belief was the direct cause of Ned's two managerial problems—morale and ab-senteeism. Unfortunately, Ned and his colleagues got caught up in their own value system and missed the major point: It makes little difference whether the belief in evil spirits is true or false. Ned was no more capable of proving that evil spirits did not in fact cause this se-ries of events than the local workers could prove that they did. What Ned and his Ameri-can staff failed to understand was that (a) the workers did believe that evil spirits were at work and (b) this belief, whether true or false, was causing a major problem for the com-pany. The only reasonable way to solve that problem is to take an action that would en-able the workers to perceive that the power of evil spirits had been neutralized and that their safe work environment had been restored.

5-4   Despite Ray's Hispanic heritage, his dramatic rise in his company's organization re-quired him to adopt the mainstream U.S. cultural interpretation of time; that is, Ray was operating under the assumption that since time is money, there is no reason to waste it. Such a definition of time assumes that the end product of negotiations between two com-panies is more important than the process that brings it about. But in Argentina and many South American cultures, the *process* is also very important. It is not enough just to make a decision on the merits of the product; to many South Americans, it is equally important that those entering into a business relationship enjoy one another's company and build a strong foundation of mutual trust. To the Argentinians, Ray's insistence on getting down to business as quickly as possible was bypassing some very important components of the negotiation process.

5-5   The scenario can best be understood by first appreciating the very different views in U.S. culture and Saudi culture concerning *locus of control*. In the United States, it is be-lieved that people are ultimately responsible for their own destiny. If something goes wrong, it is believed, it is frequently possible for the individual to *do* something (that is, to change certain behavior) to bring about the desired outcome. In Saudi Arabia and throughout the Arab world, people are taught from an early age that all things are subject to the direct will of Allah. All plans for the future (including, of course, business plans) are viewed with a sense of inevitability and will be realized only if Allah wills it. This is not to say that peo-ple in the Arab world would not work hard to help bring about the desired results. Rather, they believe that despite the effort the desired ends will not happen unless Allah is will-ing. Perhaps Stefan would have been less frustrated if he had translated *inshallah* to mean "if possible" or "Allah willing" rather than as a knee-jerk response used to absolve oneself of all responsibility for one's actions.

CHAPTER 6

6-1   The meaning of time and punctuality varies not only from culture to culture but also within any culture, depending on the *social context.* In Portugal a person of high status should never be kept waiting by a person of lesser status; a woman may keep a man wait-ing, but it would be considered very bad form for a man to keep a woman waiting; an older person can be late for an appointment with a younger person, but the reverse is not true. Although punctuality for its own sake is not valued in the same absolute sense as it is in the United States, some social situations demand punctuality, and others do not. This ex-ample should remind us that when in Portugal, and most other cultures as well, it is im-portant to understand the nuances of values, attitudes, and behaviors.

6-2 Even though Japanese women receive considerable education, they have not been accepted into the higher echelons of the corporate world. The Japanese negotiators simply were not very subtle in their efforts to disguise their displeasure with having to negotiate with a woman.

6-3 The term *parallel* has a different meaning to Japanese than it does to Americans. We think of the word *parallel* as meaning compatible, being on the same track, going in the same direction, or agreement. However, to the Japanese, it represents a lack of agreement, positions that will always remain apart, never to meet, like two train tracks. When Harold stated that their thinking was "parallel," Kushiro took that as an indication the negotiations were over because they would remain apart in their contract goals.

6-4 The Japanese have great difficulty saying no. Instead of saying no in a direct, unequivocal way, the Japanese are more likely to give a conditional response or an irrelevant tangential response, ask a counterquestion, change the subject, leave the room, or say nothing at all. Of all the indirect ways that the Japanese say no, silence is the most difficult for Americans to handle gracefully. Americans place such importance on words that the absence of words becomes very disorienting. Because most Americans feel that silence is inherently unnatural, they frequently say things that get them into trouble in their haste to fill the silence. Roger would have been better off to have waited out the silence and then come back with another proposal or a question that would have kept the discussions on track.

6-5 The unwillingness of these four Korean accountants to leave their current employer stems from a sense of loyalty felt by many Korean workers that is not shared by their U.S. counterparts. The vast literature on Japanese business practices suggests that Japanese workers have a strong loyalty to their employers because their lives revolve around the company, and they in fact gain a sense of their own importance primarily through the prestige of the company. However, Koreans, unlike the Japanese, have relatively little loyalty to their companies, per se. There is a good deal of job mobility in Korea, for employees are always on the lookout for better job opportunities. Koreans, however, have a strong sense of loyalty to their *bosses* within the company. When Korean employees do change companies, they frequently are following bosses who take them along when they move. Even though it may be every bit as difficult for foreign firms to recruit Koreans away from their current jobs as it would be to recruit Japanese, the nature of the workers' loyalty is different in these two countries.

CHAPTER 7

7-1 Although both U.S. and French culture are what Edward Hall would call monochronic (emphasizing promptness and schedules), they differ in terms of the degree to which each emphasizes the primacy of meeting deadlines. For Americans, keeping to an agreed-upon schedule takes priority, even when confronted with unanticipated contingencies. If need be, personal pleasure or even quality will take second place to meeting the deadline. The French, too, are interested in efficiency and meeting schedules, but they don't give deadlines the same top priority as in the United States. For the French, the emphasis is on quality. In the event that time runs short, the French will choose to take additional time to ensure high quality, whereas Americans are more willing to sacrifice a number of things—including quality—in order to meet the deadline.

7-2   Although cameras can be valuable for documenting a foreign culture, they must be used with care. There is the simple matter of violating one's privacy, a notion to which most Americans can relate. How would a typical middle-class American, for example, feel if someone dressed in foreign clothing started taking his picture while he was cutting his front lawn? At the very least, such behavior would be met with suspicion. For a number of other cultural reasons, many East Africans would be reluctant to have their picture taken. First, a sizable number of people living along the Kenya coast are Muslims and as such resist being photographed because of the Koranic prohibition of depicting the human form. Second, whereas the Westerner looks for "picturesque" scenes of people doing traditional things, the local people themselves may feel that the foreign photographer is documenting their "backwardness" or lack of modernization. Third, some East Africans who do not understand the technology of the camera believe that having their pictures taken is tantamount to having their soul entrapped in the camera. In a society where witchcraft is widely believed, the thought of anyone, particularly a witch, capturing one's soul can be terrifying.

7-3   Asians in general and Koreans in particular, place a high value on harmonious personal relationships. Conflicts are avoided at all costs, and every effort is made to be polite and nonconfrontational. Also, Koreans have great difficulty in admitting failure, for to do so is to be humiliated or shamed—that is, to lose face. It is therefore important to maintain a high degree of *kibun,* translated as "morale" or "self-esteem." The reporting or acknowledging of a problem is far more serious than the problem itself, for it causes a loss of face for the teller and a loss of morale for the hearer. Thus, when the Korean employees withheld knowledge about plant problems from Jim, they did so to (a) preserve his *kibun* and (b) not lose face themselves. If anything negative has to be reported it should be done, according to the Korean way, at the end of the day so that the parties involved will at least have the evening to restore their damaged *kibun.*

7-4   For the local Indian labor pool, flexibility of time was of greater significance than housing or high wages. Under the German system, which paid an hourly wage (rather than a forty-hour-per-week salary, as with Bill's company), local laborers could take time off for their festivals and ceremonies without fear of losing their jobs. The solution to Bill's labor recruitment problem required the relatively simple task of changing to a more flexible hourly wage system rather than a weekly salary system.

7-5   Dick's problem stemmed from making the unwarranted assumption that informality at the party could carry over into a business context. In fact, Japanese make a very real distinction between these two social situations. Japanese senior executives can be informal and playful at parties, but this is not the environment in which to discuss business matters. The two realms are kept quite distinct in Japan.

CHAPTER 8

8-1   This is an excellent example of what can happen if one assumes that banks in Bogotá operate under the same system as they do in, say, Manhattan. In the United States, we expect to line up in an orderly fashion and wait our turn. In most banking transactions in the United States, the teller handles the entire transaction. But in Bogotá, in the absence of a sophisticated electronic system, most checks must be verified to ensure sufficient funds to cover them. That process may take five or ten minutes under normal circumstances. Thus, it is expected in Colombia that a person will walk up to the teller directly, hand over the check, and then step aside until the check has cleared, thereby allowing others to hand their checks to the teller. When the check has cleared, the person's name will be called, and he or she will be given the money. Clearly, this is a very different system of customer service than would be found in the United States. Had Tom understood this very logical system, he could have avoided an unpleasant situation.

8-2   Among middle-class men in the United States, it is customary to shake hands as a gesture of friendship, as it is also among men in Kuwait. When communicating extreme friendliness, an American man may grasp his friend's right hand with both of his hands. If, however, an American man gives such an emphatic handshake to a Kuwaiti man, he will be sending an extremely offensive message. In Kuwait and generally throughout the Muslin world, where the right hand is sacred and the left hand is profane, touching someone with the left hand is highly offensive.

8-3   Australians take a great deal of pride in their sense of hospitality, their conviviality, and their ability to throw and enjoy a good party. No good Australian party is without a generous supply of things to drink. Native Australians take their drinking seriously and expect others to do so as well. In fact, "spirited drink" is such an integral part of the social process that most Australians do not know how to cope with a nondrinker. Frequently, they interpret a refusal of a drink as a rejection of their friendship and hospitality. Martha, a nondrinker, would have been better off to have accepted the drink, simply carrying it around with her rather than actually drinking it. And even though women are frequently included in such business affairs, they are often segregated and don't offer their own opinions. Martha, a strong proponent of women's rights, had difficulty accepting this secondary role.

8-4   Life in rural Turkey is quite different from life in Istanbul. Located in two different continents (Europe and Asia), Istanbul reflects a good deal of its past European influence. The farther one gets from Istanbul, the more traditional, non-Western, and Islamic the people become. The arrival of a foreigner in a small Turkish town is not a common event. Andy and his wife received stares not out of hostility but rather out of curiosity. In addition to the general interest in foreigners, there was another source of confusion, which many of the local people no doubt felt. The presence of a woman in the generally all-male domain of the coffeehouse was an unusual sight. Rural Turkish women (who frequently wear dark clothing, cover their faces, and have little contact with the general public) do not enjoy the same liberties as their urban counterparts.

8-5   Unlike the Netherlands, where offices generally close promptly at 5:00 P.M. and the workers go home, it is common for Spaniards to work until 8:00 P.M. or later. Therefore, a 5:00 P.M. deadline would not be advantageous to a Spanish operation. Failure to seek out cultural differences when trying to establish new territory can result in a less than successful operation.

B

Locating Revelant Cultural Information

In recent years an increased awareness has risen in the international business literature regarding the need for a fuller understanding of the cultural environment of international business. Whether one is managing a firm's overseas operations, directing an international sales force, or helping expatriate employees and their families adjust to living and working in a foreign culture, the need for understanding the cultural environment has never been greater than it is today.

The difficulty lies not with identifying the problem but rather with knowing how to solve it. Much of the literature from international business tends to be anecdotal, illustrating by endless examples how well-meaning but shortsighted businesspeople can run amok because of their cross-cultural insensitivity. Or the literature deals with general pleas for cross-cultural understanding. This approach is of little assistance to the international businesspeople who must deal with culture-specific problems as they apply to the immediate international situation. Clearly, international businesspeople need to be able to acquire culture-specific data that are accessible, relevant, and applicable to their immediate business situations.

THE TRADITIONAL ANTHROPOLOGICAL APPROACH

Although the discipline of anthropology, with its central focus on the concept of culture, is the logical place to turn for culture-specific information, most international businesspeople contend that the conventional anthropological approach to research is not particularly well suited to meeting their informational needs. Cultural anthropologists collect data in a particular culture by means of the time-consuming technique known as *participant observation*. The field anthropologist must master the language, gain acceptance into the foreign culture, and develop networks of relationships before the formal data gathering can even begin. Thus, most international businesspeople view the traditional data-gathering process used by anthropologists as so snail-like in pace that it is virtually useless for their more immediate needs.

As time consuming as traditional cultural anthropological research is, there may well be international business situations that would require such an approach. For example, a U.S. multinational corporation about to invest millions of dollars in a manufacturing facility in Colombo,

Sri Lanka, will not be acting extravagantly by hiring one or more anthropologists to conduct a cultural study of the local people, who would eventually make up its workforce. Such a study might include traditional techniques such as participant observation and interviewing, as well as drawing on the already existing ethnographic and social science literature on the region. Although conducting such firsthand research would cost thousands of dollars, it nevertheless provides the best assurances that the corporate values and assumptions will be integrated into those of the local workforce. To do anything less would be to invite serious long-term managerial problems. Richard Reeves-Ellington, a professionally trained anthropologist working for the Upjohn Corporation, illustrates how the traditional anthropological approach can inform the conduct of international business:

> When Reeves-Ellington joined Upjohn, the company was planning to expand its international operations by marketing products in Indonesia. No one in the firm at the time (including Reeves-Ellington) had experience in Indonesia, but Reeves-Ellington had enjoyed doing fieldwork in Mexico as well as living in Europe, and he felt that his anthropological training would permit him to function effectively in another culture. The company concurred, and Reeves-Ellington was sent abroad to set up operations in Indonesia, where he stayed for 10 years. While in Southeast Asia, Reeves-Ellington says he "did a lot of applied anthropology." An ability to analyze social systems from the native's point of view and to determine the interconnections among and reasons for human behavior enabled Upjohn's anthropologist to establish good working relationships with local officials and thus to move the company's products effectively into local marketing and distribution channels—a process that could have taken many times longer or failed altogether without an appreciation for local logic and custom. (Baba 1986, 20–21)

HRAF: AN UNDERUTILIZED CULTURAL DATABASE

For more than half a century, there has been a retrieval system for anthropological data that can greatly facilitate research on various aspects of particular cultures. It was not until the late 1940s that the Human Relations Area Files (HRAF), the largest and most sophisticated cultural database ever devised, was made available for comparative cultural studies. Unfortunately, this cultural database has gone largely unnoticed and unused by most people outside the field of anthropology, particularly in the area of international business.

Developed largely by George Peter Murdock at Yale University's Institute for Human Relations, HRAF is a vast ethnographic archive structured according to two basic principles. First, the materials are divided into over 310 separate cultural files, each representing descriptive information on a single culture (or a closely related group of cultures) such as the Yoruba of Nigeria, the Navajo nation, or the Koreans. A full listing and description of all 310-plus cultural groups (each with its own alphanumeric code) are found in the manual entitled *The Outline of World Cultures* (*OWC*) (Murdock 1972).

The second basic organizational principle is a highly detailed, subject classification system composed of more than 700 categories grouped into seventy-nine major topical sections. The concepts covered include such topics as food consumption, property systems, labor and leisure, age stratification, gestures, theories of disease, and in-group antagonisms. An explanation of these and other topics, along with cross-references to other categories, is presented in a second manual entitled *The Outline of Cultural Materials* (*OCM*) (Murdock 1971).

When these two guides (*OWC* and *OCM*) are used together, it is possible to have before you within a matter of minutes most of the information on a given subject for a particular cultural group. The HRAF files are well designed for the rapid and accurate retrieval of data on specific cultures and subjects. Thus, the time of the international business analyst can be devoted to the search for structural similarities and differences between the corporate and the local culture rather than to the search for the information itself.

In recent decades cultural anthropologists have glutted conventional libraries with a vast and largely indigestible number of books, articles, and field reports on specific world cultures. The major significance of HRAF is that it has organized this unwieldy quantity of cultural data into a form usable by nonanthropologists.

DOCUMENTARY SOURCES USEFUL IN DEVELOPING A CULTURAL PROFILE

Culture-Specific Associations

A particularly effective way to access culture-specific information is by contacting the many associations, both at home and abroad, that focus on a particular country or culture. A primary reference book that can be found in the reference department of any good research library is the four-volume *Encyclopedia of Associations* (Sheets 1999). Suppose you are interested in obtaining culture-specific information on Japan. By consulting the Keyword Index (Part 3) of this encyclopedia under "Japan," you will find entries having to do with Japan for approximately 150 associations based in the United States, including the Japan-American Society, the Japan Foundation, the Japan National Tourist Organization, the Japanese American Citizens' League, and the Japanese-American Curriculum Project. Parts 1 and 2 of the encyclopedia provide pertinent descriptive data on these culture-specific associations, including address, telephone number, contact person, membership, and publications.

Some Country-Specific Series

One of the best single series of culture-specific data is the *Interact* series. Edited by George Renwick and published by Intercultural Press, this series of books is designed to explore the bases of cross-cultural conflict in various countries. Each of the eleven books in this series (dealing with Mexico, Australia, Israel, Thailand, China, Japan, the Philippines, Spain, Germany, Greece, and Russia) analyzes how nationals from these countries perceive the world, how their actions differ from those of middle-class Americans, and how these differences influence their relationships. It is hoped that there will soon be more volumes in this excellent but small series.

The David M. Kennedy Center for International Studies at Brigham Young University produces a series entitled *Culturgrams*, four-page cultural orientations covering the customs, courtesies, and lifestyles in more than 170 different countries. Each *Culturgram*—now in electronic, downloadable form, which represents a condensation of a wide variety of data sources—is designed for those with more interest in cross-cultural communication than with time. Although these minicultural briefings are by design not in-depth cultural profiles, they do provide some valuable information on a wide variety of contemporary cultures.

U.S. Government Sources

In addition, the U.S. government (with its intelligence network made up of perhaps the largest research organization in the world) makes available through the Government Printing Office a number of current, thoroughly researched, and relatively inexpensive country-specific publications. By far the most comprehensive are those found in the *Country Studies* series developed by the Foreign Area Studies Group at American University for the Department of Defense and other government agencies. Formerly called *Area Handbooks*, each of the more than 100 books in the series, dealing with a particular foreign country, describes and analyzes how the economic, national security, political, and social systems and institutions are influenced by the cultural factors. Researched and written by interdisciplinary teams of scholars, each volume attempts to describe a whole society as a coherent, dynamic system. All the books, ranging from 300 to 500 pages in length, are updated on a fairly regular basis.

For a less encyclopedic approach to country profiles, the U.S. Department of State publishes periodically a series entitled *Background Notes*, short pamphlets (four to eight pages in length) on approximately 160 countries. Each pamphlet in the series includes information on the demography, geography, government, economy, history, and foreign relations of the country. Included also is a statistical profile, brief travel notes, a map, a listing of government officials, and a brief reading list. Single issues or annual subscriptions of *Background Notes* can be obtained from the Government Printing Office.

The Central Intelligence Agency (CIA) makes available basic factual information on most countries in a source called the *CIA Factbook*. Available electronically through the Internet, each entry contains three to five pages of background information on such topics as geography, climate, land use, population, birth and death rates, ethnic divisions, religions, languages spoken, government divisions, membership in world organizations, and considerably more. These brief country sketches include a map of the country and are updated periodically. Most of the government sources of country-specific information are available in printed form through the Government Printing Office, as well as on-line through the appropriate websites (e.g., the U.S. State Department or the CIA).

Sources of Country-Specific News and Current Events

It would be difficult to find any successful U.S. businesspeople in Chicago, New York, or Atlanta who was not in the habit of keeping abreast of local, national, and international news through newspapers, periodicals, and the electronic media. Hardly a day passes without something being reported that affects one's business or personal life. The same holds true for those conducting business abroad. In addition to knowing the language, history, and culture of the host country, the international businesspeople must also be well aware of current happenings. When living and working in any of the major cities of the world, procuring local English-language newspapers or news magazines would not be difficult. However, if the U.S. international businessperson is in the United States or wants to supplement the in-country news coverage, a number of very adequate alternatives are available.

Perhaps the most complete and convenient news-reporting system available is the World News Connection (WNC), an on-line search service for world current events, sponsored by the National Technical Information Service of the federal government. WNC offers timely news information gathered from thousands of media services, including newspapers, periodicals, radio and TV broadcasts, and books. Subscribers get the most extensive collection of up-to-date information (military, political, social, scientific, environment, and technical) from around the world, all of which has been translated into English. The data are organized into eight regions of the world: Central Asia, East Asia, Near East and South Asia, China, East Europe, West Europe, Latin America, and sub-Saharan Africa. Under certain subscription plans, WNC will provide custom-designed profiles, whereby the subscriber defines the type of information required (subject and geographic location) and WNC will e-mail only those media reports that fit the profile.

Sources on Business Customs and Protocols

The most specific form of country-by-country information relates to business cultures, the do's and don't's of conducting business in a specific country. For the overwhelming majority of the post–World War II era, there was a near total absence of descriptions of foreign business customs in the international business literature published in the United States. This lack reflected the very strong position of U.S. business in the world marketplace during the 1950s and 1960s. If the rest of the world wanted our goods and services, it was thought, they would come to us and play the game of business according to our set of rules. Since U.S. products and services are no longer the only or best around—our corner on so many markets simply no longer exists—the U.S. international business community is becoming painfully aware that, if we want to sell to other parts of the world, we will have to go to them and play according to their rules. In short, to be successful in today's highly competitive international marketplace, it is absolutely imperative that we understand the business customs, practices, and protocols of those with whom we are trying to conduct business.

Although there has been an appreciable amount of literature on different business customs in the last decade, it remains relatively small and uneven in terms of both quality and countries covered. Nevertheless, a number of useful sources deserve mention. First, there is a fairly wide and growing number of individually written books that deal with how to avoid "shooting oneself in the foot" when trying to navigate through a foreign business culture. The best way to find these works is to search your local library. To illustrate, a spate of full-length books have appeared recently on how to understand the often enigmatic (at least to Westerners) business customs of the Japanese. Such titles as *Doing Business with the Japanese* (Abecasis-Phillips 1992), *Doing Business with Japanese Men: A Woman's Handbook* (Brannen and Wilen 1993), *How to Do Business with the Japanese: A Complete Guide to Japanese Customs and Business Practices* (De Mente 1993), *Japanese Etiquette and Ethics in Business* (De Mente 1994), *Japanese Business: Cultural Perspectives* (Durlabhji and Marks 1993), *Doing Business with the Japanese: A Guide to Successful Communication, Management, and Diplomacy* (Goldman 1994), *Hidden Differences: Doing Business with the Japanese* (Hall and Hall 1987), *Doing Business with Japan: Successful Strategies for Intercultural Communication* (Nishiyama 2000), and *Doing Business with the New Japan* (Hodgson, Sano, and Graham 2000) all sound suspiciously similar, yet they do provide a wide variety of excellent information on the Japanese business culture. The recent interest in Japan and its strategic importance to the U.S. economy has spawned this plethora of literature. Unfortunately, the literature on the business customs of Indonesia, Kuwait, or Argentina is considerably more modest, and the literature on the business customs of some of the more obscure parts of the world is either nonexistent or so superficial or inaccessible that it is virtually useless.

In addition to single volumes on one country, several excellent books dealing with the foreign business cultural milieu in general also include helpful country-specific data. For example, Philip Harris and Robert Moran in their 1996 publication entitled *Managing Cultural Differences* discuss key insights into the business cultures of the major regions of the world, including Africa, Europe, South America, the Middle East, and Asia. As with so much of this literature, the treatment is uneven. Moreover, there is little consistency in the level of specificity or categories of culture discussed. A more uniform approach is provided by Neil Chesanow (1985) in *The World Class Executive*. In fact, the final three-fourths (220 pages) of this volume is devoted to strategies and tactics for coping with the business cultures in Europe, the Arab world, Japan, China, South Korea, and Latin America. Terence Brake, Danielle Walker, and Thomas Walker (1995) in their *Doing Business Internationally*, devote approximately sixty pages to how cultures in six major regions of the world (Africa, Asia, Europe, Latin America, the Middle East, and North America) differ on ten major dimensions of culture.

In their recent cross-cultural compendium entitled *Kiss, Bow, or Shake Hands*, Terri Morrison, W. A. Conaway and G. A. Borden (1994) examine cultural features, behavioral styles, negotiating techniques, protocol, and business practices in sixty countries throughout the world. Each country description, written succinctly in five to seven pages, deals with a standardized set of issues such as cognitive style, negotiating strategies, locus of decision making, power distance, punctuality, business entertaining, nonverbal communication, forms of address, and gift giving. Although hardly definitive, this entry into the cross-cultural business literature is a convenient and reasonable place to start.

The Electronic Library

Many of the preceding documentary sources can be located in any good research-oriented library through the card catalog or the indexing system for U.S. government documents. Within the last several years, however, the nature of libraries has changed dramatically. Today, the search for relevant literature on different cultures and business cultures has been made infinitely easier than in the past owing to on-line electronic searching, which is both fast and comprehensive. For example, the *College InfoTrac* databases include vast quantities of periodic literature, including academic/scholarly publications, business literature, and newspaper articles (all easily referenced) going back to the early 1980s. *CARL UnCover* provides access to articles from more than 17,000 journals from the Colorado Alliance of Research Libraries. *FirstSearch* is a menu-driven electronic service providing access to journal databases, newspaper articles, and government reports from 16,000 libraries. *EUREKA* is an electronic bibliographic catalog containing over 56 million items held by the Research Libraries Group, Inc.

In addition to these on-line bibliographic services, vast quantities of cultural data can be found by surfing the Internet. By using such search engines as Netscape, Google, or Yahoo, it is now possible to find a great deal of helpful information about the country/culture in which one wants to do business. It is important to say from the outset that all information found on the Internet is *not* created equal. With the advent of the mass use of television in the 1950s, anyone could become a viewer. Today, with the widespread use of the Internet, anyone can become a broadcaster: Anyone with a little bit of technical know-how can construct their own web page and put any type of information on it that they please. This necessitates that we learn to look at the sources of information on the Internet with a critical eye. There are no methods for assessing the accuracy or validity of Internet information with absolute certainty. Nevertheless, you should look for the reason(s) that a particular site exists in the first place. Do the people constructing the site have a "hidden agenda"? Are they putting this information on the Internet for the purpose of educating you in an objective way? Are they trying to sell you something? Are they trying to convert you to their particular cause? In most cases, websites that are the property of universities, libraries, museums, and governments are likely to be the most reliable. Those sites that are put on the Internet by individuals or small, noninstitutional groups and organizations require considerably more scrutiny.

HUMAN RESOURCES FOR CULTURE-SPECIFIC INFORMATION

Given the generally inaccessible nature of much culture-specific information, the successful international businessperson must be creative in his or her search for relevant information. This search of course requires the use of human resources as well as published ones. Every businessperson bound for a foreign assignment has a vast variety of experts to draw on, but it requires knowing where to look. Unfortunately, most businesspeople do not take advantage of the resources at hand, many of which are free. Here are some major sources of expertise that should be utilized.

One's Own Company

Frequently, expertise on the cultural environment of a particular country can be found in one's own corporation. Depending on the size of the corporation, people working right down the hall may have experience in living and working in a specific part of the world. Western multinational corporations are so large and decentralized, with divisions operating independently of one another, that most divisions usually do not know what types of international expertise exist in other divisions. If this is the case, the wise international businessperson will do well to contact the one division within the corporation that might have that type of information—the personnel department. Once the appropriate persons have been identified, they will likely be willing to share all sorts of culturally relevant information, if for no other reason than they have become instant experts on a subject of mutual concern.

Academia

Local colleges and universities are excellent sources of culture-specific information. Interestingly, U.S. businesses have turned to universities for technical assistance but have not by and large utilized the cultural, social, or political expertise that is also part of the academic world. Many mid- to large-sized universities have well-established area studies programs composed of faculty, and often graduate students, who have had considerable experience in various parts of the world.

For many of these faculty members, the prime purpose for living abroad was to study firsthand the sociocultural realities of the area. Perhaps the most relevant are the small but growing number of academic programs in the United States that are designed to integrate international business studies with area studies (that is, language and culture). Although it would be impossible to list them all, this type of program is exemplified by the Masters of International Management offered at the American Graduate School of International Business in Glendale, Arizona; the Masters in International Business Studies (MIBS) offered at the University of South Carolina at Columbia; and the M.B.A./M.A. in International Management and International Studies at the Wharton School, University of Pennsylvania. Yet even those institutions that do not offer programs in international business employ faculty from a wide variety of disciplines with extensive knowledge of different parts of the world. For example, a sociology professor who lived and conducted research at the University of Cairo for several years will no doubt be a valuable resource on the general cultural, social, political, and economic environments of Egypt. Such academic experts can be identified with a few well-placed phone calls to the office of the director of the International Studies Program, the dean of the Business School, or the dean of Arts and Sciences.

Foreign Trade Offices

In the United States, many foreign governments maintain foreign trade offices (FTOs), whose very existence is to assist U.S. importers and exporters. Although most FTOs are located in Washington or New York, some of the larger foreign governments may have branches in other major cities throughout the country. These offices publish excellent (and usually free) brochures, booklets, and so forth on both the technical and the cultural aspects of doing business in their countries. The extent of the services provided by any FTO will vary according to the country's relative affluence and its commitment to stimulating trade with the United States. The Japan External Trade Organization (JETRO) maintains the most elaborate services. To illustrate, JETRO makes available over 100 complimentary publications and films on doing business in Japan and employs Japanese trade experts in New York, Houston, Los Angeles, and San Francisco, to answer personal questions. Not all foreign governments provide such extensive services, but frequently helpful culture-specific information can be obtained from the appropriate embassy in Washington or consulate in other U.S. cities.

Private-Sector Consultants and Trainers

Before the 1950s there were virtually no cross-cultural consultants specializing in business. Then with the appearance of William Lederer and Eugene Burdick's *The Ugly American* (1958) and the "discovery" of culture shock by Kalvero Oberg (1960), there was an increasing awareness of the hazards involved in conducting business in an unfamiliar cultural environment. In the past several decades, an entire specialized consulting and training industry has developed. The problem today is not a shortage of qualified cross-cultural consultants and trainers but rather sorting through all their credentials to find someone with the particular knowledge and skills needed to address a firm's particular and frequently unique situation. By simply searching any search engine on the Internet by using the term *cross-cultural training,* you will be directed to the home pages of many of the leading cross-cultural trainers and consultants.

Consultants and trainers must be able to address the firm's special needs and problems. Does the consultant have the proper culture-specific experience and training? Are the proposed training and/or services designed to meet the specific needs and objectives of the corporation? Are the learning objectives clearly stated? Are the methods of training realistic and compatible with company policies and procedures? How will the program be evaluated to determine if it has accomplished what it promised? Once these questions have been answered to the firm's satisfaction, a program can be designed and executed. These may include predeparture briefings for international businesspeople and their families on such topics as customs, history, political structure, and practical matters necessary for living and working in the assigned country.

In recent years a relatively dramatic increase has occurred in the number of people claiming to be cross-cultural trainers or consultants. Many are well trained and effective, but others may be considerably less effective or just plain charlatans. Before hiring such cross-cultural trainers, insist on their demonstrating six important qualifications. First, they should possess considerable knowledge of the target area, gained through both formal academic study and firsthand living experience. Second, they should understand a number of important anthropological principles and concepts that they can apply to their country-specific area of expertise. Third, they should have personal experience with culture shock and should have made a successful adjustment to living in another culture. Fourth, they should have a sound understanding of their own culture and how their own values and attitudes influence them. Fifth, they should be experienced trainers who feel comfortable using a wide variety of educational strategies, including experiential learning techniques. Finally, they should have a "presentation of self" that corporate personnel would not find offensive.

THE SEARCH FOR CULTURAL INFORMATION UPON ARRIVAL

So far we have considered a number of possible sources of cultural information that should be consulted before one's departure for a foreign business assignment. This constitutes the predeparture aspect of one's preparation, which should provide a solid background for the most important learning that is yet to come. Regardless of how much predeparture preparation has taken place, the new arrival will be a stranger in a very different, and perhaps frightening, cultural environment. Despite occasional claims to the contrary, this is no different from the position most cultural anthropologists find themselves in when first arriving at the site of a field research project. It is now time for the newly arrived Western businessperson to become his or her own "ethnographer" by becoming an active learner while immersed in the culture. If the businessperson is serious and purposeful about mastering the new cultural environment, there should be no shortage of sources of cultural information, both documentary and human. Moreover, the quality of one's cultural learning during this on-site phase should be significant because it will be acquired *experientially*. In short, if the newly arrived businessperson realizes that the culture *is* the classroom, the amount of cultural learning that can occur is virtually endless.

In-Country Documentary Resources

Since tourism represents a welcome source of foreign exchange, most countries make considerable efforts to attract tourists and make certain that they see the sights, spend their money, and leave with a desire to return. Consequently, most foreign countries, even small third-world countries, maintain tourist information centers (at least in the major cities), where the new arrivals can obtain printed information (brochures, booklets, maps, and so on) on things to do and see while in the country. Thus, one of the first stopping places in your continuing search for cultural information is the local tourist center. However, having in your possession information on national monuments, historic sites, scenic areas, and museums is just the beginning of the learning process. Your understanding of the culture will be greatly enhanced by actually exploring these places and learning about them firsthand.

It is hard to imagine any country without a public or university library with books on national history, culture, and contemporary issues. Shortly after arrival, seek permission to use the local library and get to know the most valuable person there, the reference librarian.

Private-sector bookstores can also be valuable sources of local cultural data. Not only are you likely to find a number of valuable written sources, but also it is possible to learn a good deal about a culture by noticing how the bookstores are organized. Are some topics or categories of books not sold? Are some topics or categories unusually large? Frequently, it is possible to get a feel for what a particular culture emphasizes by looking at how much space is devoted to certain topics in local bookstores. For example, several years ago I was struck by the unusually large section of books in an all-white bookstore in Johannesburg, South Africa, dealing with self-defense, martial arts, fortifying your home, and how to use handguns.

One of the best entries into a culture, and by far the most accessible type of documentary source, is local or national newspapers, some of which will be printed in English. Not only are local newspapers the best source of contemporary happenings, but also they reflect a wide range of cultural values. To illustrate, what does it say about a society if there are no letters to the editor? If there is an editorial page, are certain topics restricted or limited? What clues might one get about a culture if male suitors advertise for "brides wanted" in the classified section? Can information be gleaned from the jobs section of the classifieds about the degree of labor specialization within the society? What can you learn about the family structure by reading the obituary pages? What insights into the culture can one pick up by reading the comics? These are only some of the questions that the culturally sensitive businessperson should raise when reading local newspapers in a foreign country.

In addition to reading in-country newspapers daily, many have found it helpful to clip and file some of the more interesting articles. Clipping articles is more convenient than taking notes and can provide a sizable amount of data that can be referred to and studied for years to come.

In-Country Human Resources

Clearly, it would be unwise to spend all or most of your time in a new country reading various printed materials. There is no substitute for people, for most of the important insights into a culture will come from interacting with local people. After all, they are the real experts in the local culture. Although cultural anthropologists do in fact draw on whatever reliable documentary materials are available, most of their data come from a combination of being a participant observer and asking questions of knowledgeable local people. These are the two best sources of cultural data for the international businessperson as well.

The stock-in-trade of the field anthropologist is participant observation—that is, immersing yourself in the culture to as great an extent as possible while making systematic observations and recording what is taking place. Although much has been written in recent years about some of the methodological fine points of participant observation, the primary prerequisite for being a successful participant observer is the desire to do so. Unfortunately, many Western businesspeople when living and working abroad all too often make no attempt to involve themselves personally with the local culture, preferring instead to spend their leisure time with their families, friends, and colleagues in a Western ghetto.

Of course, most international businesspeople operate under certain work and time constraints not usually facing the field anthropologist, thereby making a total immersion into the local culture impractical if not impossible. Yet there are a number of opportunities for expatriate businesspeople to become involved in the local culture. The critical question is whether you choose to take advantage of these opportunities. If you do, you will increase your cultural learning geometrically, and you will most likely enjoy yourself in the process.

Being a participant observer in the local culture involves making a conscious decision and taking some personal risks. As a newly arrived participant observer, you will feel very much out of control of the situation, particularly at first. Much of what will be observed will not be understood, and there will be opportunities at every turn to contract "foot-in-mouth" disease. Yet to succeed as a field anthropologist or international businessperson, you must be patient and able to live with ambiguity. Gradually, more and more of what is observed begins to make sense until eventually an increasingly logical and coherent picture of the culture emerges.

Once you decide to become a participant observer in the new culture, the question of how best to record the cultural data arises. The best advice is to always carry a pocket notebook. As new bits of cultural information are experienced, it is important to jot down as soon as possible some key words that can be transformed into more elaborate notes at the end of the day. Periodically, perhaps every month or two, your daily notes should be reviewed to discover both recurring themes and possible inconsistencies, which may require additional focused research to resolve.

When acting as your own ethnographer, participant observation alone is not enough. Bound by your own cultural perspective, you can possibly misinterpret what is observed. Thus, as a check, you should ask questions of local people. Key informants should be chosen carefully, and the sample of interviews should be as large and representative of the total society as possible.

CONCLUSION

We have explored a number of sources of information available to the international businessperson when attempting to construct a cultural profile of another country. These sources of cultural data include both written materials and human resources. They also include resources that should be consulted in the United States before entering the international business arena, as well as those likely to be found abroad. This discussion of sources certainly does not pretend to be definitive but is rather meant to be suggestive. Many valuable data sources have not been mentioned specifically.

The international businessperson should keep three major points in mind when constructing foreign cultural profiles. First, there is a direct correlation between the amount of culture-specific information a person has and the success of his or her personal and professional overseas experience. Second, it is important to be constantly on the lookout for new sources of cultural information *and* to be sufficiently creative and open minded to see how they can be integrated with other sources. Finally, the cultural learning process does not end with an orientation program or the completion of a reading list; rather, it is an ongoing process that starts before leaving home and continues throughout one's assignment abroad.

The aim of this appendix has been to explore some sources of information that can help the international businessperson acquire a measure of "cultural literacy" when entering a foreign business setting. According to E. D. Hirsch (1987), literacy requires more than knowing how to read; it also requires a certain level of comprehension of background information about the culture. Just as a U.S. high school graduate cannot be considered culturally literate if he or she identifies Karl Marx as one of the Marx Brothers or the Great Gatsby as a magician, the international businessperson attempting to conduct business in Germany cannot be considered culturally literate without knowing something about Nietzsche, Wagner, and the Schwarzwald. The sources discussed in this appendix are intended to provide the Western international businessperson with a starting point in the quest for "literacy" in another culture.

References

Abecasis-Phillips, John. 1992. *Doing business with the Japanese.* Lincolnwood, Ill.: NTC Business Books.

Adler, Nancy. 1997. *International dimensions of organizational behavior.* 3d ed. Cincinnati: Southwestern.

Adler, Peter. 1975. The transitional experience: An alternative view of culture shock. *Journal of Humanistic Psychology* 15(4): 13–23.

Allport, F. H. 1924. *Social Psychology.* Boston: Houghton Mifflin.

Anderson, David C. 1985. How to offend a Mexican businessman. *Across the Board,* June, 53–56.

Argyle, Michael. 1975. *Bodily communication.* New York: International University Press.

Argyle, Michael, and Mark Cook. 1976. *Gaze and mutual gaze.* Cambridge: Cambridge University Press.

Baba, Marietta L. 1986. *Business and industrial anthropology: An overview.* Bulletin 2. Washington, D.C.: National Association for the Practice of Anthropology.

———. 1994. The fifth discipline: Anthropological practice and the future of anthropology. *Human Organization* 53(2): 174–88.

Ball-Rokeach, S. J. 1973. From pervasive ambiguity to a definition of the situation. *Sociometry* 36: 3–13.

Barnum, C., and N. Wolniansky. 1989. Talk isn't cheap if you can't speak the language. *Management Review,* July, 1991. 52–56.

Barrett, Richard A. 1991. *Culture and conduct: An excursion in anthropology.* Belmont, Calif.: Wadsworth.

Baxter, J. C. 1970. Interpersonal spacing in natural settings. *Sociometry* 33: 444–56.

Beals, Ralph L., Harry Hoijer, and Alan R. Beals. 1977. *An introduction to anthropology.* 5th ed. New York: Macmillan.

Befu, H. 1979. Konnichiwa. Essay read at the meeting of the Japan Society, April 1975, San Francisco. Quoted in Sheila J. Ramsey. Nonverbal behavior: An intercultural perspective. In *Handbook of Intercultural Communication,* edited by M. K. Asante, E. Newmark, and C. Blake, 105–43. Beverly Hills, Calif.: Sage.

Bernstein, Basil. 1964. Elaborated and restricted codes: Their social origins and some consequences. *American Anthropologist* 66(6): 55–69.

Besner, Patricia. 1982. Watch your language. *Pace* 9(2): 53f.

Birdwhistell, R. L. 1963. The kinesis level in the investigation of the emotions. In *Expressions of the Emotions in Man,* edited by P. H. Knapp. New York: International University Press.

Black, J. Stewart, H. B. Gregersen, and Mark Mendenhall. 1992. *Global Assignments: Successful expatriating and repatriating international managers.* San Francisco: Jossey-Bass.

Black, J. Stewart, and Mark Mendenhall. 1990. Cross cultural training effectiveness: A review and theoretical framework for future research. *Academy of Management Review* 15: 113–36.

Brake, Terence, Danielle Walker, and Thomas Walker. 1995. *Doing business internationally: The guide to cross cultural success.* New York: Irwin.

Brannen, Christalyn, and Tracey Wilen. 1993. *Doing business with Japanese men: A woman's handbook.* Berkeley, Calif.: Stone Bridge Press.

Brett, Jeanne, and Tetsushi Okumura. 1998. Inter- and intracultural negotiations: U.S. and Japanese negotiators. *Academy of Management Journal* 41: 495–510.

Brewster, Chris. 1995. Effective expatriate training. In Westport, Conn.: Quorum Books edited by Jan Selmer, *Expatriate Management: New Ideas for International Business,* 57–71.

Brislin, Richard W. 1981. *Cross-cultural encounters: Face-to-face interaction.* New York: Pergamon Press.

Brown, Roger, and Marguerite Ford. 1961. Address in American English. *Journal of Abnormal and Social Psychology* 62: 375–85.

Brown, R., and S. Levinson. 1978. Universals in language usage: Politeness phenomena. In *Questions and politeness,* edited by E. Goody. Cambridge: Cambridge University Press.

Buck, Ross, 1984. *The communication of emotion.* New York: Guilford Press.

Burgoon, Judee K., David B. Buller, and W. Gil Woodall. 1989. *Nonverbal communication: The unspoken dialogue.* New York: Harper and Row.

Byrnes, F. C. 1966. Role shock: An occupational hazard of American technical assistants abroad. *Annals of the American Academy of Political and Social Science* 368: 95–108.

Cannon, W. 1942. Voodoo death. *American Anthropologist* 44: 169–81.

Casagrande, Joseph B. 1948. Comanche baby language. *International Journal of American Linguistics* 14: 11–14.

———. 1960. The Southwest Project in Comparative Psycholinguistics: A preliminary report. In *Men and cultures: Selected papers of the Fifth International Congress of Anthropological and Ethnological Sciences,* edited by F. C. Wallace, 777–82. Philadelphia: University of Pennsylvania Press.

Caudron, Shari. 1991. Training ensures success overseas. *Personnel Journal,* December, 27–30.

Chambers, Erve. 1985. *Applied anthropology: A practical guide.* Englewood Cliffs, N.J.: Prentice Hall.

Champness, B. G. 1970. Mutual glance and the significance of the look. *Advancement of Science* 26: 309–12.

Chesanow, Neil. 1985. *The world class executive: How to do business like a pro around the world.* New York: Rawson Associates.

Collett, P. 1971. Training Englishmen in the nonverbal behavior of Arabs. *International Journal of Psychology* 6: 209–15.

Collins, Robert J. 1987. *Max Danger: The adventures of an expat in Tokyo.* Rutland, Vt.: Tuttle.

Condon, John. 1984. *With respect to the Japanese: A guide for Americans.* Yarmouth, Mass.: Intercultural Press.

Condon, John, and Fathi Yousef. 1975. *Introduction to intercultural communication.* Indianapolis: Bobbs-Merrill.

Darwin, Charles R. 1872. *The expression of emotions in man and animals.* London: John Murray.

Davis, Flora. 1971. *Inside intuition: What we know about nonverbal communication.* New York: Mc-Graw-Hill.

Davis, Kingsley. 1947. Final notes on a case of extreme isolation. *American Journal of Sociology,* March, 432–37.

De La Torre, Jose. 1994. Multinational companies will need trans-national managers. *Los Angeles Times,* July 24, D-2.

De Mente, Boye. 1993. *How to do business with the Japanese: A complete guide to Japanese customs and business practices.* 2d ed. Lincolnwood, Ill.: NTC Business Books.

———. 1994. *Japanese etiquette and ethics in business.* 6th ed. Lincolnwood, Ill.: NTC Business Books.

Denison, Daniel R. 1990. *Corporate culture and organizational effectiveness.* New York: Wiley.

Downs, James F. 1971. *Cultures in crisis.* Beverly Hills, Calif.: Glencoe Press.

Driver, Harold E. 1961. *Indians of North America.* Chicago: University of Chicago Press.

Durlabhji, Subhash, and Norton E. Marks. 1993. *Japanese business: Cultural perspectives.* Albany: State University of New York Press.

Economist. 1987. *Even the British find it pays to learn languages.* May 16, 67–68.

Edwards, Linda. 1978. Present shock, and how to avoid it abroad. *Across the Board,* February, 36–43.

Efron, David. 1941. *Gesture and environment.* New York: King's Crown.

———. 1972. Similarities and differences between cultures in expressive movement. In *Non-verbal communications,* edited by R. A. Hinde. London: Cambridge University Press.

Eibel-Eibesfeldt, I. 1971. Transcultural patterns of ritualized contact behavior. In *Behavior and environment: The use of space by animals and men,* edited by A. H. Esser, 297–312. New York: Plenum Press.

Eisenberg, A. M. and R. R. Smith. 1971. *Nonverbal communication.* Indianapolis: Bobbs-Merrill.

Ekman, Paul., Wallace V. Friesen, and Phoebe Ellsworth. 1972. *Emotion in the human face: Guidelines for research and an integration of the findings.* New York: Pergamon Press.

Ellsworth, P. C. 1975. Direct gaze as a social stimulus: The example of aggression. In *Nonverbal communication of aggression,* edited by P. Pliner, L. Kramer, and T. Alloway. New York: Plenum Press.

Ember, Carol R., and Melvin Ember. 1999. *Anthropology.* 9th ed. Upper Saddle River, N.J.: Prentice Hall.

Engholm, Christopher. 1991. *When business East meets business West: The guide to practice and protocol in the Pacific Rim.* New York: Wiley.

Engholm, Christofer, and Diana Rowland. 1996. *International excellence: Seven breakthrough strategies for personal and professional success.* New York: Kodansha International.

Eve, Raymond, Bob Price, and Monika Counts. 1994. Geographic illiteracy among college students. *Youth and Society* 25(3): 408–27.

Farb, Peter. 1968. How do I know you mean what you mean? *Horizon* 10(4): 52–57.

———.1974. *Word play: What happens when people talk.* New York: Knopf.

Feldman, D. C. 1991. Repatriate moves as career transitions. *Human Resource Management Review* 1(3): 163–78.

Figg, J. 2000. Executives shun expatriate opportunities. *Internal Auditor* 57(1): 13–14.

Foster, Dean Allen. 1992 *Bargaining across borders: How to negotiate business anywhere in the world.* New York: McGraw-Hill.

Frank, Sergey. 1992. Avoiding the pitfalls of business abroad. *Sales and Marketing Management,* March, 48–52.

Friedman, Thomas L. 1999. *The Lexus and the olive tree.* New York: Ferrar, Straus, & Giroux.

Frost, Peter J., et al. 1991. *Reframing organizational culture.* Newbury Park, Calif.: Sage.

Gallup Organization. 1988. Geographic knowledge deemed vital, but many lack basic skills. *Gallup Report* 277: 35.

Gardner, Burleigh. 1945. *Human relations in industry.* Homewood, Ill.: Irwin.

Gates, Stephen. 1994. *The changing global role of the human resource function.* New York: Conference Board.

Geertz, Clifford. 1984. Distinguished lecture: Anti anti-relativism. *American Anthropologist* 86: 263–78.

Goffman, Erving. 1963. *Behavior in public places.* Glencoe, Ill.: Free Press.

Goldman, Alan. 1994. *Doing business with the Japanese: A guide to successful communication, management, and diplomacy.* Albany: State University of New York Press.

Goodman, Neal R. 1994. Cross cultural training for the global executive. In *Improving intercultural interactions,* edited by Brislin and T. Yoshida. Thousand Oaks, Calif. Sage.

Gorer, Geoffrey. 1935. *Africa dances: A book about West African Negroes.* New York: Knopf.

Greengard, Samuel. 1999. Technology is changing expatriate training. *Workforce* 78(12): 106–07.

Gudykunst, William B., and Y. Y. Kim. 1984. *Communicating with strangers: An approach to intercultural communication.* Reading, Mass.: Addison-Wesley.

Guthrie, G. M. 1975. A behavioral analysis of culture learning. In *Cross-Cultural Perspectives on Learning,* edited by R. W. Brislin, S. Bochner, and W. J. Lonner. New York: Wiley.

Haas, Mary. 1964. Men's and Women's Speech in Koasati. In *Language in Culture and Society,* edited by Hymes, 228–33. New York: Harper and Row.

———. 1966. *The hidden dimension.* Garden City, N.Y.: Doubleday.

———. 1959. *The silent language.* Garden City, N.Y.: Doubleday.

Hall, Edward T. 1976. *Beyond culture.* Garden City, N.Y.: Doubleday.

Hall, Edward T., and Mildred R. 1987. *Hidden differences: Doing business with the Japanese.* Garden City, N.Y.: Anchor Press/Doubleday.

———. 1990. *Understanding cultural differences: Germans, French, and Americans.* Yarmouth, Maine: Intercultural Press.

Hall, J. A. 1978. Gender effects in decoding nonverbal cues. *Psychological Bulletin* 85(4): 845–57.

Harris, Philip. 1979. The unhappy world of the expatriate. *International Management,* July, 49–50.

Harris, Philip R., and Robert T. Moran. 1996. *Managing cultural differences.* 2d ed. Houston: Gulf Publishing.

Harrison, Randall P. 1974. *Beyond words: An introduction to nonverbal communication.* Englewood Cliffs, N.J.: Prentice Hall.

Heron, J. 1970. The phenomenology of social encounter: The gaze. *Philosophy and Phenomenological Research* 31: 243–64.

Herskovits, Melville J. 1955. *Cultural anthropology.* New York: Knopf.

Hewes, Gordon. 1955. World distribution of certain postural habits. *American Anthropologist* 57: 231–44.

Hickerson, Nancy P. 1980. *Linguistic anthropology.* New York: Holt, Rinehart & Winston.

Hirsch, E. D. 1987. *Cultural literacy: What every American needs to know.* Boston: Houghton Mifflin.

Hodgson, John, Yoshihiro Sano, and John L. Graham. 2000. *Doing business with the new Japan.* Lanham, Md.: Rowman & Littlefield.

Hofstede, Geert. 1980. *Culture's consequences: International differences in work-related values.* Beverly Hills, Calif.: Sage.

Hofstede, Geert, et al. 1998. *Masculinity and femininity.* Thousand Oaks, Calif.: Sage.

Holmes, Lowell D. 1971. *Anthropology: An introduction.* New York: Ronald Press.

House, R. J., et al. 1995. *Globe: The Global Leadership and Organizational Behavior Effectiveness Research Program.* Philadelphia: Department of Management, Wharton School, University of Pennsylvania.

Howard, Cecil. 1992. Profile of the 21st century expatriate manager. *HR Magazine,* June.

Huebener, Theodore. 1961. *Why Johnny should learn foreign languages.* Radnor, Pa.: Chilton.

Imai, M. 1981. *Sixteen ways to avoid saying no.* Tokyo: Nihon Keizai Shimbun.

Jensen, J. V. 1982. Perspective on nonverbal intercultural communication. In *Intercultural communication: A reader,* edited by L. A. Samovar and Richard E. Porter, 260–76. Belmont, Calif.: Wadsworth.

Jessup, Jay M., and Maggie L. Jessup. 1993. *Doing business in Mexico.* Rocklin, Calif.: Prima.

Kapp, Robert A. 1983. *Communicating with China.* Chicago: Intercultural Press.

Katriel, T., 1986. *Talking straight: Dugri speech in Israeli sabra culture.* Cambridge: Cambridge University Press.

Katzner, Kenneth. 1975. *The languages of the world.* New York: Funk & Wagnalls.

Kelley, Colleen, and Judith Meyers. 1995. *CCAI: Cross Cultural Adaptability Inventory Manual.* Minneapolis: National Computer Systems.

Kennedy, Gavin. 1985. *Doing business abroad.* New York: Simon & Schuster.

Kim, Uichol, Harry Triandis, et al. 1994. *Individualism and collectivism: Theory, methods, and applications.* Thousand Oaks, Calif.: Sage.

Kluckhohn, Clyde. 1968. *Mirror for man.* New York: Fawcett.

Kluckhohn, Clyde and W. H. Kelly. 1945. The concept of culture. In *The science of man in the world crisis,* edited by R. Linton, 78–106. New York: Columbia University Press.

Kluckhohn, Florence, and Fred L. Strodtbeck. 1961. *Variations in value orientations.* New York: Harper & Row.

Knapp, M. L. 1972. The field of nonverbal communication: An overview. In *On speech communication: An anthology of contemporary writings and messages,* edited by C. J. Steward and B. Kendall, 57–72. New York: Holt, Rinehart & Winston.

Kobrin, Stephen. 1992. Expatriate reduction and strategic control in American multinational corporations. In *Globalizing management: Creating and leading the competitive organization.* edited by V. Pucik et al., 263–75. New York: Wiley.

Kohls, L. Robert. 1978. Basic concepts and models of intercultural communication. In *USIA Intercultural Communication Course: 1977 proceedings,* edited by M. Prosser. Washington, D.C.: U.S. Information Agency.

———. 1984. *Survival kit for overseas living.* Chicago: Intercultural Press.

Kottak, Conrad P. 1987. *Anthropology: The exploration of human diversity.* 4th ed. New York: Random House.

Kotter, John P. 1992. *Corporate culture and performance.* New York: Free Press.

Kramer, Cheris. 1974. Folk-linguistics: Wishy-washy mommy talk. *Psychology Today* 8(1): 82–85.

Kroeber, A. L., and Clyde Kluckhohn. 1952. Culture: A critical review of concepts and definitions. *Papers of the Peabody Museum of American Archaeology and Ethnology* 47(1).

Kuethe, J. L. 1962. Social schemas. *Journal of Abnormal and Social Psychology* 64: 31–38.

Kupfer, Andrew. 1988. How to be a global manager. *Fortune,* March 14, 52–58.

LaBarre, Weston. 1947. The cultural basis of emotions and gestures. *Journal of Personality,* no. 16: 49–68.

Lanier, Alison R. 1979. Selecting and preparing personnel for overseas transfers. *Personnel Journal,* March, 160–63.

Lebra, T. S. 1976. *Japanese patterns of behavior.* Honolulu: University of Hawaii Press.

Lederer, William J., and Eugene Burdick. 1958. *The ugly American.* New York: Norton.

Levine, Robert, and E. Wolfe. 1985. Social time: The heartbeat of culture. *Psychology Today,* March, 29–35.

Linton, Ralph. 1936. *The study of man.* New York: Appleton-Century-Crofts.

Little, K. B. Cultural variations in social schemata. *Journal of Personality and Social Psychology* 10: 1–7.

Little, K. B. 1965. Personal space. *Journal of Experimental Social Psychology,* no. 1: 237–47.

Machan, Dyan. 1988. Ici on parle bottom line responsibility. *Forbes,* 8 February, 138–40.

Mayo, Elton. 1933. *The human problems of an industrial civilization.* New York: Macmillan.

Mbiti, John S. 1969. *African religions and philosophy.* New York: Praeger.

McClelland, David C., 1961. *The achieving society.* Princeton, N.J.: Van Nostrand.

Mead, Margaret. 1961. *Cooperation and competition among primitive people.* Boston: Beacon Press.

Mehrabian, Albert. 1981. *Silent messages.* 2d ed. Belmont, Calif.: Wadsworth.

Mendenhall, Mark E., Edward Dunbar, and Gary R. Oddou. 1987. Expatriate selection, training and career-pathing: A review and critique. *Human Resource Management* 26(3): 331–45.

Mitchell, Charles. 2000. *A short course in international business culture.* Novato, Calif.: World Trade Press.

Mizutani, Osamu. 1979. *Nihongo no seitai [The facts about Japan].* Tokyo: Sotakusha.

Montagu, Ashley. 1972. *Touching: The human significance of the skin.* New York: Harper & Row.

Moran, Robert T. 1985. *Getting your yen's worth: How to negotiate with Japan, Inc.* Houston, Tex.: Gulf Publishing.

Moran, Robert T., and William G. Stripp. 1991. *Dynamics of successful international business negotiations.* Houston, Tex.: Gulf Publishing.

Morris, Desmond. 1977. *Manwatching: A field guide to human behavior.* New York: Abrams.

Morris, Desmond, Peter Collett, Peter Marsh, and Marie O'Shaughnessy. 1979. *Gestures: Their origins and distribution.* New York: Stein & Day.

Morrison, Terri, Wayne A. Conaway, and George A. Borden. 1994. *Kiss, bow, or shake hands.* Holbrook, Mass.: Bob Adams.

Morsbach, Helmut. 1982. Aspects of nonverbal communication in Japan. In *Intercultural communication: A reader,* 3d ed., edited by L. A. Samovar and R. E. Porter, 300–16. Belmont, Calif.: Wadsworth.

Murdock, George P. 1971. *The outline of cultural materials.* 4th ed. New Haven, Conn.: Human Relations Area Files.

———. 1972. *The outline of world cultures.* 4th ed. New Haven, Conn.: Human Relations Area Files.

Nishiyama, Kazuo. 2000. *Doing business with Japan: Successful strategies for intercultural communication.* Honolulu: University of Hawaii Press.

Oberg, Kalvero. 1960. Culture shock: Adjustments to new cultural environments. *Practical Anthropology,* July-August, 177–82.

Offermann, Lynn, and Peta Hellmann. 1997. Culture's consequences for leadership. *Journal of Cross-Cultural Psychology* 28(3): 342–51.

Osland, Joyce S. 1995. *The adventure of working abroad: Hero tales from the global frontier.* San Francisco: Jossey-Bass.

Parsons, Talcott, and Edward Shils. 1951. *Toward a general theory of action.* Cambridge, Mass.: Harvard University Press.

Pike, E. Royston. 1967. *The strange ways of man.* New York: Hart.

Plog, Fred, and Daniel Bates. 1980. *Cultural anthropology.* New York: Knopf.

Prothro, E. T. 1955. Arab-American differences in the judgment of written messages. *Journal of Social Psychology* 42: 3–11.

Reynolds, J. I., and G. H. Rice. 1988. American education for international business. *Management International Review* 28(3): 48–57.

Rhinesmith, Stephen H. 1996. *A manager's guide to globalization: Six skills for success in a changing world.* Chicago: Irwin.

Richardson, Friedrich, and Charles Walker. 1948. *Human relations in an expanding company.* New Haven, Conn.: Yale University Labor Management Center.

Ricks, David A. 1983. *Big business blunders: Mistakes in multinational marketing.* Homewood, Ill.: Dow Jones–Irwin.

———. *Blunders in international business.* Cambridge, Mass.: Blackwell, 1993.

Ricks, David A., 1999. *Blunders in international business.* 3d ed. Oxford, Engl.: Blackwell.

Ricks, David A., M. Y. C. Fu, and J. S. Arpan. 1974. *International business blunders.* Columbus, Ohio: Grid.

Robinson, Richard D. 1983. *Internationalization of business: An introduction.* New York: Dryden Press.

Roethlisberger, F. J., and W. J. Dickson. 1939. *Management and the worker: An account of a research program conducted by a western electric company, Hawthorne Works, Chicago.* Cambridge, Mass.: Harvard University Press.

Rogers, Everett. 1971. *Communication of innovations: A Cross-cultural approach.* New York: Free Press.

Rosen, Robert. 2000. *Global literacies.* New York: Simon & Schuster.

Rosenthal, Robert, et al. 1979. Measuring sensitivity to nonverbal communication: The PONS test. In *Nonverbal behavior: Applications and cultural implications,* edited by A. Wolfgang, 67–98. New York: Academic Press.

Rugh, William A., 1995. If Saddam had been a Fulbrighter. *Christian Science Monitor,* November 2.

Ruhley, Sharon. 1982. *Intercultural communication.* 2d ed. Chicago: Science Research Association.

Salacuse, Jeswald W. 1991. *Making global deals: Negotiating in the international marketplace.* Boston: Houghton Mifflin.

Salmans, Sandra. 1979. Industry learns to speak the same language. *International Management,* April, 45–47.

Samovar, Larry A., and Richard E. Porter. 1991. *Communication between cultures.* Belmont, Calif.: Wadsworth.

Sapir, Edward. 1929. The status of linguistics as a science. *Language* 5: 207–14.

Scheinfeld, Amram. 1950. *The new you and heredity.* Philadelphia: Lippincott.

Seager, J., and A. Olsen. 1986. Women in the World Atlas. New York: Simon and Schuster.

Serrie, Hendrick. 1986. Anthropological contributions to business in multicultural contexts. In *Anthropology and international business,* edited by H. Serrie, ix–xxx. Williamsburg, Va.: Department of Anthropology, College of William and Mary.

Shane, Scott. 1993. Cultural influences on national rates of innovation. *Journal of Business Venturing* 8(1): 59–73.

Shane, Scott. 1995. Uncertainty avoidance and the preference for innovation championing roles. *Journal of International Business Studies* 26(1): 47–67.

Sharp, Lauriston. 1952. Steel axes for Stone Age Australians. *Human Organization* 11(2): 17–22.

Sheets, Tara E., ed. 1999. *Encyclopedia of Associations.* Detroit: Gale Research.

Sheflen, Albert E. 1972. *Body language and the social order.* Englewood Cliffs, N.J.: Prentice Hall.

Shimoda, K., M. Argyle, and R. Bitti. 1978. The intercultural recognition of emotional expressions by three national groups—English, Italian, and Japanese. *European Journal of Social Psychology* 8: 169–79.

Shimonishi, R. 1977. Influence of culture and foreign language learning: A contrastive analysis in terms of English and Japanese passive based on Japanese culture. M.A. thesis, University of Kansas, Lawerence.

Shuter, Robert. 1977. A field study of nonverbal communication in Germany, Italy, and the United States. *Communication Monographs* 44: 298–305.

Slater, Jonathan R. 1984. The hazards of cross-cultural advertising. *Business America,* 2 April, 20–23.

Solomon, C. M. 1994. Success abroad depends on more than job skills. *Personnel Journal* 73(4): 51–54.

Sommer, R. 1959. Studies in personal space. *Sociometry* 22: 247–60.

Stein, Jess, ed. 1979. *The Random House college dictionary.* New York: Random House.

Stevenson, Burton. 1948. *The home book of proverbs, maxims and familiar phrases.* New York: Macmillan.

Takahashi, Dean. 1998. Doing fieldwork in the high-tech jungle. *Wall Street Journal,* 27 October B-1.

Teagarden, Mary B., and Gary Gordon. 1995. Corporate selection strategies and expatriate manager success. In *Expatriate management: New ideas for international business,* edited by J. Selmer Westport, Conn. Quorum Books.

Terpstra, Vern. 1978. *The cultural environment of international business.* Cincinnati: Southwestern.

Trompenaars, Alfons, and Charles Hampden-Turner. 1993. *The seven cultures of capitalism.* New York: Currency/Doubleday.

———.1998. *Riding the waves of culture: Understanding cultural diversity in global business.* 2d ed. New York: McGraw-Hill

Tung, Rosalie L. 1981. Selection and training of personnel for overseas assignments. *Columbia Journal of World Business* 16: 68–78.

———. 1988. *The new expatriates: Managing human resources abroad.* Cambridge, Mass.: Ballinger.

Tylor, Edward. B. 1871. *Origins of culture.* New York: Harper & Row.

Warner, W. L., and J. O. Low. 1947. *The social system of the modern factory: The strike, a social analysis.* New Haven, Conn.: Yale University Press.

Watson, O. M. 1970. *Proxemic behavior: A cross-cultural study.* The Hague: Mouton.

Watson, O. M., and T. D. Graves. 1966. Quantitative research in proxemic behavior. *American Anthropologist* 68: 971–85.

Weeks, David. 1992. Recruiting and selecting international managers. *Report 998, The Conference Board,* 12.

Whorf, Benjamin Lee. 1956. *Language, thought, and reality.* Cambridge, Mass.: MIT Press.

Wills, Stefan, and Kevin Barham. 1994. Being an international manager. *European Management Journal* 12(1): 49–58.

Wilson, Meena, and Maxine Dalton. 1996. Selecting and developing global managers: Possibilities and pitfalls. Unpublished paper, May.

Wood, Julia T. 1994. Gender, communication, and culture. In *Intercultural communication: A reader.* 7th ed., edited by L. A. Samovar and R. E. Porter, 155–65. Belmont, Calif.: Wadsworth.

The world almanac and book of facts (2000). 1999. New York: World Almanac.

Ya'ari, Ehud, and Ira Friedman. 1991. Curses in verses. *Atlantic* 267(2): 22–26.

Photo Credits

Index